Loving Yusuf

AFTERLIVES OF THE BIBLE
A series edited by Timothy K. Beal and Tod Linafelt

Recent Books in the Series

Mel Gibson's Bible, edited by Timothy K. Beal and Tod Linafelt
Faithful Renderings, by Naomi Seidman

Loving

Conceptual Travels from Present to Past

Yusuf

MIEKE BAL

The University of Chicago Press
Chicago and London

MIEKE BAL is Academy Professor at the Royal Netherlands Academy of Arts and Sciences and a founding director of the Amsterdam School for Cultural Analysis, University of Amsterdam. She is the author of numerous publications, most recently of *Louise Bourgeois' "Spider": The Architecture of Art-Writing, The Artemisia Files: Artemisia Gentileschi for Feminists and Other Thinking People,* and *A Mieke Bal Reader,* all published by the University of Chicago Press.

The University of Chicago Press, Chicago 60637
The University of Chicago Press, Ltd., London
© 2008 by The University of Chicago
All rights reserved. Published 2008
Printed in the United States of America

17 16 15 14 13 12 11 10 09 08   1 2 3 4 5
ISBN-13: 978-0-226-03586-4 (cloth)
ISBN-10: 0-226-03586-7 (cloth)
ISBN-13: 978-0-226-03587-1 (paper)
ISBN-10: 0-226-03587-5 (paper)

Library of Congress Cataloging-in-Publication Data

Bal, Mieke, 1946–
    Loving Yusuf : conceptual travels from present to past / Mieke Bal.
        p. cm. — (Afterlives of the Bible)
    Includes bibliographical references and index.
    ISBN-13: 978-0-226-03586-4 (cloth : alk. paper)
    ISBN-10: 0-226-03586-7 (cloth : alk. paper)
    ISBN-13: 978-0-226-03587-1 (pbk. : alk. paper)
    ISBN-10: 0-226-03587-5 (pbk. : alk. paper)
    1. Joseph (Son of Jacob)—Meditations. I. Title.
BS580.J6B35 2008
222'.11092—dc22   2007040676

For August and Lena
—*the future in the present*

In memory of Belgacem Mehdi Kouni
—*the past in the present*

CONTENTS

ACKNOWLEDGMENTS

This book looks back at memories, from my childhood as well as from my later life as an intellectual, some of which I describe in the text. But the texture of memory is denser than I can ever even grasp. Innumerable voices are murmuring in the background, and I feel unable to do justice to them all. In the late 1980s I began to muse and write about the story of the unfortunate passion of a woman for Jacob's favorite son. In the present book I have recycled and expanded this early material into an argument about how to study cultural material that is both strange and familiar, both ancient and current, rewritten every day by those who have a stake in presenting it in certain ways—stories from the past that shape the present and have an impact on the future.

Over the years that Yusuf's story has accompanied me, I have greatly benefited from conversations with many people. Some of their names will appear in the bibliography, some not, but all are present in the text I am now completing, explicitly or through their ideas. I keep fond memories of conversations with Alice Bach and Tim Beal in the United States, and with Begüm Özden Firat, Ihab Saloul, Athalya Brenner, and Jan Willem van Henten in Amsterdam, about how to teach ancient material with such ongoing and vivid cultural presence at a time of devastating divisions of the world.

My small Parisian world, where I take refuge when I need withdrawal from a life too full and busy to concentrate, has also been crucial. Early on in this project, I had an unexpected encounter there with a brilliant chemist who is also a playwright and producer of cultural events (not to mention his Nobel Prize for Chemistry), Roald Hoffmann from Cornell University. Roald gave me suggestions that were more important than he knew. My ongoing friendship with Tarek Mehdi and Ilhem BenAli-Mehdi and their families has brought truly inspiring conversations on the level of the everyday, lived experience of Islam as well as collective sessions of poring over the relevant Qur'anic passages. Tarek Mehdi helped with the adaptation of the translated Qur'anic fragment in this book. During the time I was writing this book, Tarek's father, Belgacem, fell ill; he passed away just as I was completing it. The end of his life as well as Tarek's dedication to his father taught me a lot about life. I dedicate this book to Belgacem's memory.

In the end, books materialize in a specific context that is indispensable for book-making. At the University of Chicago Press I have always felt greatly encouraged by Alan Thomas and Susan Bielstein. Until I met them I had been a drifter, publisher-wise. Alan and Susan know how to forge a bond between authors and publishers. I had never known that friendship could be involved in this process. In Amsterdam, Noa Roei, who did some research for me; Bregje van Eekelen, who edited the first draft; and then Debbie Knoller, who took over from Bregje, have helped with many details of the text and helped to make the book a reality. I thank Noa Roei for helping me adapt the translation of Genesis 39.

Like so many of my previous books, this one could not have come off without my toughest and most constructive critic, Ernst van Alphen. His stern refusal to spare me even the hardest comments has been a great gift.

FRAGMENTS

FROM GENESIS 39

And it came to pass after these things/words and lifted the woman of his master her eyes upon Joseph and she said, lie with me (7).

And he refused himself and said to the woman of his master: See, my master knows not with me what [is] in the house and all that [is] onto him he gave into my hand (8).

No one [is] greater in this house than me and not kept he back from me anything except you and you [are] his woman and how shall I do this great wickedness and sin against God? (9)

And it came to pass on such a day and he went to the house to do his work and no man of the men of the house [was] there in the house. (11)

And she called unto the men of the house and said to them saying: see he made come to us a Hebrew man to mock us, he has come to me to lie with me and I called out in a loud voice. (14)

And Joseph's master took him and gave him in the closed house, a place where the bound ones of the king were bound and he was there in the closed house. (20)

Translation my own, based on Buber and Rosenschweig, King James, and Hebrew text.

FROM THOMAS MANN, *JOSEPH AND HIS BROTHERS*

Again Mut-em-enet had beckoned, and he who now appeared on the scene was the cup-bearer, the pourer of wine—it was Joseph. Yes, the lovesick woman had commanded him to this service, requesting, as his mistress, that he should himself serve the wine of Cyprus to her guests. She did not tell him of her other preparations, he did not know for what purpose of edification he was being used. It pained her, as we know, to deceive him and deliberately make such misuse of his appearance, But her heart was set on enlightening her friends and laying bare her feelings. So she said to him—just after he had once more, with all possible forbearance, refused to lie with her:

"Will you then, Osarsiph, at least do me a favor, and pour out the famous Alashian wine at my ladies' party day after tomorrow? In token of its excelling goodness, also in token that you love me a little, and lastly to show that I am after all somebody in this house, since he at its head serves me and my guests?"

"By all means, my mistress," he had answered. "That will I gladly do, and with the greatest pleasure, if it be one to you. For I am with body and soul at your command in every respect save that I sin with you."

So, then, Rachel's son, the young steward of Petepre, appeared suddenly among the ladies as they sat peeling in the court; in a fine white festal garment, with a colored Mycenaean jug in his hands. He bowed, and began to move about, filling the cups. But all the ladies, those who had chanced to see him before as well as those who did not know him, forgot at the sight not only what they were doing but themselves as well, being lost in gazing at the cup-bearer. Then those wicked little knives accomplished their purpose and the ladies, all and sundry, cut their fingers frightfully—without even being aware at the time, for a cut from such an exceedingly sharp blade is hardly perceptible, certainly not in the distracted state of mind in which Eni's friends then were.

This oft-described scene has by some been thought to be apocryphal, and not belonging to the story as it happened. But they are wrong; for it is the truth, and all the probabilities speak for it. We must remember, on the one hand, that this was the most beautiful youth of his time and sphere; on the other, that those were the sharpest little knives the world had ever seen—and we shall understand that the thing could not happen otherwise—I mean with less shedding of blood than it actually did. Eni's dreamlike certainty of the event and its course was entirely justified. She sat there with her suffering air, her brooding, sinister, masklike face and sinuous mouth, and looked at the mischief she had worked; the blood-bath, which at first no one saw but herself, for all the ladies were gaping in self-forgotten ardour after the youth as he slowly disappeared toward the pillared hall, where, Mut knew, the scene would repeat itself. Only when the beloved form had disappeared did she inquire of the ensuing stillness, in a voice of malicious concern:

"My loves, whatever has happened to you all? What are you doing? Your blood is flowing!"

It was a fearful sight. With some the nimble knife had gone an inch deep in the flesh and the blood did not ooze, it spouted. The little hands, the golden apples, were drenched with the red liquid, it dyed the fresh whiteness of the linen garments and snaked through into the women's laps, making pools which dripped down on the floor and their little feet. What an outcry, what wails, what shrieking arose when Mut's hypocritical concern made them aware of what had happened! (802–3)

FROM THE QUR'AN, SURA 12

"O our Father! Why dost thou not entrust us with Joseph? *Indeed* we mean him well" (1); "we will *surely* keep him safely" (12); "*Verily,* your taking him away will grieve me" (13); "*Surely,* if the wolf devour him, and we so many, we must in that case be weak *indeed*" (14). . . . "O our Father! *Of a truth,* we went to run races . . . but thou wilt not believe us even though we speak the *truth*" (17). "And they brought his shirt with *false* blood upon it" (18).

And he who bought him—an Egyptian—said to his wife, "Treat him hospitably; haply he may be useful to us, or we may adopt him as a son." . . . (21)

And when he had reached his age of strength we bestowed on him judgment and knowledge; for thus do we recompense the well doers. (22)

And she in whose house he was conceived a passion for him, and she shut the doors and said, come hither. He said: "God keep me! *Verily*, my lord hath given me a good home: and the injurious shall not prosper." (23)

And she desired him, and he would have desired her had he not seen a token from his Lord. Thus we averted evil and defilement from him, for he was one of our sincere servants. (24)

And they both made for the door, and she rent his shirt behind; and at the door they met her lord. "What," she said, "shall be the recompense of him who do evil to thy family, but a prison or a sore punishment?" (25)

He said, "She solicited me to evil." And a witness out of her own family witnessed: "If his shirt be rent in front she speaks truth, and he is a liar; but if his shirt be rent behind, she lies and he is true." (26–27)

And when his lord saw his shirt torn behind, he said: "This is one of your [singular] devices! Verily your [plural] devices are great! (28)

"Joseph! Leave this affair. And thou, O wife, ask pardon for thy crime, for thou hast sinned." (29)

And in the city, the women said: "The wife of the Prince hath solicited her servant; he hath fired her with his love: but we clearly see her manifest error." (30)

When she heard of their cabal, she sent to them and prepared a banquet for them, and she gave each of them a knife, and she said, "[Joseph,] shew thyself to them." And when they saw him, they were amazed at him, and cut their hands, and said, "God keep us! This is no man! This is no other than a noble angel!" (31)

From *The Koran*, translated from the Arabic by J. M. Rodwell (London: Dent, 1971).

Art is less concerned with delivering information about the world than teaching us about how to stand in relation to it, how to find our place in it, and live with it: through art we do not seek to master the world so much as become its denizens. It is a teaching of love.

DIDIER MALEUVRE

1

First Memories, Second Thoughts

It was a winter afternoon in primary school, perhaps third or fourth grade. I attended a Catholic girls-only school in a predominantly Protestant village near Haarlem in the Netherlands. In the afternoon, when concentration is hard to muster, the classroom was hot, and many girls had trouble keeping their eyes open. Not me. Given my lifelong obsession with narrative, it comes as no surprise to me to recall, decades later, that I was such an eager listener to the stories the schoolmistress used to tell. I think she told at least one story every few hours, often after the break or at the end of the day. At such sleep-inducing times of the day she dished up an incredible number of stories, the sole common feature of which was their baggage of moral lessons. We never read the Bible, ever. Nevertheless, I think it was a form of religious education, as usual with religion and ideology not very clearly distinguished. With my rather vivid imagination, I tended to bring the stories to bear on my own life all the time.

With the story of Potiphar's wife's wicked attempt at Joseph's virtue this proved to be a bit difficult. Neither I nor, I expect, my classmates had any education on matters sexual at the age of eight or nine. I even remember wondering what it was exactly that the woman wanted Joseph to

do. But whatever it was, he didn't want to do it. And I understood
that she insisted and he fled. I never doubted that she was evil.
The heart of the story, of course, was her lie. This was what the
teacher was trying to convey. Potiphar's wife lied, and as a result,
Joseph went to prison. The horror was obvious, translated into
absolute silence while the teacher lowered her voice to a near-
whisper, and somehow I went home with the notion that women
can be dangerous to men.

This was a point worth making. More often than not, stories
about danger targeted men. These cautionary tales of terror concerned strangers offering candy only in order to abduct children;
bad men hidden in dark corners, so that I tended to walk close to
the edge of the sidewalk; men grabbing children who were alone
in the street against their parents' admonitions; men hiding under
my bed. Now, I learned, women could be dangerous as well. But
strangely, in ways I did not understand, they were dangerous especially or exclusively to men.

These are my first memories of the story of Joseph and Potiphar's wife. I don't recall the precise story, but I do know it was
about a woman in whose house Joseph was working. He was in
good standing; his master appreciated him a lot, and so did, in fact,
his mistress. She wanted something from him that he didn't want
to give her, and he was right in his refusal. I don't remember what
I thought it was she wanted. She then trapped him and deceived
her husband, and Joseph went to jail. Luckily, and as a reward for
his steadfastness, he went up from there like a comet because he
was so good at explaining dreams.

I tell this tale of getting to know the story not to make this
essay unnecessarily personal but because I want to understand
how books and lives hang together. I am a literary scholar by
training, and I love texts. Later I also learned to love images, to
which I relate as other kinds of texts: as objects or artifacts that
solicit me to make sense out of them. With images, I was also sensitive to their materiality. Whenever I worked on art, I yearned to
touch, to hold the actual object, and did not rest until I had seen the
real thing, wherever on earth it might be. Later in this book this
contact with the material object will prove to be as crucial as the
textual "letter" of the written stories. In this chapter, I will propose the concept of *cultural memory* as the first in a small series

of concepts I wish to put forward as relevant for the interpretation of such well-known—as well as ill-known—stories as the one of Joseph's mishaps at the hands of a woman. These stories circulate and shape minds and lives.

Perhaps because of my training, I am in sympathy with scholars who are as dissatisfied with the reliance on oral transmission as I am and who therefore seek to trace the "original" version of any given tale that goes around and around in as many versions as the world has cultures. I take this to be a standard scientific attitude. The disciplines of philology are all based on this intellectual posture. Hence, on a gut level, I tend to a qualified adherence to the tale's firm *anchoring* in the Hebrew Bible, as suggested by James Kugel in his study on biblical exegesis for which he uses this tale (1990). Kugel is a well-known, highly respected biblical scholar, and for this reason alone his book will stand for that academic field and be a constant companion for me throughout my current exploration. But as I will argue throughout this essay, living with stories requires also a constant questioning not only of their oral retellings but of written versions as well. My vague childhood memory, his expert textual study—what kind of combination is this?

Introducing the discursive genre of biblical exegesis Kugel calls "narrative expansion," the subject of his book *In Potiphar's House*, he insists that "such narrative expansions are, by definition, *exegetical* because they are ultimately based on something that *is* in the text" (1990, 4, emphasis Kugel's). How can such an affirmative assertion of positive anchoring match memories of a humid classroom so long ago yet so recent? The question is crucial for what I do with my life. The utterly subjective, fleeting memory does not come out of a cultural blue. But how can I believe that a text thousands of years old can affect my life, my flesh? I intend to make the textual approach of Kugel and others cohere—theoretically and semantically—with my childhood memory. *Cultural memory*, then, is the subject of this chapter. It is the first concept I propose for an intertextual and intercultural study of this love story and others like it.

Kugel applies the term *exegesis* to all narrative expansions that answer implicit questions raised by "an unusual word, an apparently unnecessary repetition, an unusual grammatical form" that

arouses the need to "bring . . . out all possible nuances implied in
the *precise* wording of each and every sentence" (1990, 3–4, emphasis added). He talks the talk of one who will not have the text
abducted by ideological abuse. I wish to heed this injunction, if
only as a remedy to the kinds of ideological appropriation and political misuse to which canonical religious literature is subjected
more frequently than are any other texts. But these abductions
happen all the time. They cannot be wished away, because they are
the result of texts; they are how texts *act*. I cannot believe in those
textual roots of truths that suit some purpose while damaging others. So even if a text is an artifact and if it contains words that have
meaning, each of them and in their arrangement, I take issue with
the notion that they also *contain* the questions we ask of them.

The leap from words to questions is significant. In the course
of this book I will argue that interest in the precise wording is a
reading attitude I call *literalism*, of which I am a strong advocate.
On the other hand, the idea that the texts *contain* the questions
we ask of them is, I will argue, akin to *fundamentalism*. My argument in this book seeks to carefully delineate the distinction
between these two understandings of textuality and reading. The
one treasures the cultural inheritance and opens it up for the contemporary world. The other makes a devastating appeal to an im-
mutably referential, prescriptive meaning, an appeal that is based
on a radical denial or negligence of how signs work.

However, it is not enough to align ourselves with reception theory and to simply assume the reader is in charge. I contend it is in
the questions, not in the texts as hard core, that we must understand
the texts that traditions have managed to save for us. Yet our questions are, in turn, culturally framed, embedded in ways of thinking and common conceptions of social life. Reading is establishing
a meaningful connection between these relatively stable texts and
the varying, historically shifting meanings they generate.

The practice of interpretation is not quite in step with this conception of reading. Instead, I contend, the standard question of interpretation of which Kugel's study is a prime example is, simply,
"why?" We ask questions of the order of "why?" to understand
things whose meanings have shifted and slid from underneath the
relatively stable blanket of the text. "Why did X do what he did"
(Kugel 1990, 2). These questions of "why"—why does a figure do

or say something, why doesn't the husband understand, why is the interlocutor refusing to comply, and the like—emerge not from the text but from the cultural frameworks of the interpreter, who feels the text does not fully flesh out the concerns of those who read it. In other words, it is from within our own conceptions that we wonder and ask why characters do or say what they do. These frames and conceptions change all the time, whereas the texts as artifacts retain more—although by no means total—stability. This stability is due, in large part, to the process of canonization, which is by definition conservative. The readings change faster. What I resist, therefore, is the reasoning that a "why" question is anchored in the text whenever there is something considered enigmatic "in" a text, something the reader has to contend with: a seeming contradiction, a missing detail, an unexpected form. "Seeming" begs more specific questions. Who is the person or group of persons for whom there is a seeming contradiction? For whom and from which expectation would the detail be lacking? From which horizon of expectation would the form appear unexpected? These are questions of readership, the group identities and mythologies that inform a text's readers. Given this, I take these questions very seriously but will deny them their self-evident universality. With these qualifications and specifications in mind, I will refer to such questions of readership and expectations with the shorthand phrase "why questions."

This asking of "why questions" of the text is never finished, because readers move on with the times and hence meanings keep sliding along. Moreover, they have personal baggage to bring to the text as well as the cultural framings of this baggage. This is where my personal childhood memory joins the cultural memory in which I was and am steeped. Indeed, if we take seriously the cultural situation from which the text came to us, we must assume that the "why?" comes from the reader—who is, in turn, framed by her culture—not from the text. There are two paces at work—the long-term continuity of the artifact's existence and availability on the one hand and the faster pace of changing communities of readers on the other. Between these two paces the inevitable discrepancies define what has been called "cultural memory." To put it simply, cultural memory is the gap—sometimes abyss—between the words on the page and the meanings such as the one

I took home that winter day in the 1950s. The question "Why?" is the most tangible site of that cultural memory. As such, it is neither "in" the text nor outside of it, but "into" it, toward it; it is the reader's relationship to the text.

I take Kugel's authoritative study to stand for the discrepancy between belief in the text's "precise wording"—literalism—and the belief that the questions are located in the text—a potentially fundamentalist attitude. I will flesh out what I understand fundamentalism to be in the context of readings of tradition-transmitted texts such as the Joseph story. Kugel's formulation does not address the issue of whether "why questions" can be considered based on something other than his own frame of reference, something stable that *is* (ontologically) *in* (locally) the text, although he does acknowledge from the start that the texts "exercised a central role in everyday life" (1990, 1). I will return to this issue throughout this book. For now, however, I qualify this alleged anchoring by means of my memory of primary school. School, as Louis Althusser argued long ago, is one of those "Ideological State Apparatuses" where memories are shaped to fit the cultural frame (1971). It is the site where children learn to think, and to think in certain ways. This is both necessary and unavoidable, and I am not going to argue that this kind of education shouldn't happen. But how it takes place—and what interests it serves—is worth considering if we wish to understand the intertwining of individual and social identities, as well as that between past and present. In order to understand this intertwining I will draw on three areas of study: semiotics, or the theory of sign and sign use; aesthetics, or the theory of humans' relationship to the material world; and religion, or the relationships among people and with deities.

Like so many others, I was raised to despise, hate, and at the very least blame Potiphar's wife for Joseph's mishaps. His stint in prison, which cannot have been pleasant to say the least, was brought about by her lie. And lying, I was taught, is bad. The emotion we were compelled to feel for Joseph was pity. He did not deserve his unfortunate downfall. With this firm and emotionally sustained hatred of the guilty woman I entered adulthood—becoming a woman myself. The story was safely stored away in my memory for later use. When, much later, I was led to *read* the story for the first time, I had this affective tie to the characters already set in place. I could not read the story without it. And only because I had not been raised reading the biblical stories firsthand was I able to be surprised by it. Something did not match the sources; something remained stubbornly alien to me. This book is an account of that surprise. I seek to understand and unravel that mismatch between memory and text.

Between memory and text lies a gap, or a stumbling block, and stumbling over it is the cause of my surprise. That surprise emerged from a clash between a memory and a text. Several times during my encounters with biblical literature, with retellings of biblical stories in modern Western literature, and with what, for the sake of fairness, I consider "versions" of such stories—among which the Qur'an text of 12:23–31—I have felt such a clash. These were often productive, indeed exciting moments of learning. It was always to the extent I did not recognize what I saw before me that I found the text or image *interesting*. This rather flat word, a word of politeness and often of polite dismissal, receives new meaning when we take it in the German sense awoken by such writers as Jürgen Habermas. His seminal book *Knowledge and Human Interest* (1972 [orig. 1968]) remains an inspiring source for reflection on how knowledge thrives on interestedness—the opposite of Kant's ideal of aesthetic contemplation, defined as *dis*interestedness.

I am interested in exploring the interestedness of interpretation on the level of self-evidence. The kind of self-evidence I was carrying along concerning Potiphar's wife I can now recognize as a moral, indeed moralistic lesson against love or sexual attraction. A lesson in innocence defined as abstinence. Against women, protecting men.

How, then, can I articulate the imbrications of personal memory with cultural memory—in other words, how can my memory from schooldays become relevant in a discussion of a scholarly nature? The connection lies in the self-evidence, the unspoken implications of that warm schoolroom with the story told in it. These self-evident ideas, a culture's stock of wisdom, include what we call stereotypes. This notion points to fixed ideas that articulate the self's opinion about "others," construed as a group. Mireille Rosello's book *Declining the Stereotype* (1998) discusses the mechanism of stereotyping within a culture in terms congenial to what I set out to do in this book. She constructs the notion of the "reluctant witness," which I find a very useful, productive counterpart to the stereotype as itself an artifact. This reluctant witness is someone recruited to listen to a stereotyping discourse, a listening that entails the appearance of at least partly acquiescing to that discourse. When the listener herself belongs to the group being stereotypically constructed, she may be infuriated and feel offended, but often it is easiest to just go along for the ride. And then, after a time, to forget to get off. I think this happens to girls, to women-in-the-making, in misogynistic cultures such as my own. In my memory of it, I was a witness, only slightly reluctant, to my own stereotyping through the story of the wicked woman.

Rosello introduces the concept of the reluctant witness with the following examples, which are easy to recognize:

> An overtly gay person may be invited to agree with the supposedly legitimate disapproval of a straight interlocutor. A Jewish guest may be asked to swallow his or her host's anti-Semitic stereotypes with dinner, the French relative of Arab origin may be entrusted with more or less carefully worded revelations about anti-Arab feelings in his or her immediate surroundings, he or she, of course, constructed as the exception to the rule. (1998, 1)

The exceptional status of the witness is at the heart of my story. Readers are witnesses, and as we will see, their act of witnessing is embedded in the story in one of its versions. Women are dangerous, the story intimated to me as a child, but if you do your best to be good, you can belong to the good guys. The invitation offers hospitality within the group in recompense for acceptance of the insult. The insult is mitigated. The morality that suggests the possibility of avoidance of the condemned behavior is the lesson—to stay with school parlance—that helps overcome the unease that would otherwise lead to its rejection or, as Rosello's pun has it, "declining."

In the case of our tale, this lesson, clearly, was gender specific. Told to an audience of gullible girls, unknowing about sex and inexperienced in that event referred to as "falling in love," the tale of Joseph's downfall was meant to instill in its listeners, specifically, a repulsion against lying as well as against what only later was named "love." It worked. As far as I can remember, I have tended to associate falling in love with guilt and being in love with the need to lie. Lying to the loved person, who would, without any doubt, run away if told about my thrill; lying to parents, who, without giving me the necessary information to judge for myself, told me repeatedly how bad, dirty, and dangerous all this unnamed stuff was; lying to myself, thinking something was wrong with me and I had better rid myself of that emotion that kept me awake at night.

Not that I came ever close to the specific kind of lie the woman in the Genesis story had performed. The situation was never quite like that. But associations flow in the direction in which they can go, like a river; and like rivers, they carve out an ever-deeper channel that tames the water. Speaking in very general terms, the tale was one of several stories—a corpus later supplemented by other stories, novels, paintings, and films—that prepared me to grow up into a "decent" female, ready to organize my life accordingly. Whether or not this worked is not important. It never works to perfection; it never fails to work altogether. For the cultural critic I ended up being, the point is that any reading I was later able to perform on any "version" of the story of Joseph and Potiphar's wife was always already framed by the earliest memories of a story half-understood and rapidly abducted. Where and who was I in that process, and what is this "me" to begin with, if I can be so framed?

"Me" is an individual shaped by many frames, but inescapably strongly shaped by school. In my case it was a Catholic school, in which the church participated, directly and indirectly. I remember the priests who came to teach religion, because they were the only men in the school and for a time I thought they wore robes to dress like women. Even within the relatively small village of my childhood, other children grew up in other environments, just as specific but also just as collective. *Cultural memory* is the term that has been used to theorize this togetherness of memories through which individuals are shaped as part of communities. The storytelling of my teacher and my processing of the story told would be "acts of memory" in this cultural sense (Bal, Crewe, and Spitzer 1999).

In a recent study, Jan Assmann, one of the prominent specialists of cultural memory, offers useful terms to distinguish between

kinds and aspects of memory. He refers to episodic memories as
derived from experience and "semantic memories"—a somewhat
infelicitous term—as derived from learning. In light of my starting point in my school memory, the two categories are tightly
imbricated. He further distinguishes *scenic* memories, which he
considers "incoherent and remote from meaning," from *narrative* memories that do have meaning and coherence. I find these
terms highly stimulating but his definitions disappointing because of their oppositional character. This opposition favors temporal over spatial structure: narrative versus scenic, for example.
But the notion of distinguishing different—neither opposed nor
categorically exclusive—kinds of memory is helpful. It helps us
understand what makes memory by definition cultural, and why
this recognition is important (Assmann 2006a, 2). For me, *scenic*
is a crucial qualification that helps explain the ineradicable persistence of memories through time; later on I will make a case
for the scenic quality of the key scene of the Joseph story as an
explanation for its power. Meanwhile, *narrative*, far from being
an opposite qualification, complements the scenic with a range of
events and characters that make the scenic memory articulate in
the first place.

Assmann rejects the term *social memory*, through which Mau-
rice Halbwach inaugurated collective memory studies in the social sciences in the 1920s, "because individual memory is always
social to a high degree, just like language and consciousness in
general. A strictly individual memory would be something like a
private language that is only understood by one person" (Assman
2006a, 3). Instead, Jan and Aleida Assmann have proposed the
term *communicative memory* to indicate the social aspect of individual memory. Such memory "grows out of intercourse between
people, and the emotions play a crucial role in its process. Love,
interest, sympathy, feelings of guilt and shame—all of these help
to define our memories and provide them with a horizon. Without such definition they would not imprint themselves on our
minds; without a horizon they would lack relevance and meaning
within a specific cultural context" (2006a, 3). Assmann concludes
on the same page: "Only emotionally cathected forms of communication bring structure, perspective, relevance, definition, and
horizon into memory."

Nietzsche, Assmann's source of inspiration here, has argued that one of the functions of memory is helping people form bonds. Indeed the cohesion of groups depends on it. Nietzsche explains this thesis in reference to implied promises contained in shared memories. To the extent that the bonds that have been established promote responsibility and reliability, the philosopher grounds his concept of morality in these promises. This is how the human being in culture is made predictable: he will remember what he promised. Nietzsche attributes this reliability to acts of will. I am more focused on acts of obedience, of collusion, of halfway accepting the invitations Rosello wrote about, accepting them with reluctance. What Assmann's view foregrounds in this context is the possibility that the cultural production of shared memories stabilizes group identities and "a point of view that span[s] several generations" (2006a, 11).

For Assmann, religion is just such a form of shared remembering. This view makes my case against the anxious claims that the "why questions"—the alleged oddities—are in the text. I contend that these questions are nowhere but emerge, as a promise, from the cultural memories that make us "remember" to raise them. Returning to Kugel, then, I would like to propose a reading that qualifies the text-as-anchor with my memories and my memories with the texts—plural. Instead of relying exclusively on scholarly skills and bodies of knowledge, I seek to establish a dialogue in which my memories are as seriously involved as the memories that, I presume, have filtered into the most scholarly of exegeses. How can I be so bold?

Well, look again at Kugel's formulations, now through the lens of Assmann's concept of cultural memory. Bringing out "all possible nuances" suggests an openness that, if it is to be comprehensive, must be hospitable enough to accommodate my personal nuances as well. The word *implied* begs the question of the source of the authority that proclaims a question to be relevant. This authority belongs, in the present, to professionals such as priests, rabbis, imams, and the schoolmistresses doing their bidding. It belongs also, in the past, to the texts that result from processes of canonization. This is how personal memories fit into cultural memory: the figures of authority in the present draw on the authority of the past processes of canonization. They derive their present authority from the resulting canon, while the past is given ongoing, hence present, relevance by their compliance with what they take to be immutable truths.

The authority of the canon is just as difficult to dismiss as that of the text. As I will argue in the final chapters of this book, I don't wish to dismiss it but to understand the way it works, not to undermine but to delimit its power over the present. Further, the phrase "in the precise wording of each and every sentence" suggests a philological desire that I share, but it is also invoked to circumvent the question of relevance and *its* anchoring in interests. I will begin to examine this issue in chapter 2. The tension between literalism and fundamentalism, the recurrent theoretical theme in this book, will be more fully explicated there.

To anticipate this work: The grounding of Kugel's confidence in the textual basis for exegesis is his formalism expressed in the words "an unusual word, an apparently unnecessary repetition, an unusual grammatical form." Yet in his own formulation I find the reasons to take my small-girl memories seriously and consider them relevant for an understanding of the story. Sure, words, repetitions, and grammatical form are textual features. However, "unnecessary" and "unusual" are judgments derived from habits—cultural, collective, informing personal ones—in relation to which words, repetitions, and forms are unusual or unnecessary. These habits are important in Kugel's standards but then are glossed over in his methodological reflection. In contrast, I put them at the center of this study.

According to this wording, the issue of the questions attributed to the text belongs to the realm of aesthetics, at least according to my conception of that domain. For me, the term *aesthetics* suggests a connection to the senses, through which the object "binds" itself to the reader. In a story whose themes concern a strong sensual appeal, this old and broad definition of aesthetics is quite suitable. For it suggests that one way to read the story is to consider Joseph, the figure who is constantly extolled for his beauty, as an aesthetic object. Such a framing of the character is easier to understand through a consideration of visual art that retells the story in its own medium—through line, color, and composition. This, at least, is what I have been led to do. Although the memories attached to my interest in Rembrandt's works around this

delimit

story are more specific than that, it is against the background of an aesthetic of the senses that the story gains much of its thrill. On the condition that this binding be complicated by the fantasy aspect of all aesthetic experience, as I will argue in chapter 3.

That fantasy aspect lies at the heart of another experience of rereading that left an indelible memory of surprise. At a much later moment I was led, by my reading of a modern novel about the Joseph material, to look up what the Qur'anic story had to tell. It was astoundingly different, so much so that in a resulting publication I claimed that, far from being a version of the same story, this was an altogether different one. In terms of historiography, the move to look at the Qur'an to see where Thomas Mann had gotten his material was profoundly *preposterous*, in a double sense. This term, which I have developed at some length elsewhere (1999), indicates a literal turning upside down of the order of time: pre- becomes post- and vice versa. Any exegesis, then, is pre-posterous by definition, and no appeal to the "original text" can change that. Qua text, the Qur'an postdates the biblical text, and modernist literature cannot but anachronistically distort any reading of either text that one might venture to perform. Granted. More than granted: foregrounded. As I will argue, this preposterousness is necessary as an antidote against the infusion in the alleged textual basis of exegesis of other people's memories, just as personal, unexamined, and "doxic" as mine.[1]

My schoolteacher was convincing and had such lasting influence because she was gentle and seemed to speak from her heart. Obviously, she was also simply transmitting a version of the story she had been told and had remembered, because she was a Catholic too and hence didn't read the Bible. Even if she had, she would have read it with her interpretation framing her reading *beforehand*. Cultural memories such as this one predate any

1. Footnotes in this book will be sparse and always keyed to the end of paragraphs. I will limit footnotes to either a further explanation of terms or the framing of an idea with references for those who wish to pursue it further. *Preposterous* is the term I have introduced in a book-length study for the willful and thoughtful deployment of anachronism in the interpretation of historical artifacts (Bal 1999). The idea is to draw attention to the productive potential of asserting the interpreter's position in the present as an entrance into understanding the past insofar as it is relevant for the present.

reading. For this reason, they are the heart of what I just called, apropos of Mann, a "preposterous" view of the past.

The collective cultural nature of such unimportant little memories as the one of that afternoon in primary school makes me want to declare cultural memory itself a text, with the same right and with the same status—dubious, polymorphic, interested—as the texts proper. Not my personal memory, mind you, but the collective memories that, diffuse and ungraspable, make themselves known in such personal experiences. The schoolmistress's as much as mine; her parents and mine, her advisers in school and church as much as mine. This is my starting point, always up for dispute of course, but relevant nevertheless. What "the text" is remains elusive in this approach, but the gain is that reading becomes more diverse, yet not subjective in the individualistic sense. The corpus I have composed, although not at all comprehensive, allows me to set "versions" in relation to one another as mutually illuminating rather than competitive.

Once this earliest of my consciously retrievable memories of a love story is given its rightful place, it is time to engage Kugel's position—a predominant and scholarly one—and acknowledge the textuality of my "sources." I have six major and some minor ones I wish to confront with one another. The biblical text of Genesis 39, the relevant passages of Thomas Mann's novel from 1932, and the Qur'anic story of 12:24–35 mark the successive stages of my incorporation of the story I read, and therefore I cite them in that order. But this is only half the truth. Sometime before, during, and after these readings I saw depictions of the key scene of the story, of which a small etching by Rembrandt is the first I remember, while two of his paintings came a bit later. Numerous other paintings followed, but I prefer to limit myself to these three images. Conversations, whether casual and incidental or goal-oriented, with various people who also had their own memories of the story to contribute were just as crucial to shape the view of the intertextuality of Joseph-and-Potiphar's-wife I am laying out in this book. I will not trace too many details of this muddled "influence" but will do some tracing only when it is theoretically relevant.

This relevance does not lie in the truth of the interpretation but in the process of interpretation itself. This process is framed by, while also an instance of, canonization. The fact that we are dealing with at least four canonical traditions concerns me most of all. For the sheer number of traditions that are intertwined here calls into question the concept of canon along with that of interpretation. It also complicates the view of cultural memory as Assmann's book represents it. While I am interested in showing the adventures of reading in the encounter between different "versions," I am keener still to demonstrate how each reading, even confined to one person's lifetime and framed by her scholarly training and lack of it, of necessity revisits and transforms the earlier ones.

Thus the outcome, if any, of my itinerary is self-reflection. Again, the reflection I propose as an inevitable key to cultural analysis in the present is not a reflection of and on me as an individual but on my activity as a scholar and writer within a culture that is plural. Not only is my culture—say, Western Europe—composed of an enormous number of different traditions, including religious ones, but it is also constantly being reshuffled into categories whose importance shifts with issues and situations. Sometimes age is more important than gender; sometimes class overrules all other groupings. At the present moment, religion, always politically inflected, is gaining renewed prominence as a tool for group formation. But never, in no situation, is that culture homogeneous. Reflection hence occurs along with other activities, as one among many. It holds me responsible for my own errors, indebts me to others for my insights. And ultimately it leaves me both alone and surrounded, framed, by the murmurings of the discourses of others. This makes "me" a porous subject, both temporally, in relation to the child who first experienced this story, and socially, in the sense that I was, and am, not alone with that experience. I will elaborate on this porousness in chapter 3, devoted to the great but frequently underestimated importance of *fantasy*.

Only after discussing the two extremes of literal words (chapter 2) and fantasy (chapter 3) will I feel comfortable analyzing what was for me the maddest, wildest instance of this tale's cultural life: Rembrandt's etching. On the one hand, I use this image to discuss form. That is, I will analyze how visual images can also be held to their "words," their detailed form. On the other hand, that form, without producing a particular fantasy, solicits the production of fantasy. In this case it does so by means of a fantastic ambiguity. *Ambiguity*, then, is the topic central to chapter 4.

The possibility of mobilizing words and forms for the production of fantasies is predicated upon an aspect that is also at the heart of the cultural nature of memory. This is the issue of *identification*. I will first discuss Thomas Mann's narrative expansion of a single verse of the Qur'an to establish the connections between words and forms, which at first sight appear too distinct. Then, in chapter 6, I will stop to consider what that single verse in the Qur'an does to me, how it changes the story compared to what my memory had told me it "meant." The difference goes beyond the textual and theoretical topics discussed so far. My discussion of the Qur'an verse ends in a specifically Qur'anic version of semiotic theory, the theory of *signs*. This result will help me to overcome a sense of competition between the versions.

This semiotics, while derived from the Qur'an, need not be confined to a Qur'anic specificity. That would turn it into an exotic conception of signs alien to the Western sensibility. Instead, I consider the understanding of this semiotic conception a moment of intercultural learning. Hence the point of reading across the four different canons is to interact without merging, to develop a sensibility to cultural difference that avoids reifying difference as much as imposing assimilation. The Qur'anic semiotics is the tool to break open the enigmatic nature of two paintings by Rembrandt in chapter 7. For a long time I have been looking at these paintings with some intensity and always found one more appealing than the other. Invoking Qur'anic semiotics, I am now better able to read each of these paintings in their own right, on their own terms.

But this outcome may give the wrong impression: that a point of view that combines cultural memory with philology ends up in a wildly subjectivist mode of interpretation. This impression would be wrong; I argue instead that these processes of enlivening the artifacts at the expense of their cultural stability are framed and enabled by claims to the truth, equally culturally framed, in their rhetoric and their contents alike. The final three chapters each deal with an aspect of this truth claim, or as I call it, *truth speak*.

First, in chapter 8, I will unpack the rhetoric of Mann's metacritical commentary on his own fabulations, or, as I should say in the context of a reflection on shared memories, *con-fabulations*. Mann neither reiterates myths as he knows them nor invents the stories. Rather, he turns them into fictions that are fabulous. He does this *with*, as the prefix *con-* indicates, the fictions that the multiple cultures through which he read had already produced before him. This rhetoric encompasses vastly different claims to truth. One of these is, of course, the rhetoric of truth itself, which I consider an instance of *realism*.

The question of the texts' status as the truth in their respective traditions inevitably leads to a discussion of canonicity, the process of canonization, and the authorities involved. This is the subject of chapter 9. In the face of so many canonical artifacts, no claim to higher canonicity can be accepted for any of them. But, I argue, the issue of canon does not lie in such a competition. Nor can it be dismissed with an appeal to cultural relativism, that all-too-easy refusal to think through what others think. Instead, the canon is, as its etymology suggests, a measuring stick along which every one of us must judge. Not too fast, and not lightly, because judgments have a real influence on the lives of those we judge. But judge we must nevertheless, for the sake of ourselves, if we are to extract from our readings even a tiny grain of wisdom. The texts of the various canons—religious, literary, artistic—that make up pluralized public culture can be taken seriously only, I argue, when taken together, in dialogue. Only then can they exceed their canonical fixity and come to life again, even if that life plays itself out against the setting of a particular centripetal canon.

But unfixing canons is not so easy. For their authority defeats attempts to liquefy their borders. In chapter 10 the nature of authority itself is up for scrutiny. Only if we are willing to analyze and understand authority can we accept chosen forms of authority, in order to live by them. At the heart of authority lies a tenacious belief in what we call, perhaps too easily and too polemically, "patriarchy." While sharing the critique of this all-too-handy term—especially in its tendency to blame Judaism and Islam for all that is wrong in the ways past and present cultures deal with gender, and its lumping together of widely divergent social structures—I keep the term here, in scare quotes, to foreground the still-rampant power of fathers and father-figures, metaphors of fatherhood, and authority itself as "fatherly." The automatic authority of fathers—and one look at the registers of names of the leaders of the world makes it difficult to deny that this authority is indeed automatic—is grounded in misconceptions concerning procreation and is extremely hurtful. Ultimately the story of Joseph and Potiphar's wife is framed by attempts to affirm that authority. But, as I also demonstrate, this frame is nevertheless undermined, or at least challenged, by the slightly liquefied state of this authority. To make these arguments I will revisit earlier publications, all somewhat locked into disciplinary scholarship. My earliest publication on the story is in a book of art historical reflection, *Reading "Rembrandt"* (2006 [1991]). I will rearticulate those arguments in a more accessible manner. The later self-critique of this piece, recently published (Bal 2006a), will help me shift the focus from the issue of canon to a larger issue of culture. Together, these sources sustain, but do not confine, the essay offered here. This book is an essay in the literal sense: an attempt. I aim to explore concepts that I find particularly helpful in the understanding of classical, overly known, and thus doxically misread or unread cultural artifacts. It is an essay in methodology, but one that, in line with some of my earlier work (esp. 2002) seeks to establish in concepts the standards no longer self-evidently anchored in specific disciplinary knowledge.

As with other issues, it sometimes happen that I feel I need to be more explicit about my own position. This is the case here concerning my relationship to religion. Having been brought up a Catholic, I have declined further participation in that or any religious culture. I didn't care for the institutionalized power, the authority on which the invitation to be a reluctant guest—to reiterate Rosello's terms—was based. Since then, I have become more aware of the cultural importance of religion for many people with whom I interact. This awareness has increased the urgency to think through what religion can mean. It can be seen as a form of binding, a social effect that connects people to one another and their private lives to the cultural environment. This brings me back to Nietzsche and his conception of cultural memory. It also brings me back to a certain conception of aesthetics, also conceived as binding. Religion is not aesthetics, but it does have an aesthetic dimension. The primary difference is that in religion, the bond is based on the assumption of a prescriptive deity or deities; in aesthetics, on an object. Moreover, in religion, the senses are often put under suspicion; in aesthetics, they are central. These are major differences. But then, when I think of the Qur'anic semiotics that keeps the sign unsplit, I can see how the fields in which this essay is anchored have more in common than I had realized.

As I just mentioned, all three concern a form of binding. Aesthetic binds the subject to the aesthetic object through the senses. This appears to be an individual experience, although it is impossible outside of a social frame offering the objects and the terms of the experience. Semiotics presupposes a social framework within which communication by means of signs is possible. This is a crucial form of binding—one without which human life cannot be sustained. With religion, the binding occurs among members of the group that share the religion but also between the individual and the deity he or she feels connected with. Thus, if I may be forgiven the simplification, while aesthetics and semiotics concern primarily horizontal relationships, in religion the bond is both horizontal and vertical. Here the trick is to realize the need for the horizontal bond, not only to form a group of "selves" as distinct from "others" but also to counterbalance too strong a vertical bond. The trick, to put it bluntly, is to unbind, so to speak, the notion of binding from the *akedah*, the binding of Isaac about to be killed by his father.

This father had to submit so totally to the vertical relationship that he was willing to sacrifice what defined him as a father. It is rarely noted that horizontally he had already done that when, on the instigation of his wife Sarah, he had cast out his firstborn son, Ishmael, and the lad's mother, Hagar. Ishmael made it, and is said to have become the father of the Arabs. Then, vertically, God asked Abraham to prove his faith by sacrificing his "only" son—"the one you love." This figure Abraham is supposed to be the model of religious life. This model has a lot to account for. I consider this ideology of sacrifice the utmost illusion of a subject desirous, above all else, to be alone—a subject in fear of binding. What these three fields help us reflect on, instead, is the kind of subjectivity we wish to live by: either an autonomous one, fearful of dependence on others and invested in authority as a way of safeguarding an autonomy one knows to be untenable, or a porous one that accommodates others as part of the self, or others as models, spectacles, masks of the self. The three theoretical domains most

1ˢᵗ born

2ⁿᵈ born

prominent in this essay—semiotics, aesthetics, and the study of religion—attempt to grasp the modalities of that porousness.

The three conceptions of semiotics, aesthetics, and religion that emerge from these reflections join in a cultural field that, paradoxically perhaps, I can only indicate as a form of "abstraction." By this word I do not mean the opposite of figuration, for stories like the one central here are nothing if not figurative. Abstraction, instead, is a field of possibility, delimited by a threshold below which no form has yet emerged, hence no meaning is yet being produced. This leaves the field wide open for all manner of meaning production. Abstraction, then, is the *potential* of new forms, hence of new meanings, not the existence of them.

The French psychoanalyst Jean-Martin Charcot, Freud's master, is rumored to have said that for years he just walked through the wards of the hospital La Salpétrière, seeing only what he had been taught to see (Balmary 1999, 19). It was giving up this disciplined eye that allowed him to make the discoveries he did. In turn, these discoveries opened the way to psychoanalysis. But both Charcot and Freud also learned to open their eyes because the cultural moment they lived in was getting ready for such opening. It wasn't quite yet, which is why these doctors were able to invent such innovative ideas. But without the cultural moment allowing it, they both would have succumbed to the pressure of the kinds of ideological belief that constituted their livelihood. In this respect, psychoanalysis as a paradigm has come to stand for the openness that was halfway in the air. If today this is no longer true of the practice of that discipline, this can be attributed to the institutionalization and unquestioned authority that are the price to pay for canonization.

That non- or anti-discipline may have become a discipline in the strict sense, with its own rather closed training program and societies, but at first it was a lesson in seeing, including in the biblical sense: seeing what we have *not* been taught, as an entrance to insight. A seeing that allows surprises. This lesson of psychoanalysis is stronger, more productive, than any disciplinary closure can allow. As French psychoanalyst Marie Balmary keeps reiterating, Freud taught us to turn against him—the Freud of surprised seeing showed us how to see, to read, his own writings as, inevitably, also caught by his time. This is why it seems imperative to me to balance surprise with what has become "cultural memory"—the acknowledgment and study of the way memories can be shared, including across generations. Including, also, across cultures and their respective canons. From these two directives I will retain the strengths of each and try to avoid the pitfalls: opening myself up to surprises while remaining aware of the memories that inform them as well. Or, conversely, I take memory seriously as a treasure of knowledge without letting it predetermine what to see and how to think. I wish, then, to be a reluctant witness to memories, my own and those of others.

2

Falling in Love: Stumbling Words

Le discours amoureux est aujourd'hui *d'une extrême solitude.* Ce discours est peut-être parlé par des milliers de sujets . . . mais il n'est soutenu par personne.

ROLAND BARTHES

Love, it is said, is a kind of falling. How did sex enter the story for that girl ignorant of such matters? What turns the story of lying and wicked trapping into a story of sex is that strange sensation on which it is based that today we call "falling in love." The notion, apparent at my first rereading of the story, that the woman known as Potiphar's wife falls in love with Joseph makes her acts sexual in nature. The metaphor demands a literal reading. Didier Maleuvre writes: "To fall is to experience the pull of physical reality—the law of gravity, matter, weight, bodily existence. A person who falls is caught in the thingness of her body and surroundings" (2005, 82).

The phrase "falling in love" occurs in many Western languages, yet it is by no means universal. It does not occur in any of my sources. Nor, I hasten to add, did I know it when the story came my way in school. The phrase is romantic,

representing love—also, but not exclusively, another word for sexual attraction—as something sudden, an event beyond the control
of the lover. It is also contemporary, Western, anchored in a long
tradition, ranging at the very least from antisex courtly love through
romantic idealization of passion to contemporary media imagery. It
is also, in some ways, gendered. Even though the suddenness implied is not gender specific, and while both men and women use the
phrase and experience what it purports to describe, the suggested
weakness, dependency, and powerlessness link up with ideas about
femininity as weakness and women as the weaker sex.

Falling in love, being in love, is easier to describe, or at least
invoke, than falling out of love. The verb *falling* is more suitable
to express the former event than the latter, which is most frequently not an event but a long process of wear and tear. Falling
in love, by contrast, happens all of a sudden. And when knees feel
like jelly and throats run dry, the accident-prone human individual can easily experience that sensation as "falling." The phrase
makes sense, and this reinforces its use as if it were an ordinary,
some would say literal, word. "Where do we fall when we fall in
love?" asks psychoanalyst Elisabeth Young-Bruehl (2003). That is
the question, at least for this chapter. At stake is the use of words.
Focusing on what I call here "stumbling words" in analogy to the
etymological sense of scandal as stumbling block or stone, I begin
to stage words and metaphors that must be neither neglected nor
turned into laws of meaning making.

"Love" is not only a key issue in interhuman, intersubjective
relationships. It is also at the heart of what such cultural dwelling places as "art" have to offer. Maleuvre has tersely formulated
the function of art in an article the title of which, "Art and the
Teaching of Love," despite its Platonic overtones, suggests a fitting epigraph to the present essay:

> Art is primarily, not a subjectivity giving shape to a private vision,
> but a form of sanctifying the human conversation, that is, the
> *encounter* between subjectivities. (2005, 77)

The relationship between art and love underlies the story I am
considering in more ways than one. The primary form this re-

lationship takes, however, is the seriousness, yet elusiveness, of words. I have often thought that the success of Roland Barthes' *Fragments d'un discours amoureux* (1977) was due to the banality of its insights, combined with their almost shocking clarity. The breathtaking sight of the person, the slightly depressing but also exciting waiting for the telephone that fails to ring, the endless pondering over what to do, wear, or say, it is all so utterly familiar. That the author who, in his seminal book *S/Z* (1974), renewed our awareness of cultural clichés and their narrative structure should go on to refresh our somewhat worn knowledge of the beginning of erotic interest—to use yet another phrase for it—does seem appropriate.

Barthes began his book with the statement that the discourse of love, or sexual passion, is not "supported" (*soutenu*). Instead it is mocked, depreciated, or ignored. The memory of the story I have been invoking proves him right. Without even knowing it was "about" sex—hence ignoring it—I knew it had to be depreciated and mocked. Thus Barthes' book is both banal—addressing a discourse spoken by thousands (I'd say by millions) and yet not taken seriously—and exceptional, to the extent that he does justice to that discourse. In so doing he unwittingly vindicates the main character of the Joseph story. He also integrates the point of seeing-with-surprise and being embedded in cultural memory when he writes a book on the most banal discourse around and makes it strange, surprising, and exciting. Moreover, his book is called *Fragments*. This title, unfortunately not retained in the English translation, suits me as a model. What I like to think about the present essay is that it consists, also, of fragments. Combining insights and associations borne by surprise with recollections borne by cultural memory, I collect fragments of different "versions" without pretending to make them cohere. I bring concepts from cultural analysis to bear on those fragments. In this chapter, the question of "love," straddling the personal and the cultural, the private and the political, will be the starting point for a reflection on issues of text, image, signs, and meaning developed in the later chapters.

Barthes has no entry on falling in love, because his book begins when that fall has already taken place. This chapter, by contrast, reverts to that early moment when the subject loses power over

his or her self because he or she falls. I find the verb *falling* relevant for our encounter with the woman who suffered such an
accident. Not that the word occurs there, but perhaps "preposterously," I contend that it should have. It most certainly relates to
what has become known as the story of the Fall, the first transgression that cost humanity its unrealistic dreams of grandeur,
immortality, and celestial bliss.

Many interpretations of this most commonplace or, in relation
to dogma, most "doxic" story of all blame the fall on the woman
who could not refrain from "eating" (say, consuming) the fruit
(say, enjoyment) offered by the phallic serpent (say, sex). I see both
the act and its consequences in more positive terms, as a canny
endorsement of the inevitable human condition, with ineluctable
death and the potential for pleasure and procreation as a consola-
tion (Bal 1987). I will not reiterate that argument here. What is
relevant, though, is that the story that goes by this title and by this
doxic negative interpretation is always already present in people's
memories when "falling in love" is mentioned or takes place. In
other words, a negative connotation lurks even in the most blissful
accounts. And that negativity, I contend, is connected to the gendered aspect of the weakness the verb intimates.

When we fall in love, we fall into dependency, narrow-minded
obsession, and the bleak feeling of insufficiency, of falling short
(to use another fall-phrase) of the standard of our love object.
This has been explored in a rich field in psychology (see Young-
Bruehl 2003; Doi 1973; Fisher 1992). Psychology, just like falling
in love as a concept, is a historically specific domain. I will refrain
from invoking it to understand the feelings of an ancient character. Nevertheless, this field, and the contemporary conceptions it
works with and takes for granted, casts its shadow on our readings
of the stories in which such characters act and appear to "feel." I
will, therefore, resist it. Instead I first focus on words and the way
these linguistic, semiotic units work to bridge the gap the time of
history has dug between these characters and "us."

For words work. Taking words seriously is the primary task of
literary criticism. French novelist Marguerite Duras tends to take
words at their word, so to speak (Biezenbos 1995). A man who
comes to cut off water supplies to people who have outstanding
bills is held to the verb-derived noun that indicates his profes-

sion, *coupeur-d'eau*. In the story of that title in *La vie matérielle*, Duras makes the most of the idea that metaphors and the literal use of words cannot be distinguished (1987). Indeed, she uses the exceedingly literal sense of the word that indicates the man's profession when the woman, no longer able to drink after the water has been cut off in her flat, exposes herself to having her throat cut by a train. The verb *couper*, this episode tells us, indicates a measure of violence. Cutting off comes close to cutting, for example someone's throat, when this woman the *coupeur* visits does end up dead by suicide. Duras also elaborates the metaphorical verb *falling* and takes it literally. In *Le vice-consul* she uses it in connection with a tragic pregnancy. The young girl who ends up a mad beggar had "tombée enceinte, d'un arbre, très haut, sans se faire du mal, tombée enceinte" (fallen pregnant, from a tree, very tall, without hurting herself, fallen pregnant; Duras 1965, 20).

The "literalization" of the metaphor is foregrounded here. Accumulated exaggeration draws attention to it. To "fall pregnant" is just a French phrase, but "from a tree" makes it literal. The height of the tree and the notion that the girl didn't hurt herself add *couleur littérale*—literalizing flavor. In this tendency, Duras has inherited the classical French tradition led by Jean Racine, who explored in great detail the implications of the clichéd metaphor *feu*, fire, for love. In his masterpiece *Phèdre* from 1677, the passion for her stepson "really" consumes the main character, as a real fire would do. These metaphorical words are important instances of dead metaphors' second lives, a renewed chance at literary striking force with which their *literal* use infuses them. I find attention to such words a good guide to the contestation that defines live culture, or cultural life. Taking words seriously is the only way to counter a rather general tendency of ideological manipulation or, more innocently, "linguaphobic" haste to lump together different stories as "versions" of the same one. Such a reading attitude, I will argue below, is also the best antidote to fundamentalist readings. In the kind of literalism I am seeking to advocate, the signifier is taken seriously, not only for the nuances or shades it puts forward, and to which I recommend remaining attentive across cultural time and place, but also as mobile, shifting and slipping along, yet stable in its "letter." In contrast, "fundamentalism" neglects the signifier's primacy and takes an arbitrarily fixed signified as law.[1]

The example of *Phèdre* can demonstrate the importance of literalism. This woman's unfortunate adventure appears to be one "version" of our story, at least if we are to believe scholars of folklore who usefully open our eyes to affiliated stories with (vaguely) similar plots, connecting fairy tales of wicked stepmothers with stories from religious and literary canons about women in parental positions. In spite of the obvious differences between stepmothers and adoptive mothers, the similarity is assumed, fixed, and considered primary.

In themselves, such generalizations are useful for two reasons. First, they remind us of those dormant memories that have set us up to become who we are—see the preceding chapter. Second, seeing *Phèdre* as a version of the Joseph story is useful because it demonstrates the cultural importance of such memories across two classical dividing lines. Such memories work between religious traditions as well as between religious and secular ones, or high-cultural and popular-cultural ones.

Yet this thinking in versions is also problematic if the acts performed to do these things remain unexamined. For our case, the generalization must be examined when it moves a little too easily from the master/mistress love relationship, as in Potiphar's case, to family relationships, as in Phèdre's case. After all, a slave or servant is not identical in structural function to a stepson. To remedy this problem while taking advantage of the useful aspects of such folklore studies, taking words "literally," even without believing that the opposition between *literal* and *metaphorical* holds, engages that thinking in versions critically. That is, in the context of thinking in versions I will think of words as "literally" motivated metaphors.

1. With the concepts of literalism and fundamentalism I am trying to respond to two problems in the interpretation of the kind of culturally remote artifacts under scrutiny here. One is the facile dismissal of textual detail with the argument of copyist errors (texts) or later additions (visual images). Literalism is meant to safeguard the integrity of the artifacts as they have survived their migration. The other, opposite problem is rigid adherence to allegedly original formulations and their equally rigidly preserved meanings, often even acted upon as if they were referents, so that art became law. This definition of fundamentalism is exceedingly succinct. I will have more to say on fundamentalism toward the end of chapter 3.

One example out of a flurry makes this clear: "The universal story of the Chaste Youth and the Lustful Stepmother is best known to Western readers in the biblical account of Joseph's temptation by the wife of Potiphar and in the Greek myth (later embodied in drama) about Hyppolytus and Phaedra" (Yohannan 1982). The universality of the story is declared not argued. And once this declaration has passed, it seems obvious that Euripides, Racine, and our texts and images are "really" talking about the same story. Surely Racine's Phèdre's famous confession, first to her attendant Oenone, then to Hyppolite himself, would even justify the sense of falling. Phèdre's fantasized sojourn in the labyrinth infuses the story of her love's beginning with an underworld, perhaps to be read as an underbelly. But the verb *falling* does not occur. Nor does it in our three textual "versions."

The naming of the stories together, as a set, is further substantiated performatively in the writing of the critic, who capitalizes roles and thus turns them into proper names: Chaste Youth, Lustful Stepmother. The tender age of the man earlier said to be seventeen years when his adventure started, is not really mentioned, and given his long and intricate previous adventures, it is not so obvious either. Chaste, well, yes, that's the point. Sometimes, though, the chastity is simply interest in another woman, as in Racine's tragedy, where Phèdre's fury is unleashed by jealousy when it turns out Hyppolite is himself also in love, forbidden as it is by his father. From this I learn one important thing: the culture of chastity is not universal.

The stepmother element, inevitably roaming around somewhere in the afterlife of the story, is hardly appropriate for the story of a mistress putting upon a slave. Except, of course, when we consider the sense in which domesticity is the backdrop of the drama. The young man was a house slave. He not only had access to the privacy of the woman but could also be put in danger in that private realm. The house, not the kinship relation—the second sense of the noun *house*—will have to be retained for further literalizing scrutiny. The insistence on the house as the site of the power structure in which the adventure is set throws a thin thread to what later histories of imperialism have taught us. It is in the domestic sphere that slavery and colonial subjection produced the contradictions of relationship. It is the site of intimacy in inequality (Stoler 2002).

With these thoughts in mind, let me look at the words of the story that initiate the woman's love. Both to do justice to these words and to suggest why certain wordings have caused translators as well as exegetes to fill in what they considered ambiguous or elliptic, I translate as literally as I possibly can, with the help of my friends. Please bear with me when translations are awkward; I attempt to literalize in order to denaturalize smooth translation, and thus defundamentalize the text.

I don't recall the words of my teacher but it is safe to assume none of these explicitly referred to love. The Genesis text uses words that might also contain a stock phrase, but it goes in the opposite direction:

> And it came to pass after these things/words and lifted the
> woman of his master her eyes upon Joseph and she said, lie
> with me. And he refused himself and said to the woman of his
> master . . . (39:7–8)

To lift up one's eyes upon: this appears to be what Western modern culture would call falling in love. I wish to literalize the phrase. Taken at face value, the phrase suggests three important ideas. First, it suggests seriously looking someone in the face, becoming aware of what someone looks like, and liking, feeling attracted to, what one sees. Instead of falling into endless moral misery, the expression simply states that looking takes this risk of attraction. Moreover, and second, the phrase implies that the sense of sight entails distance, but it may also solicit a touch that nullifies these distances. Hence, a look can generate adventures and narratives of adventures. It can also generate emotions followed by actions. Third, the phrase presents falling in love as an act of elevation—of the eyes—that may also imply elevation of the one looking, who through this act becomes a subject, or reconfirms her subjectivity. Hence looking can make art, and thus inflect or even create reality; as Maleuvre puts it, "The aim of art is not art. Its destination is elsewhere; its aim is reality encountered and lived with" (2005, 77).

Refraining as much as I can from filling in what is not made explicit, I keep the word *woman* and do not use the more common *wife*. Not to put too fine a point on it, I do wish to keep in mind anthropological variation and consider what kinds of relationships go by the marital term *wife*—a special word not extant in the Hebrew.

For today's readers, the word *wife* conjures up marriage in the sense in which contemporary Western habits of living have set up the socioeconomic organization of procreation. This sense of marriage, with its romantic justification, cannot be simply adopted for our story. The possessive adjective *his* indicates property, and soon Joseph will speak to the issue of property in justifying his refusal. But mainly, the indication of sex in *woman* is relevant here, whatever the structures of affiliation and property might have been, or might have been seen as valid. It is in her capacity of woman belonging to Joseph's master that she braves her condition and lifts her eyes upon him. It is as this woman that he turns her down.[2]

Seeing, in the Hebrew Bible, is a strong and frequent verb. *See* or *behold* (*hinneh*) is often used to introduce a new fact. It has epistemological meaning. To see is to know—and we all know what knowing can amount to in biblical parlance. I like to think of the phrase used here as an elevation, not only of the woman's eyes to Joseph's face but also of her as a subject to a status not reducible to being someone's property. Whatever her domestic status and life, and whatever else the phrase implies, she *is able to see*. And *seeing*, although it is not equivalent to a (forbidden) biblical knowing, attributes to this woman a status of full subjectivity, capable of knowing. The speech act of the command—"lie with me"—fits this status.

This moment of recognition of the woman's subjectivity, then, must be the moment of naming. Indeed, in the older versions she remains nameless, Potiphar's property. Like many others, Kugel calls her, without a trace of irony at this anachronism, Mrs. Potiphar, with a frequency that suggests insistence. I remember I also called her by that name when feminist friends and I discussed this text. But for us it was a nickname, tongue in cheek, meant to foreground rather than naturalize the projections we tend to put onto the story from this side of the Romantic period. In an account of a class taught about the story, Athalya Brenner and

2. For a range of anthropological approaches to the Bible, see Lang 1985. I have contested the translation of *isha* as "wife" at length elsewhere (1988a).

Jan-Willem van Henten call her "Madame Potiphar" and discuss
the name issue explicitly (1998). Brenner goes even further in a
witty book that tells stories of biblical women in the first person,
simply speaking with the woman's "I" (2005). Alice Bach adopts
Mann's name Mut-em-enet (1997). All these texts perform the
act of naming in acknowledgment of the woman's love.

Since she acts here as "woman"—with the word for "wife,"
as in "wife of," being the same as "woman," as in human person
of the female sex/gender, no matter the relationship—I too must
name her. Elsewhere I have named nameless biblical women in
the book of Judges with nouns that characterize their stories. One
of them I named Beth, since her house was the place that trapped
her. This makes that obvious name unavailable for our woman.
In addition, such a name would be unfitting, since it is a Hebrew
word and the woman, as far as we know, is Egyptian. This also
makes the name by which she goes in some later versions, Zu-
leikha, less appropriate. Moreover, that name is too much filled
with negative connotations poured in by these traditions. And it
is an Arabic name, which makes it anachronistic as well. Instead
I go for the name that is both an attempt at adapting the name
to the *Sitz im Leben* and a blatantly preposterous one: Mut-em-
enet, the name given her by Thomas Mann.

This name sounds Egyptian in a way tourists would imagine it, it sounds ancient in a way viewers of Hollywood movies
about pharaohs and pyramids have come to expect it, and it can
be shortened to Mut, as Mann does. Mut is close to the word for
death in Hebrew, *mot* (Koelb 1978). Mann never said he meant
the name to allude to its Hebrew meaning (Kenney 1983). Nor is
there any reason to project this association into the biblical story,
where death is not an issue.

Instead, expressing sexual attraction to men, declaring love,
requires courage. For such frankness does not become women, I
learned while growing up between my two memories of the story.
I have transgressed that rule, but always in keen awareness that
it was a transgression. And I vividly remember the fear—of rejection, of ridicule—and then the courage it took to proposition
nevertheless. In German, *Mut* means courage, and it resonates
with *Mutti*, the familiar term for mother. Not only was Thomas
Mann German but he also wrote his long cycle on Joseph, the

Hebrew hero of turbulence, foreignness, and unsettlement in German, for a German audience, at a historical moment of great precariousness, when courage could and often did entail death. I adopt the short version of the name he chose to honor his dare. So from now on, and in full acknowledgment of the preposterousness of such a speech act, I will refer to this woman as Mut.

The second phrase that is somewhat ambiguous in the story is the one denoting Joseph's response, "he refused himself." Many interpretations easily shift from the meaning that he simply refused to "give himself" to the notion that he was tempted. To be sure, if he is to be a model of chastity, the embodiment of the seventh commandment, he needs to have at least a challenge, a test to pass. This is plausible only if a lesser mortal would have fallen for the temptation. Hence it is easy to see why refusing his body, his person, shifts to refusing his inclination, seduction, temptation. This is one of those instances in which sexual feelings just slip in.

Like many others, my *compagnon de route* Kugel finds the notion that Joseph is tempted so natural that he doesn't stop to consider how it got there. And the same holds for many of the exegetes he cites. So many assume this, in fact, that it would sound pedantic to question it. I don't wish to question it; I find it plausible enough. I just wish to denaturalize a seeming self-evidence from logical deduction to readerly import. Instead of taking the mutuality of the attraction for granted, I consider this "natural" fact instructive for the view of sexual attraction put forward in the story. Such an assumption inevitably colors the story in various ways. To put it simply, it makes the woman less guilty as well as less alone.

Preposterously speaking, if we consider that Joseph was indeed attracted, the story can be seen as one of a mutual attraction that, for reasons external to the emotional interaction between the two figures, is prohibited. The woman has the *Mut* to take the initiative. She can do this because she has higher status (although she is of a lesser sex), and the man, for reasons that he is about to disclose but that say nothing about his feelings, turns her down. Nothing, here, of the horror and repulsion conveyed by Hyppolite's rejection speeches in *Phèdre*. This is the reverse of a marriage of convenience; it is a refusal of convenience.

The word *convenience* puts a bit of a gloss on Joseph's uncontested virtue. He does not allege his chastity at all, nor is there any indication that he is bound by a vow of chastity of any sort. He "refused himself." Instead of putting chastity forward as a value or a promise, he alleges his loyalty to his master, a loyalty that in this version remains unrequited. But "loyalty" substitutes one sentiment to another. The words he says do not translate easily into such virtuous notions. He begins his explanation, his reasoning, with that word *see*. Again, my translation sacrifices poetry for a literalism that will turn out to offer a poetry of its own.

> See, my master knows not with me what [is] in the house and all that [is] onto him he gave into my hand.

> No one [is] greater in this house than me and not kept he back from me anything except you and you [are] his woman and how shall I do this great wickedness and sin against God? (8–9)

The reason for my somewhat awkward translation is to bring to the fore the paratactic structure of sentences stringing together clauses connected through *and*. This structure leaves it to the reader to fill in logical connections. Usually, this fragment runs as follows:

> See, my master knows not with me what [is] in the house because all that [is] onto him he gave into my hand.

> No one [is] greater in this house than me and not kept he back from me anything except you because you [are] his woman, and how shall I do this great wickedness and sin against God? (8–9)

This filling in of the causal conjunction *because* turns parataxis into syntax. This change is the translator's implicit response to the implicit "why?" question. It leads to the logic that the woman is the possession of the master; hence sleeping with her would be a great sin against property. The idea that giving in would be a sin comes last, following up, and thus explaining, the consequence of the primary reason: Joseph's lofty position bestowed on him by his master. The total confidence he enjoys as first steward of the house is limited only by forbidding of one item of property. This is the logic of the Fall: the fruit from all trees in the garden—

another enclosed space—may be eaten except for one. The logic entails monogamy for the possessed.

But nothing prevents us from reading it slightly differently, merging the two translations:

> See, my master knows not with me what [is] in the house because all that [is] onto him he gave into my hand.

> No one [is] greater in this house than me because not kept he back from me anything except you and you [are] his woman, so how shall I do this great wickedness and sin against God? (39:8–9)

Now Joseph warns her that he, not the master, knows what's going on in the house. He is boasting about his power. This is reiterated when he boasts about his superiority. Only then does a new idea come in: she is Potiphar's woman, in the sense of "married," not necessarily belonging to him as a possession, and thus his sin would be not against the master but against the law of God that regulates the marriage bond.

The nuances are small, but the point is, the reader must perform the logic and is thus responsible for the nuances selected. The mere act of filling in the blanks, of turning the free-floating prose of parataxis into a structured syntax, is a crucial act of reading, a performance of reading as inflection. It is where the reader can and must claim her freedom.

It is easy to explain this by way of traditional notions of (unilateral) monogamy. Again, I would not wish to be pedantic and deny this explanation. But something lingers in the echo of these words with the previous ones. *Woman* is a word that indicates a human subject, however appropriated by patriarchal power relations. It is the only part of the explanation that has the causal conjunction in all standard translations. Potiphar did draw the line at giving his woman to Joseph. He did so but, I speculate, not, or not only, because doing so would nullify his marriage to her. After all, what does such a noun, *marriage*, mean in the context? Rather, although she is "his," being a woman she is not his to give. Not that he would refrain from such a gift—many figures from antique literature do so without qualms when it suits them—but because she is not "givable." Here I use literalism to explore possible meanings on the fringes of the canonical. This is my speculation concerning the specification brought in through the word *see*: this word performs the woman's status as subject. Against the backdrop of Joseph's refusal of himself, there is a possible parallel at stake. This involves Potiphar as the third party in this harrowing tale.

As we will see later, the question of Potiphar's role, Mut's relative solitude, and the function of the house recur in fascinating ways in some of the other versions. In the tissue of words of Genesis, the house is surely a motif of great importance. The plot needs the house in many more ways than as just a location. It is inside the house that the event occurs, that Mut "knows" because she "sees" Joseph's beauty. It is in the house that, in our preposterous terms, she falls in love with him, propositions him, tries to seduce him, slanders him, and then traps him. I consider the house a motivator, a near-actant. It is in the house that the two of them are alone one day, a circumstance that moves the plot along. It is also in the house that Mut enacts one other nasty thing by means of words that has received precious little attention and to which I will attend in a moment. But the word *house* duplicates itself when we keep in mind that the invisible parallel is with *prison*—that is, closed-house or guarded-house.

It has been frequently noted that verse 14 is a bit surprising, as it is for me, but for different reasons. Kugel traces many versions that have taken exception to the unexpected plural pronoun:

> And she called unto the men of the house and said to them saying: see he made come to us a Hebrew man to mock us, he has come to me to lie with me and I called out in a loud voice. (Gen. 39:13–14)

After this follows the account of the alleged attempt at rape. The text shifts to a masculine plural here. In Kugel's account, the shift to a plural signifies the appeal to the other women of the household and their jealous husbands to also accuse Joseph (28–65, esp.48–49). Otherwise, some versions explain, her husband would not believe her. This interpretation requires a specification of the "men of the house" to consist almost exclusively of women, which begs the question of the generic masculine term. What might motivate such an unnecessary filling-in?

In some later versions a story has been inserted, a story not mentioned in Genesis at all. I will revert to this episode, which is developed in the Qur'an, some exegetical texts, and Mann's novel. It has traditionally been referred to as "the ladies of the city" or, in attempts such as Kugel's to claim its "origin" in Genesis, as, according to a section title of his, "The Assembly of Ladies" (1990, 28–65). This claim needs to obscure the city in favor of the house— a distortion I will show to obscure an extremely relevant intertext. But in Genesis no trace of it can be detected; there is a shift to plural, but in the masculine form. Unless, of course, one is all set to claim temporal priority of all elements in later versions for the canonical Hebrew text. Kugel performs some gender bending in his interpretation of what the Genesis text names "the men of the house" as the "ladies" of later versions. Such figures of "ladies" are absent from the Genesis text but not from the Qur'an; the Qur'an text, however, explicitly calls them "ladies of the city."

Kugel's interpretation that turns men into women seems far-fetched on three counts. It is an instance of an unwittingly preposterous interpretation, informed by the later version that the critic needs to attach to an earlier one. He needs to perform this reversal because, I speculate, he has already decided to give priority to the earlier version, the one that for him is the canonical source text. But to suggest foundational or qualitative primacy as a feature of temporal priority is a second, equally unwarranted step. This logic is emphatically not in accordance with biblical logic. I have argued against this conflation of temporal priority with qualitative primacy in my interpretation of the creation of woman in Genesis 1–3, an argument I will not reiterate here (1987, 104–30).

A third reason Kugel's interpretation seems far-fetched and even damaging to the richness of the text is the double meaning of the key word *house*. All through biblical narrative the word *house* resonates with the meaning we would now, anachronistically, call "family" or "ancestry." The most important house in this sense is the House of David. The genealogical lists of Genesis in particular are at pains to tie this house backward to the earliest names, while Christianity tries to link it forward to the birth of Jesus. A house is not only a building and a household but also a lineage. In the case of Potiphar's house, we are clearly dealing with a house of some importance. "The men of the house," then, can certainly refer, at least as an additional, overdetermined allusion, to the men of the house of Potiphar, who wield the power over the women and servants alike. To call out to those men is also to call out to the men who can judge the woman, the men who have the legal power to confirm or inform her claim of assault—with all the consequences such a judgment would entail, for her as much as for Joseph.

As a result of his eagerness to assign priority to Genesis for the inventive addition of the "ladies of the city" episode, Kugel ignores a key element through which the Bible asserts both its coherence and its importance—an element on which this scholar has even based the title of his book. Instead, inclined to take the text at its words, as I have argued we should, I see no contradiction in this plural at all. Nor do I see a possibility of ignoring the words "the men of the house" by turning them into "ladies." This shift neglects the strong sense of *house* as a key word. All these accumulative interventions are the result of a *projected* contradiction where there is none "anchored in" the text. This, on the condition, of course, of taking the rest of the verse literally—hence seriously—as well. And that remainder is what disturbs me more. The play of pronouns is not really strange and certainly does not solicit the kind of projection Kugel performs. I quote the passage again, now specifying the pronouns and verb forms according to number and gender. If we refrain from getting excited about the possibility of recuperating this passage for a "why?" question— the "why were the men in the house while Joseph was supposed to be alone with the woman?" question—we might avoid getting as distracted as practically all exegetes have been from a matter that, for me, lies at the heart of the story of Mut and Joseph:

> Then she called [singular, feminine] unto the men of her house, and spoke [singular, feminine] unto them, saying, See [plural, masculine], he hath brought [singular, masculine] in an Hebrew unto us [plural, no gender] to mock us [plural, no gender]; he came in [singular, masculine] unto me [singular, no gender] to lie with me [singular, no gender], and I cried [singular, no gender] with a loud voice.

The first word of Mut's direct speech is, again, *see*.

And again, this imperative form of the verb of visual perception indicates that Mut arrogates to herself epistemic authority: "see he made come to us a Hebrew man to mock us." She has the power to use the imperative and the capacity to see, which she shares with the men on whom she bestows this power by means of her order to see. The power she claims through her use of words has different possible meanings. The imperative *see* is a strong word. It is frequently used in this imperative form to make claims, including truth claims and political claims.

The imperative or exclamatory of *to see* can be related to power, as in Deuteronomy 1:8, where it bluntly turns seeing into colonization: "See, I am granting you the land; go in and take possession." The French verb *pouvoir* that doubles as a noun to mean "power" and as copula to mean "being able to" is best retained here in all its ambiguity. For, in the same vein, the biblical act of seeing is not necessarily bound up with a physical act of visual perception. In the case of Deuteronomy 1:8, it is doubtful that the land is visible when God utters this order, but it can be known, since there has been a promise and a lot of talk about it.[3]

Physical seeing would be the case when the epistemic meaning goes hand in hand with the kind of words linguists have termed *deixis*. Deixis, in reference to the here-and-now of speaking, is a spatial pointer that physically binds seeing to the subject in spatial proximity, as in "look here." At this point in the plot, this could well be the meaning in Genesis 39:14. Mut is holding, after all, the physical trace of her encounter with Joseph. This, then, is a vividly theatrical scene, an image. It is worth considering how deixis makes images more memorable—in both personal and cultural memory.

In her theory of the formation of subjectivity and the place of the body therein, Kaja Silverman argues that "one's apprehension of self is *keyed* both to a visual image or constellation of visual images, and to certain bodily feelings, whose determinant is less physiological than social" (1996, 14, emphasis added). This

3. This is a neat instance of power-knowledge à la Foucault. I write this concept with a hyphen instead of the slash that is more common in Anglo-Saxon criticism. In this I heed Gayatri Spivak's injunction to reconsider the French meanings of *pouvoir* (1993).

statement explains how the relationship between the individual
subject and the culturally normative images is bodily without
being "innate" or anatomically determined. Its insistent inter-
rogation of the indexical relationship between image and viewer
has a basis in a cultural myth of which this instance provides
an indication. It is an instance of such bodily interaction "from
within" subjectivity with the outside culture; of the inextricable
conflation of the speaker and addressee in deictic binding.

In this statement by Silverman that I just quoted, the issue is
feeling: how the subject *feels* his or her position in space. What
we call "feeling" is the threshold of body and subjectivity. It is
around such feeling that "falling in love" can happen and can take
the form of lifting one's eyes up to become a subject *in relation to*
the other seen. The external images are "attached" to the subject's
existence, which is experienced as bodily, locked together; the
subject is "locked up" in the external world. In the musical sense
of the word *key*, the external images and the body are adapted,
harmonized; the one is "set into" the tonality of the other. But
the term *to key to* can also be understood through the notion of
code, the key to understanding, comprehending, communicating
between individual subjects and a culture, a communication in
which "abstract space" is practiced.

In a spatiotemporal flow, which temporarily and provisionally
conflates the subject's body to the space it occupies, this event of
falling in love can occur. The usefulness of this "carrying along"
or this connotative use of a key concept from semiotics becomes
obvious when Silverman, a short time later and while still writing about the bodily basis of the ego, writes about proprioceptiv-
ity (the sensation of the self from within the body) that it is the
"egoic component to which concepts like 'here,' 'there,' and 'my'
are keyed" (1996, 16). She reuses the linguistic concept of deixis
in the way it was given currency by Emile Benveniste, to theorize
the construction of subjectivity in language (Benveniste 1971).
Strictly speaking, by placing deixis "within" or "on" or "at" the
body, she decisively extends into materiality and physicality the
meaning and importance of Benveniste's thought that deixis, not
reference, is the "essence" of language.

Hence language is unthinkable without bodily involvement.
One can even go on to argue that words can cause pain or harm

and arouse sexual and other excitement and that bodily effects thus form an integral part of linguistics. Conversely, this proprioceptive basis for deixis comprises more than just words. It includes the muscular system as well as the space around the body, the space within which it "fits" as within a skin. Abstract space becomes a concrete place within which the subject, delimited by its skin, is keyed in, into the space she perceives and of which she is irrevocably a part. Silverman uses the felicitous term "postural function" to refer to this place of the "keyed" subject. This interpretation of deixis opens up a space for a bodily and spatially grounded semiotics. *Deixis* can become a key term for a semiotic analysis of the visual and the literary domains without the detour via language. No longer restricted to the domain of language, deixis is a form of indexicality, one that is locked into (keyed to) the subject. This bodily-spatial form of deixis—this orientational form of the index—provides greater insight into those forms of indexicality in which the postural function of the subject—its shaping "from within"—sends back, so to speak, the images that enter it from without, but this time accompanied by affective "commentary" or "feeling."

In the verse just quoted, the first "he" is clearly Potiphar, who has brought the slave into the house who is the object of the verb *make come*. The second "he" is Joseph. The woman is the center of deixis. There is one way to read this that leaves the words intact. This will clarify why I advocate literalist reading. The woman appeals to the (other) men in the house, presumably Egyptian, to share her indignation that he, Potiphar, has brought a *Hebrew* slave into the household and put him in a position where he can "mock" or "laugh at" them all. Why would the plural here be so "anomalous" (Kugel 1990, 58) as to require linguistic and literary as well as fantasized amorous gymnastics to turn the men mentioned into "ladies"? Because, I presume, standard translations render the verb as "to sport with us," and that, of course, is unthinkable for men. Well, in my book it is not so, but then why do we need a dirty mind to make sense of this verse?

Perhaps—and this is just as purely speculative as Kugel's interpretation, mine based on literalism, his on an unacknowledged "why?"—the critic cannot "see," in the sense of understand, and face, the nasty implications of the word *Hebrew*. For clearly, in the mouth of the Egyptian first lady of the house, Hebrewness makes the mocking even more humiliating. In other words, the Hebrew text puts a racial slur into the mouth of the Egyptian woman, triply abject for being foreign, female, and full of deceit. The text thus imputes a form of what later came to be called anti-Semitism to a woman driven to incriminating, indeed criminal, lies by what now becomes interracial passion. "Loving Yusuf"— to reverse the ethnic differentiation—is the greatest transgression, sin, or crime, imaginable. The horror, the horror.[4]

For me, this verse is the key to the Genesis version of the story and, I speculate, its aftermath, all the way up (albeit not consistently) to that winter afternoon in the 1950s when I was turned into a reluctant witness to what I did not understand. Why is intercultural love such a problem that its occurrence turns critics against words and, in the same move, women into monsters?

Timothy Beal writes about monsters in the context of religion, in terms that suggest an affinity between ambiguous words and "monsters": "Monsters are in the world but not of the world. They are paradoxical personifications of *otherness within sameness*. That is, they are threatening figures of anomaly within the well-established and accepted order of things. They represent the outside that has gotten inside, the beyond-the-pale that, much to our horror, has gotten into the pale" (2002, 4). This is, I submit, the core of Mut's monstrosity, the thing that makes her alien: she loves "the other." This indeed is a crime. When I say "crime" in my characterization of interethnic, intergenerational, and inter-class passion, I am anticipating what follows. For Mut's portrayal of Joseph's rejection as assault is construing *it* as a crime. And as a crime shall it be punished.

The men of the house are called upon as witnesses. This in spite of, or thanks to, the fact that at the key moment they were not there. Verse 11 intimates this: "and it came to pass on such a day and he went to the house to do his work and no man of the men of the house [was] there in the house." This has led to mighty speculations about where everyone was, and many versions allege

---

4. Esther Fuchs (2000) among others has picked up on this ethnic slur. Needless to say, today, the importance of paying attention to the different ethnicities involved in the different versions makes the slur quite relevant.

literalism – antidote to fundamentalism

a religious festival. The tendency to fill in what is considered lacking information—the phenomenological term *gaps*, or *Leerstelle*, comes to mind—goes against the grain of my desire to convey some of the surprises in my first rereadings of the words, neither more nor less. That pernicious question "why?" says more about the exegete posing the question than about the text's allegedly omitting information. It is primarily a psychological question, derived from the habit of reading realistic novels à la Dickens, Balzac, and beyond. It is a profoundly preposterous question, which I can accept only if it is reflected upon, not if it is passed off as "natural."

The primary anachronism, or what narrative rhetoric calls retroversion, a figure that is time and again applied to ancient texts without critical examination, is the assumption of psychological motivation. But neither the Bible nor any of the objects at stake here is a Dickens novel. Instead of asking for a psychological motivation for figures to say or do what they do, I think this kind of literature is better served when estranged a bit from our habits inspired by romanticism and its aftermath. Here, there are the words. There, there is the story. The former create the latter, the latter needs the former to exist as a story, not some doxa floating around without the material support that specifies it. Some narrative elements are necessary not to explain the figures' motivation but to meet the story's narrative needs. This, as I will argue several times in the course of this inquiry, is where we must first look to understand sometimes strange events and situations.

The men have to be absent, I submit, because only then can the woman be exonerated from collusion in adulterous sex. This is the meaning of what Mut says in verse 14: "I called in a loud voice." Deuteronomy 22, stipulating the Jewish law on sex, frames these rules in terms of property among brothers. It begins with the obligation to rescue the cattle of your brother if you see it go astray. This is followed by food laws, then by the issue of virginity, climaxing with the penalty for premarital defloration—stoning to death (Deut. 22:13–21). The rest of the chapter concerns (alleged) rape. This passage is a case for literalism as an antidote to fundamentalism. The former is about life, the life of the text, the German meaning of *Mut*; the latter is about death, killing in the name of a rigid signified, the Hebrew meaning of *Mot*.

The last verse of the chapter in Deuteronomy shifts from brother to father and, amazingly, mentions the interdiction against uncovering the father's shirt. This can only be a reference to Noah's drunkenness and its aftermath. This story is worth re-reading for its literal casting out of the act of seeing the father's less than satisfactory genitals. Ernst van Alphen wrote an exceedingly amusing commentary on this story (1992). For my purposes here, it is more relevant that the story also implies the exile of the brother who transgressed the taboo on looking at the father's nakedness. This was Cham, who, as a consequence of his exile, became the father of the black race. Just as in the comparable case of Ishmael, and here Joseph, the shirt cannot but resonate with Joseph's plight in Genesis 39. In addition to the precariousness of the father's fatherly powers, the father line in Genesis definitely harbors an element of ethnic strife folded into a potential shaming of the father. As early as this text, "patriarchy"—the unquestioned authority of the father—was not exempt from doubt. And given the narrative place of shame, this ethnic strife among brothers is not without sexual overtones. This brings us back to the story of Mut and Joseph.

In the context of Mut's alleged cries, an intertextual detour is in order. The following verses regulate rape, phrasing it in ways rather similar as what Mut says here, and explaining her need to do so. In view of the commentary by Tony Tanner which I will discuss shortly, I quote the translation Tanner uses of the relevant section of Deuteronomy 22:

> 22 If a man be found lying with a woman married to an husband, then they shall both of them die, both the man that lay with the woman, and the woman;
> 23 so shalt thou put evil away from Israel. If a damsel that is a virgin be betrothed unto an husband, and a man find her in the city, and lie with her;
> 24 Then ye shall bring them both out unto the gate of that city, and ye shall stone them with stones that they die; the damsel, because she cried not, being in the city; and the man, because he hath humbled his neighbor's wife; so thou shalt put away evil from among you.

25 But if a man find a betrothed damsel in the field, and the man force her, and lie with her; then the man only that lay with her shall die;

26 But unto the damsel thou shalt do nothing; there is in the damsel no sin worthy of death; for as when a man riseth against his neighbor, and slayeth him, even so is this matter;

27 for he found her in the field, and the betrothed damsel cried, and there was none to save her. . . .

30 A man shall not take his father's wife, nor discover his father's shirt.

The house, here the stage of confinement, in a near-Aristotelian unity of place, requires the emptiness to become, potentially, both the city and the field. If the house was not empty of its inhabitants, Mut's alleged calling out would be implausible. They would have heard her. A full house would be like a city. An empty house would be like a field. Since everyone was gone, she might have called her heart out, but no one would have heard. This, not her propositioning in itself, requires the house to be empty.[5]

I have quoted the rather traditional translation above because Tony Tanner's seminal study *Adultery in the Novel* (1979) quotes it when he begins his book with a consideration of these verses from Deuteronomy. His book is on the novel, but instead of treating the Bible as a novel, he treats the novel as similar to the Bible. This refocuses the obsessive preoccupation with psychology in the novel to a more anthropological interest. He points out a few aspects that are crucial to our story.

> Within the city the prescriptions of the law extend to both sexes because theoretically everyone can be *heard*. . . . Language has total authority, and within it individuals have total responsibility. The architecture of the city—which includes not only buildings but the related edifices of law, rule, and custom, all of them interrelated

5. This metonymic extension of the house resonates with Edward Said's comments (2004, 47–48), based on Abu El-Haj 2002, on the overlap between archaelogy and biography—on the former as a spatial version of the latter. This connection raises a host of extremely important issues concerning the meanings of *house* evoked above.

by language—"architectures" the relationships between the sexes with complete explicitness and the wrongfully assaulted woman is obliged to "cry out" according to her categorization (damsel, virgin, betrothed unto a husband). (1979, 19)

I retain from this passage in particular the appeal to hearing, not seeing; the gender equity before the law; and the specific importance of the city, overdetermined as the site of regulation or, as Tanner will call it, civic contract.

In the Qur'an, rape likewise wavers between (potentially consensual) adultery and coerced intercourse. Here, too, witnessing is key to the legal status of the event (Norman 2005). Scholars such as Amira Sonbol (2000) and Asifa Qurashi (1997), each in terms of their own society (Pakistan and Egypt respectively), have researched an impressive number of Qur'anic verses that complicate the contemporary Western notion of rape. Still, the need for witnesses or other forms of incontestable evidence remains at the heart of the legal status of rape, including in the Montesquieu-based legal systems of Western Europe.[6]

Tanner focuses on the bond between witnessing and the city. I will return to the city in greater detail later. For now, I stress the performative activity of textual detail. In the opposition between city and field through the (im)possibility of hearing, contractual binding is *established*, not simply reported; this makes the words performative. And with this binding comes transgression. As Tanner has it, "Contracts *create* transgressions; the two are inseparable, and the one would have no meaning without the other" (1979, 11).

When, as I claim, something on the order of rape is at stake, there is an issue regarding the use of words over time and across cultures. When I first heard the Genesis 39 story, I hated the woman for the violence she did to the innocent man. Then and now, I see the story as having a "moral," a lesson about decent conduct. Precisely for that reason, the resonance with "rape"

---

6. The legal issues are never far when the ancient texts narrate such crimes as lying or lying-with. But with them emerges the fundamental uncertainty of the law itself, never unambiguous in its "causal" but deconstructible sequentiality of rule and interpretation. See Smith 2008.

counts, albeit not at all in a simple way. False accusations of rape
happen, they are culturally overdetermined, and in general their
questioning supports men. Our story cannot but resonate with
this problematic of, among other issues, "false memory syn-
drome" (Sturken 1999). The word *rape* does not occur in the texts
of Deuteronomy or Genesis. We must not too quickly dismiss as
a mystifying euphemism the phrase that is translated as "laugh-
ing at us," "mocking us," or "sporting with us," for it suggests an
act of contempt, here ethnically inflected before being folded into
sexual innuendo. "Lying with" refers to sex, but the question of
consent or violence is raised neither in Deuteronomy nor in our
Yusuf story, other than by the reference to crying out loud.

Some scholars, sensitized to historical and cultural difference,
have commented on the difficulty of pinpointing a phenomenon
such as rape. This poses a dilemma we encounter all the time. It is
important because, as will become clear in the next chapter, it is
also potentially an argument against fundamentalism—the kind
that kills, specifically, rape victims. Susanne Scholz's study on the
rape story of Genesis 34 is an excellent case in point (2000). Care-
ful to avoid anachronistic projections, Scholz lays out the cultural
differences in the interpretation of sexual violence as rape and,
conversely, of rape as not so violent. She opens her study with
a consideration of the cultural specificity yet transcultural and
transhistorical occurrence of this sexual form of violence.

In an earlier article in *Semeia*, Susan Niditch discusses this
problem as well (1993). She struggles with the difficulty of ethical norms that vary according to time and place, whereas the language with which we write about cultures is also bound to time
and place, but different ones. In that context she raises the question whether "just war," called "holy war" in a biblical framework—and, I would add, in a Qur'anic one—is possible, and if so,
whether in such a war the practice we call rape can have a place.

Thus she writes about the book of Numbers: "Of course, en-
slaving the enemy (20:11) and forcing its women into marriage
are the terms of an oppressive regime and difficult to imagine
under the heading of what is just" (1993, 42). The result of her
reflection is not my point here. I am interested, first, in the notion of "oppressive regime." The word *oppressive* is anachronistic in terms of the object under analysis (the book of Numbers),

and the stake of the struggle described is hostility over land, not disagreement over human rights within the United Nations. The context in which Niditch's words were written makes the notion very much to the point: I first read her paper during preparations for the first Gulf War and reread it during the escalating violent occupation of Iraq. Over the years since this article was published, the word had come to refer almost inevitably to Saddam Hussein. In other words, the description "oppressive regime" has moral echoes and an imaginative and imagelike resonance daily fed on television—like a dream image. The obscenely broadcast images of Saddam's execution are a case in point. Thus, without either author or readers' being aware of it, the words take on metaphorical garb. The phrase "oppressive regime" is at risk of becoming a metaphor by means of which the Western present collapses its own norms and values with the Middle Eastern past, and this happens in a paper, indeed, within a sentence, in which an explicit attempt is made to avoid such anachronisms.

Perhaps it is the attempt to avoid anachronism that most threatens to cause such distortion. In contrast, I claim that it can be positively useful to boldly endorse anachronistic terms. I would endorse such terms as conceptual metaphors that serve to analyze, rather than take in wholesale, the phenomenon one is at pains to understand both in its own right and for today. This is clear, for example, in Athalya Brenner's chapter on (and concept of) "pornoprophetics," in which the modern concept of pornography is deployed to grasp the textual sexual violence of selections from prophetic discourse (1997). I submit that anachronism is actually useful, as some contemporary art historians argue, but on the condition that it be used as overt anachronism, as a kind of temporal metaphor (Wesseling and Zwijnenberg 2007). In the context of my inquiry here, what concerns me most in Niditch's somewhat tense avoidance attempt is that something in this attempt is carried over: a description, equally anachronistic, of rape.

The author wishes to avoid that term because of its anachronism, and the concessive clause in which the description "oppressive regime" occurred was meant to help that avoidance. "Forcing women into marriage" is Niditch's attempt to avoid the anachronism "rape." She doesn't wish to call it rape because, she argues, in the culture under discussion it was not perceived as such. Even if the war cannot be called just, the taking of women is culturally acceptable and therefore cannot be called rape. This is a relativist argument, the not-so-felicitous alternative to ethnocentrism. This dilemma has a precise parallel in the social and political dilemma of moralism versus relativism (or "tolerance"), the imposition of one's own norms versus the unquestioned acceptance of those of others, even if the latter are perceived as—or used as—"oppressive." I would like to allege Mut to, at least, disturb that dilemma.

Niditch replaces "rape" with "forcing into marriage"; elsewhere it is called wife-stealing. I can see how "rape" would obscure the action and fail to address the cultural status of the event. This includes, obviously, the notion of "marriage" that remains unquestioned. Also, it seems pointless to accuse a culture of thousands of years of violating human rights and thus to feel better about our own behavior. This dilemma colors my memory of the automatic condemnation of Mut. It also promotes a reading attitude that skirts fundamentalism, as the reading posture that rigidifies the word-meaning, or signifier-signified unity, but also, dangerously, fixes it to a prescriptive referent. Rather, in the awareness that the term is "ours" I would like to take a closer look at the contested term, *rape*.[7]

But rather than a semantic analysis, I wish to foreground the narratological issues involved in the notion of rape. And the first thing I notice about it is that it is a noun. Like many other nouns, it implies a story. As a noun, rape summarizes an event. The underlying story tells about that event's happening to someone, by the doing of an agent. Erasing that story posits precisely the dilemma that needs to be overcome. By alleging that she cried out, Mut at least puts it on the table. Its meaning depends on the status of men and women and their relationship within a culture.

Cultures different from "ours" tend to look more homogeneous and more coherent at a distance than they probably are for those who inhabit them. That deceptive vision is, precisely, the basis of ethnocentrism as well as of fundamentalism. Fundamentalism is the fixation of a signified, by definition slippery, from within the culture; ethnocentrism is something similar but done

7. Others have done this before me, among whom Sandie Gravett has offered an analysis that is nuanced and detailed (2004).

from outside the culture, as in racist slurs. Fundamentalism is intolerant of differences-within; ethnocentrism cannot see those differences. Instead, within each community, ancient or recent, perception of differences-within increases as one's vision comes closer. Rape implies an event that happens within a culture, involving people who are likely to differ as much as they share, and this internal divisiveness matters.[8]

To forge a noun out of a verb—a noun of action—forfeits the active character. What is restored in the phrase "crying out loud" is all that remains. Of course, I am not suggesting that Mut *was* raped. Only, what she says resonates with a discourse that erases the violence of rape. A discourse that "sounds" different for men than for women. And so does the discourse of rape's opposite, "falling in love." These two discourses are merged here, and I attempt to suggest their copresence in a cultural context where both implied actions tend to be experienced differently according to gender—it's the least we can say. The resonance of that difference, then, also inflects the sense of Mut's "lifting her eyes upon" this man called Joseph. To put it bluntly: if rape is different according to gender, so is falling in love. And for both, the house is the setting.

Empty and confining, field and city both, the house is also an echo of the closed-house or guarded-house to come. The needs of the story, what David Herman (2002) calls story logic, require it, not some woman's psyche. "And it came to pass on such a day": a temporal marker, like "once upon a time," or rather, a blander "and then" that indicates the story's passage to a following episode. It came to pass: and then this happened.

The near-chiastic contrast between Joseph's and the other men's movements—"he went to the house to do his work and no man of the men of the house [was] there in the house"—predicts, according to the same story logic, that Joseph is soon going to be on his own. The house, for him, is not a safe place. Let's not forget that he is there involuntarily; he was purchased as a slave, sold by his brothers. He, the lone Hebrew man, is not free to move where he wishes. Hence, the moment he is being pressed by the lovesick Mut almost reduces him to the object-status that so often is the lot

8. This is the main tenet of Said's inquiry into the "foreign" foundation of Jewish identity in Freud's *Moses* (2004, 54).

of slaves, and women. But like Mut, he saves his subjectivity. He flees—escaping the danger, or the temptation, or the one through the other—and leaves ambiguous evidence in her hands. Mut reiterates to Potiphar—his master—the racial slur used to mobilize the servants on the basis of what we would now call class identity. "The Hebrew slave which you made come to us to mock me."

The house, place of confinement for so many women, dangerous for so many children, is a prison for the slave. No wonder he ends up in jail:

And Joseph's master took him and gave him in the closed house, a place where the bound ones of the king were bound and he was there in the closed house. (39:20)

In this allegedly original or oldest version, Potiphar accepts Mut's lies tragically easily. Why? Not because he is stupid, or has class and ethnic prejudice, or believes his beloved wife at her word. All these interpretations would be preposterous, informed by the tradition of the Western realist psychological novel. No, he does so because the story needs Joseph to end up in prison, so that he can rise from the basest position. This is *story-logic*.

But the life of stories cannot be reduced to their logic, even if it helps to start there. Of Mut we hear no more. She remains, presumably, in her closed house, a house I, from my own "why?" questions, imagine as cold and lonely. For now, I only wish to keep the words and their resonances in front of me, as well as the logic of the story qua narrative. In the story Mut is just an instrument to make "come to pass" what must happen for the greater glory of the grand narrative of patriarchy. In this sense she, too, is a slave of the story. If this is so, there is no need to judge, let alone prejudge, Mut for her desperate and failed attempt to consummate her passion. Yet I did, even without knowing she had fallen in love. And so did, and continue to do, all manner of exegetes, popular rewriters, painters, and filmmakers. Meanwhile, Mut fell in love, and out of the story.

3

Dreaming Away: On Fantasy

> The unconscious is also referenced, that "other
> place" which is both known and eternally foreign.
> STEPHEN FROSH

Joseph is a bit of a dream specialist. In the Bible he had a
dream that he told his father and, against his father's advice,
his brothers. As it was a dream of his personal grandeur and
of being his father's preferred son, it set off the envy that
inaugurated his adventures. He literally learned his lesson
and became a specialist in dream interpretation. In Thomas
Mann's novel he is frequently depicted as fantasizing and
daydreaming. He is also notorious as a performative exegete
of the dreams of others—performative in that his exegeses
have real consequences. While his good looks make others
dreamy but get him in trouble, his way with dreams, his
hermeneutic skill, gets him out of it.

Dreams, daydreams, fantasies, and related activities have
in common that they don't have a clear subject, a definite
agent, as their instigator. They are acts, they can be phrased
by means of active verbs, but they share the subject's

passivity. They happen, that is, on the condition that the subject let go of reason and mastery.

My exploration of useful concepts to deal with Joseph and the woman who loves him against all odds continues in this chapter with a few concepts that foreground this ambiguous nature of the subject of dreaming. First and foremost, I wish to foreground the concept of *fantasy*. Before I begin discussing fantasy, I emphasize that I consider fantasy as a particular part of reality, not its counterpart, and similarly as attached to signs, not a flight from them. As a consequence, the reflection in this chapter will lead me to a provisional definition of fundamentalism as a reading posture to which I oppose literalism, rather than free play—the bad guy in antideconstructionist rhetoric. I will argue that in order to give reading its rightful place in culture and cultural memory, literalism is indispensable.

Fantasy is of crucial importance in even the most rational process of cultural life, science. To make the point of fantasy's real relevance I am inspired by a study of its place in scientific discourse. In Evelyn Fox Keller's examination of scientific discourse and its consequences for the cultural power of science and technology, *Secrets of Life, Secrets of Death* (1992), she offers a lucid critique of the devastation wrought on the cultural imagination by key metaphors in scientific discourse. Taking these metaphors as literally as possible—as literally, that is, as I advocate we should—Keller detects in them elements of a rivalry between scientists and the imagined subject of the creation of nature—a subject many call "God." This rivalry is so deadly that from the desire to give life it moves to the decision to give death—the compulsion to make ever-deadlier weapons. For this chapter, the importance of Keller's analysis lies in the connection she establishes between the practices of "hard science" and the utterly subjective, indeed infantile fantasies that contribute to informing it. If metaphors have serious, real consequences in science, then, to be sure, we must take them seriously in canonical, hence influential, narratives as well. She establishes, that is, not a deterministic pattern of "influence" but a culturally thick carpet of contributing elements that contain not sufficient but certainly required conditions for the practices to be sustained.

The key term, then, in the articulations of the threads that compose such carpets, is *fantasy*. This concept has been elaborated in psychoanalysis, but it is also a more common term, much used in everyday life. It is used to question the truthfulness of what people say or the illusionary nature of their desires. In those uses it is a rather derogatory term. Far from wishing to make it more conceptually tight, my purpose in this chapter is to connect the everyday usage of the term *fantasy* with its psychoanalytically more precise definition, as well as the realization that it has real consequences (as in science). The result is not a fixed concept but, in line with what I have proposed as a methodological alternative to such discipline-based fixities, a "traveling concept" (Bal 2002). In the following chapter this traveling concept will be an inroad into the difficult but exciting activity of "reading" visual art. Here I seek to explore the term in the cultural genre most readily associated with fantasy, the novel. But if the novel exemplifies fantasy, science demonstrates the importance of taking it seriously, including, therefore, in the novel.

At first sight, fantasy seems to stand at the other end of the spectrum from words or, more generally, signs—those visible, tangible things that produce and carry meaning. But in fact, fantasy is made up of signs, just as much as any other cultural semiotic system. Literature is made of words upgraded from casually and routinely used conventional signs to both acts (as in speech act theory) and tangible things (as in the double meaning of the Hebrew word *dabar*, word and thing). It is also a repository of fantasy. In the previous chapter I made a case for the decision to take words seriously as a method of reading. Now I seek to do justice to the way words produce fantasy. Rather than attempting a complete reading of all the verses of the Genesis text (impossible anyway), in chapter 2 I focused on a few words—*see, house, men, mocking*—selected for their centrality in the story as well as their neglect or distortion in criticism. This method will stand us in good stead for reading a novel, a work of literary art that is premised on the value of words as well as fantasy.

But if a twenty-four-verse "short story" cannot by any means be commented on comprehensively, how do we analyze Mann's novel of more than twelve hundred pages? Yet I have selected this novel as the key to the deployment of fantasy as a "real," that is, historical, social, and artistic, element in the collective life moved forward by negotiation and contestation; that collective life we call "culture." One reason for this choice is historical. The crucial parts of Thomas

Mann's *Joseph and His Brothers* were written in the historically ominous year 1932 and published at an even more dramatic moment, 1943. With the hindsight of today, this novel is impossible to read without taking its historical moments into account. I use the plural *moments* to foreground the moment of reception—for me, in 1990 and again in 2006—as much as that of production.

Fantasy in history, dreaming away in moments when rational action is needed: this is the theme of the present chapter. Mann, an author I reencountered rather late in my life, had a penchant for dreamy, fantastic situations that rub against the mythical. His *Magic Mountain* is the most famous of such works. I read long novels only during vacations when I have time to dream away on the waves of many words. And so it happened that I read his *Joseph* during a vacation, when my interest had already been awakened in the story of the woman whom Mann named Mut. In line with the dreamy character of the entire story but also the specific passages fleshing out the main characters, the novel has been accused of escapism, taking up an ancient myth in times of historical trouble. A writing that, spinning an engrossing tale of significant length, copious detail, and fantasy-inducing words out of a tiny episode of a total of fourteen verses (Genesis 39:7–20), can and has been construed as fantasy where reality would ask for commitment. A reality of madness that needed reason more than anything.

I argue, instead, that the fantasy character of the novel is the genre's primary target, its mission, to take as seriously as words. This seriousness of fantasy is indispensable for the cultural domain, both in order to maintain its life and to retain its capacity for change, which forces in the historical moment of Mann's writing were attempting to stifle. Ours is also an era in which boundaries are reinforced and cultural negotiation is encouraged to disappear, to be replaced by a rigid cultural identity that increases hostility. This similarity between the two moments of threat and subsequent increasing retreat toward the kind of cultural fixity Johannes Fabian so convincingly rejects is, of course, not strictly an identity (2001).[1]

1. I am referring to Fabian's reflection on and rejection of the concept of "culture." For him, any attempt to define a culture is doomed to reification. Instead, he proposes to see culture—or "the cultural"—as moments of negotiation and even polemics between cultural groups.

For, hopefully, the present still has a future, whereas Mann's present's future has become the past of horror we know. But the similarity is nevertheless unsettling, perhaps inspiring. I take it as an entrance into the reflection on historical interpretation I have called pre-posterous. The second goal of this chapter, then, is to begin deploying fantasy for a demonstration of such preposterous history.

Mut-em-enet, Mann's main character in the episode, confronts an exceedingly handsome but neurotically narcissistic young man with whom, indeed, she falls in love. But he belongs to men: to his father and to his God. This is, of course, my interpretation of him, for which I will account as well as I can. In order to foreground the fantasy status of this character—for Mann as well as for me—from now on let me call the figure Yusuf. This name helps to distinguish this figure somewhat from the character Mann created and whom the author called Osarsiph. The name Yusuf also helps us keep in mind the cultural difference that Genesis has already intimated and that is crucial for a preposterously historical reading of the novel. I adopt the name for these reasons even if, for Mut, the name would have to be "Joseph" according to the Hebrew character that traveled through history. For Mut the Egyptian, this name foregrounds his foreignness. Yet to reinforce this difference for the Western readers this essay addresses, the name Yusuf keeps our cultural mind fitter than the more familiar Joseph.

The name Yusuf also helps keep in mind the fantasy character of all (re-)reading, which Mann forcefully foregrounds in his re-reading of his sources. My deviation from Mann's chosen name, therefore, is an attempt to stay loyal to Mann's conception of fantasy as that which text and reader fabricate together. From now on, then, Yusuf is the name of the character with whom Mut falls in love, in the various "versions" our culture has canonized. I will call him Joseph only when the context in which I cite him demands it in a kind of cultural "free indirect discourse."

For most of the novel, Yusuf is the narrative center, living through many harrowing adventures. These adventures are (structurally) tests of his autonomy as a subject and demonstrations of his difficulty of reaching that autonomy; he is a bit of an eternal son. These adventures include moments such as being cast in a pit by his brothers, being separated from his father at a premature age, and, as in our episode, being seduced, threatened, and falsely accused by the woman who loves him (and whom, as Mann ambiguously suggests, he might have loved), and being imprisoned, and later confronted with his brothers as strangers. In the episode on which I will zoom in, however, he is not the narrative center; Mut is. This shift alone already embodies the main point I see this novel making. This point concerns shifting subjectivities and the cultural importance of a fluid and moving—temporally as well as emotionally—collective subjectivity, or, as I prefer to call it, intersubjectivity.

The itinerary begins with the individual subject's struggle to be just that: an individual. It also ends with that individuality, successfully accomplished, but at a price. Toward the end of the novel, Yusuf appears to lose his charms. When he achieves social prominence as viceroy of Egypt, he becomes fat, physically middle-aged, sure of himself, eager to have and exercise power. Of the old Yusuf "no semblance did remain": Mann demonstrates that subjectivity is not fixed and shifts through time and social interaction. This phrase "no semblance did remain" I quote not from Mann but from Shakespeare's *Rape of Lucrece*, a text in which a young woman's subjectivity is destroyed, also by the hand of male power (verse 1453).

I cite this phrase to counter the principle of Kugel's study of exegesis. His book is titled after Yusuf's misadventures because, the scholar contends, even after the terrible tests put to him, Joseph remains the same, true to his origins, the embodiment of the seventh commandment (1990, 7). I submit that he remains the same in reference to what he had been destined to be in the end, perhaps, for the needs of the story of his glory as one of the powerful patriarchs, but not the same as, all along the story, he really was. For Mann, at any rate, the character achieves this self-sameness only at the end, after the story has let go of its fascinated readers and becomes boring. So what can be the meaning—in the sense of importance—of Mann's opposite representation? Surely *not* the opposite of remaining loyal to one's origins—a relinquishing we now call assimilation. An in-depth discussion of this tricky version of intercultural integration is not possible here but should be considered a relevant backdrop for the contemporary side of my argument.[2]

---

2. The literature on intercultural relations—a term I prefer to the fraught one of *multiculturalism*—is growing rapidly. I am referring specifically to the issue—the Western demand—of integration. A recent discussion is offered by Janssen (2006).

Many times in the novel Yusuf is called "the true son"—one of those phrases that need to be taken seriously. He is called the true son in three ways. First, he is identified with his mother, the beautiful and beloved Rachel. This makes him attractive for men and women alike. As such, second, he is the true love object of his father, who had plunged into black melancholia upon the death of Rachel. Jacob focuses on Yusuf with an obsession that will turn against the possessiveness it bespeaks, as it drives Yusuf away from him. This keeps Yusuf in the position of the son long after circumstances should have ushered him into adult manhood. Third, he is jealously guarded by God, who clearly favors him. The love of his "jealous creator and lord, insistent upon sole possession," dictates the implicit vow of chastity.[3]

The thrice-ambiguous sexuality of Yusuf is also, Mann suggests, part of his sense of self, since he identifies with the mythical world he embodies. For example:

> Then his quick mind had clearly understood the allegory of the star which one evening is a woman and in the morning a man and which sinks into the well of the abyss as evening star.
>
> It was the abyss into which the true son descends, he who is one with the mother and wears the robe by turns with her. (390)

"The true son" is a highly ambiguous term to indicate the character, a turn of phrase that inevitably prefigures Christ. It is one of innumerable hints at Yusuf's megalomania, a sin compared to which any sexual transgression he might have contemplated pales. Mann is more explicit although less introspective when he writes, early on in the novel, "The bond of faith with God was sexual in its nature, and thus, contracted with a jealous creator and lord, insistent upon sole possession, it inflicted upon the human male a kind of civilizing weakening into the female . . . chastity as a sacrifice; in other words, a female significance" (48). The word *sacrifice*—here related to circumcision—is intertextually relevant when we consider the many instances of near or real human sacrifice in

3. In terms of contemporary psychoanalytic theory, he appears as a "trisexual" subject, universally attractive but through that very attractiveness barely mastering his own subjectivity, his desires (Bollas 1987).

the Hebrew Bible. Human sacrifice is a laboriously exorcised taboo that returns like a genuine instance of repression in many stories of which Isaac's near-sacrifice is only the most obvious case. The feminization so boldly put forward may well be, in turn, a repression of the true source of child sacrifice. For according to the "surprised" view of psychoanalysis as well as narrative analysis, the source of sacrifice is intermale, paternal rivalry (Balmary 1986; Bal 1988a). Mann suggests as much himself, at several places in the novel.[4]

Yusuf as a feminine man: the configuration addresses a commonplace about Jewish men in Nazi Germany that it proceeds to refute. Narratively, rather than reiterating the effeminate cliché, the general attraction of the figure turns the feminine character into a positive feature. To portray the figure in these terms and then show him to inspire great passion in a powerful woman can be seen as a political act, or at least a political gloss on German stereotyping. In the context of biblical narrative, the feminization of the main character is also of (gender-) political importance (Boyarin 1995).

Yusuf the feminine man of trisexual appeal is not the only version of the figure. Sometimes he is not at all appealing to me, certainly not as much as he was to Mut. Much as I was set up against the latter, I was also set up against the former. I recall one of my indirect encounters with the story of Yusuf. My father, who had turned from a moderate Christian-democratic position to a more leftist position under the influence of his growing children, once said, speaking of Joseph's explanation of the dreams of fat and lean years: this is the inventor of capitalism. In my family capitalism was a bad thing, and my father said it with disgust. I remember I was somewhat shocked, because for me the figure of Joseph had rather positive connotations. For me, informed as I had been up to that moment, the name resonated with victimization and steadfastness. Whether my father's interpretation of the figure made sense, and how, is not the issue here. I am grateful for the moment he offered to allow surprise in a way of seeing a story I thought I knew. It rendered the figure strange, different from what I assumed to be true or what I had been taught to see. What I read in Mann's novel, as a first rereading through which my

---

4. See, for example, 65, 125–27, 155, 391, and most explicitly, in a long digression, 575–87.

father's voice resonated, is that he became disgusting, although much later in the novel.

Yusuf the trisexual, attractive, ambiguous figure lost himself so profoundly in achieving social, hence economic, success that he all but lost all continuity between his attractive self and the later man. This is even reflected in the novel, which itself loses its appeal after Yusuf's rise to power. Gripping until the last quarter, it became boring to me toward the end, in the way Emily Brontë's *Wuthering Heights* fades out. When they lack what Frank Kermode called the "sense of an ending" (1967), long novels can simply be too long. Proust's *Remembrance of Things Past* never becomes too long; it is never soporific. But then again, it never invites the kind of fantasy-induced reading that feeds novels of adventure. Its appeal to fantasy is of a very different order, its appeal to other literature of a different kind (see Bal 1997).

Yusuf also loses the love of his father. This happens when he becomes a father himself and thus loses his sonship. Yet it happens only after the father has won the competition between father and mother, female and male lovers who struggle for the possession of his beauty. What can be the point of this simultaneous loss of self and of loveliness? To understand this we need to return to the notion of fantasy, as the opposite of what myth criticism claims to be the universality of myth. Fantasy, then, becomes yet another tool to counter fundamentalism, the alleged certainty and fixity of meaning. As we have seen in the interpretation of Yohannan, the universality of the mythic story is posited, not argued. Mann, in contrast, writing at the same time as a myth rewriter and as a myth critic, contests this universality. He says explicitly in his preface that he wishes to vindicate the woman, cast into the role of irrecoverable wickedness by the generalizations of myth. He counters: "*Joseph in Egypt* [the section of the novel that depicts our episode] seemed to me unquestionably the artistic zenith of the work, if only on account of the humane vindication that I had undertaken in it, the humanization of the figure of Potiphar's wife, the mournful story of her passionate love of the Canaanite major-domo and her *pro forma* husband" (1948, xi). What Mann is claiming here is that his ideological stance has at the very least contributed to the artistic success of his book; his politics constitute his art.

I remember that when I first read this, it seemed dubious. This was during the heydays of ideological criticism, and I resisted the conflation of ethics and aesthetics, which I considered a bit of a cheap shot. I now wonder, upon reiterated rereading, if I wasn't somewhat defensive in my doubt. I find, on the contrary, that any *separation* of ethics from aesthetics is subject to doubt. Important as it is to "protect" art from political appropriation and censorship, I resist generalizing on their relationship. The point, for me as a feminist inclined to activism, is to read aesthetically and politically in the same act, not to claim that the qualitative merits can be conflated. Art can be artistically successful *and* politically fraught—it happens all the time. Still, I do not consider this possibility a reason for ethical indifference. Hence when, like others before me, I draw critical attention to the way the Genesis story presents the Egyptian woman as, to use a somewhat anachronistic qualifier, "anti-Semitic," I do not imply an aesthetic value judgment. But neither does my resistant reading put up with the way this small word has been glossed over in favor of an assumed superiority of the text. Ethically, we would now say that if only we are willing to take the text at its words, the text is nasty here.

In Mann's assertion, then, I read sensitivity to the integration, but not necessarily conflation, of art and politics in a book of fantasy. He intimates that reading is one of those activities where the cultural acts out its polemical nature. The remainder of his sentence confirms this. His politics are "humanizing"—a term demonstrating a keen awareness of the historical moment, which was one when cultural "others" were created out of the blue, by means of *de*humanizing. Completely assimilated Germans were suddenly turned Jewish, their religion and cultural affiliation turned into a "race." They were first constituted as "others" and then dehumanized. Mann calls his creation a "vindication," hence a form of activism—against dehumanization, one may presume. Mann's willful conflation of art and politics can be taken further, and in chapter 9 I will do just that. In one sense, to which I will return toward the end of this book, the Egyptian woman Mut with her German-sounding name comes to stand for the German Jews who were being recast as "others."

For the examination of the cultural importance of fantasy, the words of the juxtaposed explanation, "mournful story," deserve attention. Why the story is mournful remains to be seen, but elements needed for our understanding are already available. I have mentioned that Yusuf's father has difficulty exiting melancholia and reaching the reparative process of mourning his beloved wife. The qualifier *mournful* may also inform the following qualification of Potiphar as a "pro forma" husband only. This phrase, it seems to me, appeals to a sentiment close to sympathy with the woman's right to desire and fulfillment. Calling her love "passionate" is qualifying it as both irresistible and fatal. The irresistibility is in line with the ideology of romantic love and hence makes her subsequent actions somewhat forgivable. The fatality is in line with tragedy, predicting disaster.[5]

What remains, then, is the noun *story*. Is this the same story as the one Yohannan characterized apropos of the same novel? Most certainly not; that would be an example of fundamentalist reading. Here is no fixed structure of which the terms have already been filled in—Chaste and Lustful with capitals, as proper names, given names, bestowed on the figures whose surnames are Youth and Stepmother, rightly called in linguistics "*rigid* denominators." Instead, Mann presents the story as yet to come. The temporality of reading, filled in a priori as rereading, is also a *becoming* in the act of reading. He sets the terms of the starting point: Canaanite, majordomo, and husband. In other words, he frames the story in terms of foreignness (Canaanite), domestic functioning (majordomo), and within that domesticity, hierarchical importance. He also frames it in terms of triangularity in the presence/absence of the husband—a social role that remains empty. The dual presence/absence of the husband—present as binding, absent as fulfilling—triggers the story and makes it "mournful." In this single sentence of the preface written afterward but read beforehand, then, we encounter Mann's first rereading of his novel, a direction that we can take or refuse, but that cannot remain completely absent. For it too is a memory, Mann's memory of what he had done.

Myth criticism is strongly inclined to projection of critics' fantasies and memories onto what they have already decided to be one

---

5. Lest this seems defensive, just think of the French notion of *crime passionnel*—an excuse primarily for men who, as scorned lovers, hurt or kill women. This notion is still very much alive in the present.

version of the same myth (e.g., Kirk 1972; Vickery 1966). Barthes associates this tendency with the desire to arrest time when he writes, "The very end of myth is to immobilize the world," playing on the double sense of *end*—both in French and for us in English, meaning goal and arrest (1972, 155). One way of putting this is to say that once you reach your goal, life is over. "Happily ever after" ends the fairy tale. Yusuf's success is his end as a subject. It also ends the novel on a spun-out slowness, as if in fear of the ending. In connection to the novel's primary appeal to "reading for the plot," this long, flat ending feels like a refusal to let go of Yusuf the unfinished character. In connection to (preposterous) history, this is likewise deadly. According to Philip Rahv, interest in myth in the commonplace sense is informed by a persistence of romanticism in its conservative mode, occasioned by the fear of freedom, change, and choice. "The craze for myth is the fear of history," he concludes (1953, 109–18). Between history and its end, where does that leave the fact that myths tend to be primarily transmitted—hence endure in cultural memory—through narrative, that dynamic mode of discourse? This question requires unpacking beyond the confines of this chapter.[6]

We remember the importance of words. Saying that the craze for myth is a fear of words is another way of addressing Rahv's point. Here I will call on the concept of fantasy to envision a countermove. Fantasy, particularly "primal fantasy," is a concept rich in psychoanalytical connotations; I prefer, however, to keep present an everyday idea of fantasy. Not as the opposite of truth, reality, and history but as a realm of relative freedom from those constraints, as a resting point where subjectivity can run wild. Fantasy, I like to suggest, can be seen as the realm where our cultural existence cannot be suspended but, on the contrary, can be endorsed with greater power, played with creatively. In fantasies we are being loved, able to do things, daring to transgress. For in fantasizing we are not confined by the strictness of rules and laws. Again, this is not to say that laws are being suspended but that they are somewhat loosened, and, while still lurking on the horizon, they are less daunting. In his fantasiz-

6. Peter Brooks (1984) discusses "reading for the plot" as a desire for a postponed but always anticipated ending.

ing moments, Mann's Joseph, Mut's Yusuf, questions the laws but sees them in soft focus. As he sees himself in soft focus, the delimitation lines of his subjectivity blur—he imagines himself in dreamy sepia colors.

Without going into the detail of psychoanalytic discourse on fantasy, as I have done elsewhere (1991, 108–13), I will quote nevertheless a definition of fantasy by a psychoanalyst. I quote this passage because it points to the issues at stake in Mann's novel: its relation to Genesis, on the one hand, and the limits of subjectivity on the other.[7] I also quote this passage for reasons of methodology. In the interest of interdisciplinary analysis I am taken by the fact that the passage uses the vocabulary of the theater. This is quite common in psychoanalysis (e.g. Weber 2000; Bollas 1987). Theater, as Maaike Bleeker has it, is a "critical vision machine" (2006). For me, this vocabulary has the double attraction of making the theory concrete and visual, like a play on stage, and of giving it a cultural rather than an individual status—a play is seen by the collectivity of theatergoers. Theater and subjectivity, the utterly public and the hard-core private, become each other's conceptual metaphor. This is key to the preposterous impact of Mann's novel.

In his book on mimesis and identification, psychoanalyst Mikkel Borch-Jacobsen writes:

> The fantasy . . . is there in front of me, in the mode of *Vorstellung*: I (re)present it to myself. Better still, I (re)present myself through some "other," some identificatory figure who enjoys in my place. But the point from which I contemplate the scene—the fantasy's "umbilical cord," we might say, through which it is linked with what is invisible for the subject—is not offstage. I am *in* the fantasy, there where I am the other "before" seeing him, there where I am the mimetic model even before he arises in front of me, there where I am acting out before any distancing, any drawing back: a nonspecular identification (blind mimesis) in which consists (if he/it consists) the entire "subject" of the fantasy. (1988, 44–45)

7. The relation of the novel to other sources, most notably the Qur'an, will be discussed in chapter 6.

This passage can do with some unpacking. The fantasy is there: it is primarily represented and presented, given shape and pointed at, as a thing: visible, tangible, concrete, and detached from "me." The author insists on the separation of the fantasy from the subject performing it. This is the first difference between fantasy and, say, reflection, where the subject knows she is thinking. There are, in fact, two different differences at play here, of levels and of kinds. First, reflection can be a simple mirroring, a specular throwing back to the subject what he or she has put forward; or a self-scrutiny, an intellectual and critical endeavor. Second, it can reflect (in both senses) either the subject or the object onto which the image is projected or the ideas brought to bear.

The distancing of the act positions the content and form of the fantasy away from the subject, thereby bestowing on it a status close to a cultural artifact. Fantasizing, the author suggests, involves a doubling of the subject, who thereby creates an "other" to "do" the fantasized things the subject feels attracted to doing. This split-off other character is not inhibited from doing, desiring, and acting out what the subject may hesitate to dare. The result is a "scene," something that happens at some distance, perhaps on stage. Away from the subject cowering in a corner, the fantasized subject stands in the spotlight. But, and this is the difficulty of this insight, the fantasizing subject is not cut off from the scene. He or she is both onlooker and actor, self and other, "I" and "he." This will become relevant in the discussion of Rembrandt's little etching of our story and the scene in Mann's novel where Mut stages, as a theater director, just such a fantasy.

Both love and hate are emotions that extend the self beyond its own boundaries. Love, in this sense, challenges the autonomy of the subject, that hobbyhorse of rationalism. But, still echoing Rahv's view of myth, the craze for autonomy is the fear of love. Yusuf's general attractiveness, his lovability, in itself already calls into question the individual delimitation of the subject, the limits between self and other. In view of Borch-Jacobson's conception of fantasy, it is possible to make this more drastic and read this character as an embodiment of fantasy. His gender position as well as his own desires is thoroughly ambiguous, all the time, and this makes it possible to say that he functions as a screen on which all others project their fantasies, especially those who "image" their most problematic feelings. But since the subject is inside the fantasy, inside the scene as well as seeing it, Yusuf can be said to *make* the boundaries of the subject permeable. The use of the verb *making* acknowledges the agency of Yusuf as a character of fantasy. He "is" not simply a subject drawn in soft-focus lines; he opens himself up to the blurring of those lines. He shines out from within. But as opposed to Kugel's conclusion that he retains his core self, the lack of sharp lines cancels out that core. He has no hard core. Instead of a drawing, he becomes a colorist or impressionist painting.

This feature—of being a subject-in-extension—turns Yusuf into a hub that brings the novel close to a discourse later known as postmodernist. According to Brian McHale (1987) modernism is defined by epistemological skepticism. The question "what can we know?" predominates. Postmodernism radicalizes this doubt. If we cannot know what we can know, then how do we know "it" exists at all? Thus epistemological doubt when radicalized becomes ontological doubt, or skepticism. Uncertainties about perception, the projected nature of interpretation, its nature as always-already a rereading, and the various descriptions of entities like characters are modernist features, all quite noticeable in Mann's novel. But the suspension of the limits of being, the identification between characters that are normally distinct, such as Borch-Jacobson's formulation of fantasy suggests, would point to postmodernist tendencies. As would discontinuities within one character—most clearly, the attractive Yusuf and the self-satisfied power broker.[8]

A certain metanarrative status bestowed on this character, a status derived from his emphatic elusiveness and the subsequent impossibility of pinpointing the story as a universal myth, is also a proto-postmodernist feature. This does not mean the novel "is" postmodern but that from the retrospective vantage point of our later insight in postmodernism it can be seen as extending its historical existence forward, toward that future. Such was the project of the Bible and Culture Collective, which published a "postmodern Bible" (Aichele 1995).

8. This discontinuity can also have implications of identity, as Murat Aydemir has demonstrated (2006).

McHale does something similar when he rightly emphasizes similarities between postmodern poetics and Renaissance poetry (1987; 2004). He was able to see the metapoetic elements in Renaissance poetics more clearly after thoroughly studying postmodern fiction. Hence his view of Renaissance poetics is preposterous, in the best sense of the term. Later I would like to extend this preposterous historicizing act to visual art of the seventeenth century, in this case, Rembrandt's depictions of the allegedly universal myth. For now, and finding support in Stephen Frosh's preposterous rehistoricizing of Joseph (2005), I recall the epigraph to this chapter. "Joseph," for Freud, stands for a screen protecting him from his egomaniacal dreams of grandeur. In his dream book he wrote, "It will be noted that the name Joseph plays a great part in my dreams . . . My own ego finds it very easy to hide itself behind people of that name, since Joseph was the name of a man famous in the Bible as an interpreter of dreams" (1900, 624). Joseph was the eternal foreigner, going where he would not be able to settle, spelling trouble as soon as Jacob his father thought he could finally settle down in life—and in Canaan.[9]

Several scholars have taken Freud up on his suggestion. As a screen image of fantasies of identity, Joseph is indeed a key figure. The figure facilitates the construction of identity in fragmentation and instability. Frosh describes Jewish identity and, indeed, identity in general through the difference between Jacob and Joseph, the former attempting to achieve closure, the latter the wanderer and troublemaker. Frosh's discourse is willfully preposterous. He takes the canonical books as metaphors, hence as "living books," in the case at hand, as guidelines for identities that are by definition "broken" (2005, 181). This fragmentation is a positive feature, and counters Jacob's attempt to settle, which, as Zornberg has it, is fatally flawed (1995). Frosh, who refers to Zornberg's view, sees the fragmented nature of identity as both narrative and positive, and has me on his side: "Each one of us, that is, continually tells, reworks, and retells the story of our lives, with the notoriously unreliable nature of memory contributing to our ever-fertile capacity for reinvention" (2005, 186). What he does

9. The fact that both Yusuf's father and Freud's were named Jacob may not be entirely irrelevant to this identification.

not mention is the other metaphorical aspect, visible only when we take metaphors as literally as I have argued we should: that Jacob's wish to settle is geographically and politically specific. If anything from this postmodern view of identity has contemporary resonances, it is the local placement, the appropriation of a place as "home," that Joseph's adventures counter.

Place is not only a geographical and political bone of contention but also a psychic one. The privileged place of dreams, the unconscious, is both familiar and foreign—which, obviously, also underlies my choice for the ambiguous (between Hebrew and German) name Mut and the differently ambiguous (between Western and Arabic) name Yusuf. I glean from Borch-Jacobson's definition of fantasy, along with McHale's preposterous postmodernism, a view of Mut as a character who steals the show—a noun to be taken at its word!—from Joseph during the episode under scrutiny.

Mann's "vindication" of this woman has led him to give her a function that is fundamentally different from that in Genesis. There she is merely a motivator, an element that moves the plot forward. Joseph has to fall in order to rise. Mut is as necessary to make this happen as is the house that confines her. Once that has happened, she is made redundant. Mann, by contrast, strengthens her position, depicting her as a full, dense character. As we will see later, she is at her strongest as a character when she stages and acts out a fantasy. Narratively speaking, she becomes Yusuf and Yusuf becomes her. Thus the text calls into question not only the identities of characters but also the distinction between the sexes that is their primary feature. Mann's myth is not the myth of the young man, the Chaste Youth. He uses the story of the son, triply sonlike, to open our eyes to the hitherto foreclosed story of the woman, in ways that will become apparent, by also "giving" her the status of daughter.

In this way, the novel can be seen not as a version of the (same) myth but as an instance of "versioning." This term, developed by Esther Peeren in a response to Bakhtin's theory of culture, indicates an active intervention in prior material. The gerund includes the activity of the verb as well as the result, "a form of agency that keeps identity in motion" (Peeren 2005, 212). And Peeren adds to this exercise in taking words seriously: "The element of continued transformation is strengthened by version's affiliation with variant and varying, derived from *varius*, changing or diverse" (212). Moreover, *versioning* comes close to *montage*, a term that in turn recalls flatness, the lack of hard-core stability I invoked above. Versioning is a rereading that alters its alleged model radically. Versioning is turning—in Mann's case, turning away. The resulting antiversion takes up, examines, and alters the three elements that structure the Genesis text. These elements, in my rereading of that text, are talk, possession, and the house, in a triangulation close to strangulation.[10]

In Genesis, Mut talks a lot. But on closer scrutiny, she constantly fails in her speech acts. She performs the speech act central to Shoshana Felman's discussion of literary speech acts, namely seduction (Felman 1983). It is an act in which she notoriously fails, perhaps because her speech act wavers. It remains ambiguous, between order and invitation. Grammatically, "lie with me" is an imperative form, but clearly the order can misfire. She also performs the speech act that undermines speech act theory, namely the lie, the one that appears to be rigorously constative—answerable to as assessment of truth or falsity—but results in such heavy consequences that it clearly defeats the distinction between constative and performative that J. L. Austin, the theory's architect, had first proposed (1975 [1962]).

She also uses reported speech—still lying—when she says she had cried out loud when Yusuf assaulted her: "when he heard that I lifted up my voice and cried" (Gen. 39:15). But reported or indirect speech is itself a flaw in the theory of speech acts, because it pretends to report the precise words of the earlier speaker, while it cannot guarantee that precision. Intertextually, this lie performs the speech act of self-defense, in a biblical-legal sense. It clears Mut of the possible accusation of adultery. But the reiteration of the verb *to cry* also points to the insufficiency of speech, due to its unclear distinction from mere sound or noise. The verb used in this pack of lies is the same, reiterated three times in two verses. She calls the men, summoning them, then she cries out with a loud voice, then she reports that she lifted her voice and cried.

10. Theorizing identity construction as intersubjectivity, Peeren develops the concept of versioning through an analysis of the Notting Hill Carnival (2005, 228–36).

Her (constative) reportage of her crying will later be reduced even more (39:19), as if the text needed to display a fear of narrative styles. Nevertheless, or because of the indirection of her speech, her lie will be effective.

Yusuf also talks, primarily performing the speech act of refusal. But when it comes to deploying the many possibilities of talk and reported speech, Mut in Genesis is a champion. Yusuf refrains from legal speech when he is accused and does not defend himself. After the succinct rendering of the lie, the master—who doesn't speak at all—simply gets angry and acts. As if speaking and acting remained separate activities. Of course, Mann has all the words of the world at his disposal. Talk is carried out plentifully in his exceedingly long novel. Compared to the nameless woman in Genesis, Mut is much better equipped linguistically, carrying out her speech acts with greater skill. Yet she, too, needs to act when speech is insufficient.

Possession does not have the relevance in the novel that it has in Genesis. The Genesis Joseph keeps repeating how his master has put into his hand all it can possibly contain and more, only to deduce how absolutely Mut belongs to the master, not him. This limited speech is significant if we look at it as a deployment of relations. The giving and taking is clearly a business between men, the woman being only one more item to be given or withheld. But Mut's speaking qualifies this objectification. Yusuf ignores her self-assertion and accepts the power of the father placed above him. In short, the explanation of his refusal lies in his savvy handling of his position as a social climber. This fits well with the invention of capitalism for which he will later be credited, at least by my father.

In contrast to Genesis, the novel gives possession a different role to play. It concerns not so much earthy goods or capitalist skills as the relationship between Yusuf and the fathers. Mann keeps returning to this relationship, fleshing out what the focus on father-son relationship does to subjectivity. Here the fathers are more ambivalent than in Genesis. The father-god claims his sexual abstinence and shows a jealousy preposterously reminiscent of the biblical jealous god in other stories, not Genesis 39. I was reminded of the jealous god of Genesis 3, who couldn't stand humans' equality to him. But in the novel this jealousy is sexually colored and is also related to Yusuf's narcissism and his lack of realism.

The third element, the house, is the place where Mann acts in the construction of his antiversion. In Genesis the house, as we have seen, is a place of bondage and a site of power. Joseph goes back and forth between inside and outside. With Potiphar tactfully exiting and entering at the key moments of the drama, the house becomes the signifier of the two relationships in which Joseph is involved. In the house Joseph evolves, slowly, after three births, to become a worldly man of power. He is born, with great difficulty, from his mother's womb. He is born again when taken out of the pit in which his brothers had cast him, out of jealousy for his position as favorite son. And he is delivered from the third "womb," the prison or closed-house in which Mut has him confined. The house, always-already a closed-house, is the condensed image of this confinement, birth, and ascension. But it is not his house. The words that act are not his words.

The house—I have written elsewhere about the deep ambivalence that permeates that motive (1988a, 169–97). The house that promises safety but doesn't deliver, that curtails freedom and makes inhabitants prisoners: that house houses monsters. This might well be so because there is a metaphorical analogy between the house and the self it houses. Beal wrote about this: "They [monsters] stand for what endangers one's sense of at-homeness, that is, one's sense of security, stability, integrity, well-being, health and meaning. They make one feel *not at home at home.* They are figures of chaos and disorientation *within* the order and orientation, revealing deep insecurities in one's faith in oneself, one's society and one's world" (2002, 5).

The house as place and frame, as symbol and structure, is a closed, limited, and limiting structure where safety and danger coexist and freedom skirts confinement. The function of the house in establishing and reinforcing divisions of labor, and in particular the divide between private and public as a means of keeping women in their place, has been studied by anthropologists. A well-known study is an early feminist collection edited by Shirley Ardener in which many different aspects and cultural contexts are confronted (1981). A house has the additional virtue of being able to be visualized. This will happen in the visual art that projects onto the story its own versions, or antiversions. In Rembrandt's works the house is reduced to the bedroom on the one hand and to the frame on the other. Both visual elements act narratively and serve to confine not only Joseph but the three members of the strangulating triangle. Not so in Mann's novel.

While the sparse, short story in Genesis uses repetition of the word *house* as a structuring device, both narratively and stylistically, Mann's wordy novel seems almost to dispense with the house. Yusuf needs no house, and he talks enough, even too much. Early on, though, he once decided not to talk when it most mattered, but to act—negatively—instead. On his way to Egypt, he has an opportunity to send a message to his father. He prefers not to. He is so convinced of his power that he acts arrogantly. Demonstrating hubris, he thus breaks with his father before his time. This attempt to break away from the son position fails; he is thrown back into that position right away. Having been forced into the pit by his brothers, the emergence from which into slavery represents a renewed birth with increased dependence, he voluntarily assumes the position of the newly born once more, the fatherless child in search of parents. But he does so under the assumption that he needs no father—his utter fantasy. Mann's decision to attack, to diverge radically from what he also takes to be his model, shows the function of the myth as screen for the projection of fantasy. As we will see in the next chapter, this fantasy character is also deployed, literally mise-en-scène, in Rembrandt's tiny etching.

I have set up the importance of fantasy for many reasons, one of which is to cast it against the backdrop of fundamentalism—*bien étonnés*, perhaps, *de se trouver ensemble*. So far, I have used the term *fundamentalism* to indicate a mode of reading, a semiotic posture, being well aware that this term invokes hot debates, suspicion of others, deployment as a slur, implying an accusation of violence and political strife. It is also a modern concept. I wish to maintain the connection between what is often seen in such contested terms and what seems—but only appears to be—an "innocent" cultural posture. Only by suspending the many connotations and implications, yet keeping these available, can I substantiate my case for the importance of shifting reading attitudes.

Precisely because this chapter deals with fantasy do I briefly evoke fundamentalism here, so as to keep it far removed from the suggestion that this anti-semiotic mode of reading is inherently Islamic, Christian, or Jewish. Nor, I hasten to add, is the rampant fundamentalism in the contemporary world a reason to dismiss religion as the cause of this logical, cultural, and semiotic aberration. Instead it is a reading posture that, as I have already suggested, takes signs as transparent and meanings as eternal. That this mode of reading is heavy with political consequence need not be emphasized.

Fundamentalism is averse to modernization, at least in the standard view of the issues it raises. But even that is a simplification. As Herman Beck has convincingly argued, if we are to understand the politics of religious movements in a more nuanced way that is adequate to their specific principles, the opposition between modernist and fundamentalist Islam should be suspended.[11]

The same, of course, would hold between modernist versus fundamentalist Christian and Judaic movements. Beck's analysis seeks to demonstrate that features of modernism and features of fundamentalism coincide in the same movement. Thus, the author counters the notion that fundamentalism is inherently, rather than sometimes coincidentally, antimodern (also B. Lawrence 1998). Similarly interested in breaking up the cluster of meanings attached to the term, I wish to foreground fundamentalism as a reading posture, whether or not political consequences are alleged to be derived from it.

Beck sums up five features of fundamentalism that he then confronts with the principles of the Islamic movement he is studying, to come up with a convincing assessment that this movement shares some features with fundamentalism but not all and can therefore not be cast in the category of fundamentalism. For him, the five features must all be present in order for the label to apply. To summarize Beck's own synthetic overview, these features are the following:

11. For the standard view, see, for example, Moaddel 1998. This more nuanced argument is developed in an analysis of the tenets of the Islamic Muhammadiyah movement in Indonesia (Beck 2001). The seminal overview by James Peacock and Tim Pettyjohn makes the same point, alleging the same movement and the different labels attached to it (1995).

1. oppositionalism (especially against modernization and
   relativism)
2. the belief in the infallibility of divine inspiration (of scripture,
   but also represented in the canonical tradition of commentary)
3. authoritarianism, with resulting exclusivism and intolerance
4. anti-individualism
5. finally, reactive, defensive (against modernization and secular-
   ization), and selective (only certain aspects of the tradition are
   kept current)

Beck was writing about a religious-political movement; I am
concerned with modes of reading. With these five features in
mind, though, it is easy to realize how a fundamentalist reading of
Yusuf's adventure with Mut can obscure all the features of the text
that clash with such a mode of reading, and those are the features
that a literalist reading will bring to the fore. Hence literalism is
not a form of fundamentalism but a tool to hold the latter in check.
Against words as weapons, literalism liberates words from their
rigid imprisonment in fundamentalist selective hostility. It turns
them into words again—conveyers of ever-shifting meanings,
sustained by the fantasies of porous subjects. As it happens, those
features obscure precisely the indicators of the fantasy character of
the scenes—both the seduction-and-betrayal scene and the scene
with Mut's women friends, on which more in the next chapter.
There I will revert to the clash between fundamentalist reading
and a more semiotic reading that I have therefore called, somewhat
provocatively, literalist, in a variety of cultural specifications. For
now, I stay a bit longer with the importance of fantasy, to substantiate my claim that literal reading does not oppose fantasy but,
on the contrary, sustains it. Through fantasy, literature, including
canonical and religious literature, can do its work.

Fantasy is an indispensable ingredient of any cultural event,
such as reading or looking at an artifact. The fivefold definition of
fundamentalism cannot dispense with fantasy either. The fantasy
of fundamentalism concerns words: the belief that words can be
killed, so that they can become deadly in death. But words cannot, must not, be stopped in their flight. Of Borch-Jacobson's rich
description of fantasy, then, I'll make two different uses. First I

will look at Rembrandt's etching and bring up some consequences of the notion that fantasy is about splitting, on-looking and looking-in, and acting at the same time. It is only because Mann has opened up the story so widely to fantasy that this reading of Rembrandt's etching becomes possible, preposterously. Then the second element of Borch-Jacobson's description, the theatricality of fantasy, will inform a return to Mann's novel.

4

Looking In: Outrageous, Preposterous

"Reading into," like the German *hineininterpretieren*, is
something like projection. It means overinterpreting, reading into a text what isn't there. Literally, the German word
suggests that what is not "in" the text lurks behind (*hinein*)
it—behind the screen, behind the veil. But what can be said
to "be" there? In spite of claims to the contrary, it is hard
to prove that a text "is" or "means" something. "Looking
in," by contrast, means to peep in, to take a peek into a space
where you are not physically located. It can mean illegitimate peeping, but it can also mean simply standing at the
edge and looking into a space, a scene, or a situation. That
is, I will argue, what is at stake in the image central to this
chapter. But whether this act is over the top, as in reading into, or illegitimate, as in peeping, remains to be seen.
Anticipating what follows, I assume it can be both, depend-
ing on the commitment or complicity of a viewer willing to
transgress in either direction, or both.

This chapter, then, is about projection, but not in a
straightforward, simple manner. Projection is part of any
form of processing signs, in reading, looking, listening, and
talking alike. As with fantasy, I wish to give projection its

legitimate place in cultural processes. Without these activities, usually dismissed as unserious, any account of cultural and intercultural interaction is simplistic and disingenuous. I will propose my own projections as a guinea pig. Some readers may find my interpretation of the image a case of looking-in in the sense of reading-into. Others may consider the act of looking along with the invitation extended by the image and the situation in which it is to be viewed an act of peeping. The collusion I will stage is meant to be performative: each reader will have to say yes or no every step of the way. The freedom to decline or go along with invitations to bow to authority or to transgress is at the heart of the moral education embedded in the storytelling of which I have such vivid memories.

Another memory—powerful, significant, and with lasting impact, although its occurrence much later in my life must transform the nature of its formative quality: I was going to a conference in Jerusalem. The conference was devoted to psychoanalysis and discourse. I had prepared a talk on Rembrandt's etching between the Bible and Dutch art. I had chosen that topic because I thought it would be impolite to go to Jerusalem and give a talk on the Bible. Talking about a Dutch and a Hebrew versioning of the story, in contrast, seemed a nice acknowledgment of my position as a foreign guest. The Rembrandt analysis was my first foray into visual art. It had come about by chance. I was looking for an image for the cover of my first book on the Bible, and my partner suggested I look into Rembrandt's etchings (see Bal 1986). I found this particular image so outrageous that I chose it for what was to be received as, I speculated, an outrageous book of feminist readings written by a non–biblical scholar, that nonexpert position I have so frequently enacted in my work. So it was with some trepidation that I prepared myself for the trip.

The way I recounted this memory here is an instance of analepsis: back, further back, and back again; first I "was going," then—before—I had consulted the book of etchings and decided to perform the outrage of putting that particular image on the cover, then—before—I had written a book that might be perceived as outrageous. At the end of the paragraph the timeline of the story joins the beginning. This mode of storytelling is quite ordinary. It does justice to the structure of memorization. First an incident happens to occur to you; then the circumstances that explain it come to mind. The increasing awareness that comes with the transformation of memories from something popping out of the unconscious into a conscious recollection is the secondary elaboration Freud theorized about dreams and their interpretation.

But the story continues with a memory of something I could never have been aware of—something that happened in the mind of my brother. Here the memory comes close to what is often understood as cultural memory: the capacity to "have" the memories of other people or, as the case may be, to see what other people see. The latter is as good an instance as any of looking-in. The evening before my departure to Jerusalem, my brother came by. He asked what I was going to talk about, and I showed him the etching. I remember laying it flat on the dining-room table in front of him. He took one look, blanched, fell silent, then said: No way! You can't do that! I thought he was overreacting. Surely he had seen a female nude before? The tradition of art history is full of them. No, that's not what shocks me, he replied. After I had lived with this image for weeks, it took me another ten minutes of my brother's excited pointing and redrawing to finally and, I suppose, reluctantly see what he saw. I was not able to integrate it into the talk, not only because I had already fully and tightly written my presentation but because it was my brother's vision, not mine. It was his act of seeing, with which, even after being totally "converted" to it, I could still not completely identify. Seeing what he saw seems a bit like free indirect discourse, where it is impossible to figure out whether the words used are those of the narrator or those of the character (see fig. 1).

The memory serves here to keep in view the widely and radically divergent things we see when looking at the same object. It makes any attempt to determine "the right interpretation" simply ludicrous. I have made the point frequently, before and after this moment, and so have many others. Where does that leave my claim for the culturally powerful impact of fantasy and the "scholarly" value of personal memories, that is, their relevance for the production of knowledge? In order to further substantiate that claim, not in spite of but thanks to the subjective nature of all reading, I will keep my brother's reaction and my resistance to it present during the inquiry into the performance of fantasy I

Figure 1. Rembrandt van Rijn, *Joseph and Potiphar's Wife*, etching, 9 × 11.5 cm, 1634; Teylers Museum, Harlem.

see in this etching. For if this etching is "faithful" to the biblical figure of Joseph while also in line with the Yusuf of this essay, it is the projected quality of what "he" supposedly sees that is the subject of this chapter.

This chapter is being written under the aegis of Borch-Jacobson's first quoted sentence about fantasy: "The fantasy . . . is there in front of me, in the mode of *Vor-stellung*: I (re)present it to myself." There, on the table, flat, a small piece of paper. I see its lower edge first, then move upward—that is, further back. Paintings on a museum wall are seen differently, frontally. Moreover, the etching is tiny, soliciting a minute, detailed mode of looking, as well as a kind of visual privacy. This was, I thought later, perhaps an aspect of my brother's shocked reaction. Perhaps sensing some of this but without being aware of it, for the lecture in Jerusalem I had purchased a great number of photographic prints on hard photographic paper instead of a single slide of the etching. I intended to put an image with the best possible quality in front of my interlocutors, not project it large on a screen. It had to be in front of everyone as it had been for me; I wanted everyone to experience it as I had—as "me."

The etching is in front of its viewer in the mode of *Vorstellung*, a representation put or set (*Stellung*) in front (*vor*) me. This terminology recalls Freud's fourth mechanism of dream censorship, *Rücksicht auf Darstellbarkeit*, usually translated as "considerations of representability" but more adequately rendered by Samuel Weber as "considerations of staging," related to mise-en-scène. In order to end up in dreams—or fantasies—latent thoughts must not only be imagined, that is, fictionalized, but also "imaged," turned into pictures. It is also a re-presentation, presenting to me an action, a drama, or a story I always already knew. The etching presents the story-action anew, pointing it out to me as physically available to, even bound to, my eyes.

At the same time it is a representation in the more ordinary sense. It gives a "version" of the story. It represents the figures. It speaks "about" them. But, Gayatri Spivak has insisted, in this ordinary sense there is always also an element of the other sense of representation (1999). The other sense, the political sense of representation—as in elected officers speaking for the electorate they represent—is never far away. This sense makes it so tempting to slip in the universalism of myth: one woman standing in for, as if elected to represent, all women. Lustful Stepmother elected to speak for all women—or, rather, *about* all women. This universalizing tendency emerges out of fear of this particular woman— of acknowledging her individually.

I tried to counter this universalizing tendency with the paper photographs, asking everyone in the audience to put their copy "in front of me" so as to "(re)present it to myself." Trying to approximate the situation where fantasy can perform itself, I hoped to put my interlocutors in a position to turn from the political sense of representation to the aesthetic one, where the scene in front of "me" figuring another "me" is attached, with an umbilical cord, to "me" the onlooker. This splitting-cum-binding of the subject in fantasy prepares the ground for the insight that fantasy is cultural, not (simply) individual; subjective but produced by a porous—not individualistic—subject. The split also helps me understand that fantasy is a good place to look for an integrated analysis of both what a viewer sees, including the projections

inevitably informing that vision and how that projection happens. In other words, I seek to demonstrate that a reading can be
at the same time totally, outrageously subjective and analytical,
metasubjective so to speak, albeit necessarily "preposterously."

I mean to undermine the either-or opposition between subjective and objective, universal, general; between looking-in, along
with others, and looking at what's out there. Instead of main-
taining a false dichotomy between subjective and objective readings—a dualism I strongly reject—I wish to demonstrate three
other possibilities. One is the possibility of articulating the idea
of "wrong reading." While the right interpretation cannot be
claimed and misreadings are pervasive, useful, even necessary to
reconnect past to present, mistaken readings can be pointed out,
while they can be both productive (Bloom 1980) and foreclosing
(myth). This pointing out of "wrong" readings would be the feed-
back loop between interpretation and its triggers. This loop protects the artifact—here the etching of Joseph and Potiphar's wife,
of Yusuf and Mut—against utterly alien projections that sever
the tie between looking and image entirely. Second and as a consequence, I contend that readings cannot be proven right but can
be proven possible. Third, if interpretation is to have any value
for (academic) knowledge, it must be in the dual sense of demonstrating what can be seen in the image and through what process
of projection this seeing develops (Culler 1981; 2006). One can
see the features of our image, but their status as sign—conveying
meaning—remains to be decided. Showing what the image does,
to put it simply, interpretation helps further our insight into interpretation as a cultural negotiation. Only if it does so can it also
contribute to a further understanding of art, both in its aesthetic
working and in the specifics of the particular artifact that is also a
test case.

I have not yet disclosed what made my brother so excited and
troubled. I will get there in due course, but to get there I must first
explain the way I had prepared to present the etching: as a "Dutch
Bible" responding to a Jewish one, a Dutch image that, according
to my reading of it, had taken the Hebrew text literally. In Rembrandt scholarship, the etching is not always treated as a biblical image but rather as a "nude" (White 1969) or an "eroticum"
(Ostermann n.d.). There is not much speculation about the artist's

intention in making it, other than a generally assumed somewhat "dirty mind," especially in the small etchings and drawings. That intention or mindset is of no import for our discussion. Instead, I am interested in the interaction between the alleged myth which the etching presumably illustrates but which it, in fact, rewrites, and the image itself, as both relatively empty screens on which projections can be cast. We must accept that there is no way to distinguish the artist's projections from the viewer's. The artist has projected fantasies onto the screen of his empty etching plate, then on the pictorial space delineated by the frame. This is distinct, but not distinguishable from what the fantasizing "me" projected. I did this as a scholar compelled to write a lecture for a particular circumstance, and now, years later, reflecting back on that moment. I am projecting, no less, in my attempt to argue for the instability of myth and the cultural importance of a subjectivity made up of blurred lines without a heart or hard core.

Even if these projections cannot be distinguished, acknowledging them makes it possible to look without a fear of history, of words, and of the specificity of fantasy—as well as without fear of media. If the image is more overtly sexual than the paintings I will discuss later, this difference must not be seen without taking the medium into account. This is the reason I offered the photographs instead of projecting a slide, why I put the photograph in front of my brother on the table, and also why I had been able to spend weeks in the company of this image prior to my triangular confrontation with it, myself, and my brother. To clarify my case, I first attempt to offer a reading that can easily be mistaken for formalist. Without making the formalist claim that what I see is "in" the image, I do attempt to follow a rhetoric of intersubjective persuasion. To that effect, I appeal to the most easily recognized visual elements. For example, the composition—that is, the distribution of lines on the available surface—the body, and the represented act of looking are all elements I can describe for you, and you can follow my description, checking it against what you see for yourself.

The composition consists of different lines: horizontal, but primarily vertical and diagonal. The strongest line is that of the vertical object beginning at the bottom right. Over against this are the weak lines of what appears to be a door in the upper left

corner. From lower right to upper left the image is further filled
with curving, diagonal lines, which also affect the only figure that,
standing, could have been expected to be made up of verticality.

The woman's body is part of the curving diagonals that characterize baroque aesthetics. It is also twisted. The upper part is
turned toward the man we call Yusuf, the lower part is turned
away from him, toward the viewer "coming into" the image,
drawn by Borch-Jacobson's umbilical cord, and helped by the
position of the sheet of paper lying flat on the table. What the
viewer thus entering is offered is simply this: a twisted body, a
play of lines, straight and curved. Even these simple and ostensively formal elements cannot be attributed to the artist's intention. The twisted body, for example, might simply be the result of
a bad day, a Monday-morning job. From my first encounter with
the image I found the woman's body strange. It was what drew
me to the image, what rendered it provocative, challenging, indeed outrageous to me. It made no sense, neither artistically nor
realistically, and that nonsensical quality attracted me, forcing me
to stay with the image and think as hard as I could.

I also see in the image propositions for viewing, points offering
positions where a viewer might take up position, letting himself be
guided by what I see as lines of sight leading up to as well as led by
the figure of Yusuf. Such lines of sight in no way guarantee that
this is how people actually look, obeying the indications offered.
All we can say is that viewing positions are being represented, but
whether actual viewers accept being thus represented is beyond
the image's control; the two meanings of representation are not
to be conflated. Such lines do facilitate experiments. For now, I
conduct such an experiment. I position myself at the lower edge,
at the bottom of the bedpost, enter the image, and taking the light
as my guide, the interplay of light and dark that makes up a black-
and-white image such as this etching, let myself be directed from
bottom right to middle, then to top left. Reaching the other end
of the flow, perhaps, in terms of strength of lines drifting toward
the thematic center of the image, I stop at Yusuf's eyes. And here
my trouble begins.

A first clash occurs here between commonsense projections,
the assumptions culturally available about the universal myth,
in other words, the fear of the signifier, the fear of history, and

Figure 2. Detail of figure 1 (Joseph's head).

the determination to take the image at its words—or signs, or lines. We "know" that Joseph fled the bedroom or the house, at this point of the story. Christopher White asserts that he looks away from the scene, toward the door for which he seems to be heading (1969). But a line or blot is like a word, to be taken seriously. The black blot in the corner (from the vantage point of the viewer) of his eye does not fill up the entire eye; the left corner remains white. This can only mean—if it doesn't mean an artist's mistake—that he is looking back. His head is turning to the door, his eye looks back (see fig. 2).

Of course it is no mistake or haphazard blur. Without that bit of white the image would have had a simple story line, depicting one movement, to be processed in one sweep of the eye. And the viewer would have had no reason to be stopped, as I was, and compelled to return, spend more time with the image, and embark on a narrative reading with more episodes than one. But to what are those eyes looking? Here our possibly consensual rhetoric is stopped in its tracks. The black blot in the eyes can be formally pointed out, but not the direction of the figure's look. This remains stubbornly ambiguous. Is he looking back to the woman's body, or to the vertical object I see as a bedpost? Or to the bottom of that object, the place where the represented, or my imagined, viewer enters the image? Indeterminacy, Derrida responded to critics accusing him of political indifference, is not undecidability. On the contrary. It is because signs remain indeterminate that the user of the sign is—also politically—responsible to decide (Derrida 1988). Instead of unreflectively projecting (only), then, I take it upon me to decide that the eyes look, at least possibly, or also, in the direction of the (imagined) represented viewer, at the bottom of the bedpost. That is, I can meet his eyes. This meeting of looks, both furtive, on the order of the glance—rather than the gaze—as Norman Bryson's distinction would have it (1983), substantiates Borch-Jacobson's umbilical cord. Here, that is, the "me" who fantasizes is stitched to the fantasized "me." This stitching positions me doubly in relation to that strangely twisted woman's body.

This move of in-looking does not destroy the ambiguity. On the contrary, it takes the latter at its word, accepting the blot's status as a shifter. The blot in Yusuf's eye allows me to freely move from his eyes, where I am also positioned now, to Mut's body on the bed, the bedpost, and my own entering position. Thanks to these ambiguous eyes the image is now mine to play with, and in. Not as in a liberal "free play" but as in fantasy's scene, upon which I must take my role, daring and bold because it is "only" a fantasy, yet responsibly, as a porous subject who must contend with the "other" on stage. From here on, then, the (re)reading of the image becomes outrageous, because it no longer claims formal reliability, although I maintain my position as a subject bound to the fantasy that the image has now become and to the intersubjectivity that sustains my writing. And it becomes preposterous, recasting the past as the present's possibility, its future. It seems fitting that the material to which I remain bound in doing this is the trace of the etcher's burrow. For the trace, as Derrida contended, projects forward as much as pointing back (1976).

I return to the spectatorial position I had seen, or projected, on the bottom right, suggested by the line of sight. I decide to follow these directions and accept the emphasis on diagonal lines this beginning or entry point reinforces. As a result, the woman's body appears to turn away from me. Of it, I see the genitals first, the protruding belly second. I don't yet dwell on its strangeness; I continue my travel to Joseph's face, his eyes, and look back with him, furtively, with a glance. This joint look—of "me" in the scene of the other, Yusuf, and of "me" looking on—is, strictly speaking, a visual equivalent of what literary scholars call "free indirect discourse." This is a form that leaves the speaker of the sentence ambiguous, indeterminate. The words can be those of either the narrator or the character or both at the same time. Identifying with a character who is "in" the scene—text-internal or "diegetic" hence fictional—looking "with" him amounts to what in terms of narrative theory would be considered a conflation of two forms of looking-with, technically called focalization. It means looking with the embedded focalizer, the one represented within the scene, and with the embedding one that "directs" the scene.[1] Between Yusuf's furtive glance turned back and my immodest identification, the fat, protruding belly of the woman (Mut) is visually caught. Seeing it "with" Yusuf, from inside the story, its present in that confining bedroom without knowledge of the future, I also see the bedpost, that unmovable vertical thing that had allowed me to peep in. Hitting my own spectatorial position and arriving thus at the beginning, I am set on a course of back-and-forth between the two "me" positions in the fantasy. Somewhat dizzying, this movement also enforces an awareness of that double position that allows me to act out and understand that position at the same time. However, while the umbilical cord keeps the two glued together, it is still impossible, according to the logic of ambiguity, to see the two at the same time (Rimmon 1977).

How can we go from this utterly fantasy-based ambiguity to an exercise of cultural-political agency? I will seek an answer to that question by bringing together two seemingly disparate issues, the political one of voyeurism and the academic one of historical (support for) interpretation. For the former, I recall the frequently depicted case of ambiguity: Freud's head morphing into a woman's body. "What's on a man's mind?" it is called, I believe. In that case, clearly, there is a hierarchy. Freud is the subject of fantasizing, the woman the "other," the fantasized subject. To muddle the waters a bit, let me emphasize that in our etching there is no direct eye contact between Yusuf and the external viewer, or between the fantasized "other-me" and the fantasizing "me." We cannot meet his eyes directly. We see his eyes; he doesn't see ours. The external viewer is invisible, yet omnipotent when it comes to looking. This turns her or him onto a voyeur.

This role is strengthened if the viewer follows my suggestion—or the image's?—to enter the image on the bottom right. This is not required; it isn't even conventional, since in the West, following the direction of alphabetical reading, looking from left to right is

---

1. I am using the terminology of narrative theory, my primary field of training. For all these technical terms, see Bal 1996.

routine. The possibility to follow that convention is made slightly uncomfortable in two ways. First, it is easier to move from darker to lighter portions of the surface. Second, the narrative dynamic, underscored by the lively scene, the "known" story, and the undulating diagonal line of the composition, counters the alphabetic mode of looking. I mention this to denaturalize the voyeuristic position and its consequences, on which more below. The occupation of the bottom-right position is a choice, but one which makes sense in terms of the image when laid out flat before the viewer—a measure of freedom gently proposed. Once taken, the identification with that vertical object becomes easy, because of the object's contiguous contact with the outside edge. This makes it a suitable mediator, an element in the image that mediates among the viewer, the work, and an outside frame of reference.

What frame of reference would you like to call on here? Let's face it. Its strong vertical presence, as opposed to the weak line of the other vertical object—the door at the other side—suggests, to "me" at least, a psychoanalytic frame of reference. Let me dare the leap, then, and see this object as phallic. Here you have it! More specifically, it comes to symbolize both the outsider position and the scepter, the latter signifying both power in general and the particular power of the voyeuristic position. The latter is characterized by noncommunication. The position is attractive because of its safety: one is looking without being seen. Thus the object is suggestive of the outside viewer in absentia. Needless to say, that position is also gender-specific, at least traditionally. The voyeur becomes a man who looks right into the woman's genitals. Is this "me"? If so, it is a "me" who, in spite of my feminist convictions, endorses a male habit, as a reluctant guest. This is one of those moments, then, where acting out the fantasy must go hand in hand with reflection on it.

Becoming aware of the masculinity of the external outsider's position tends to also make me aware of a significant absence in the image. There is no sign of Potiphar. Or is there? Well, yes, literally so, the sign of the symbol of power. The pro forma husband absent from the fantasized scene of seduction must return in the story for the sequel, the denunciation scene, to take place. Perhaps the bedpost casts a symbolic shadow of the husband already into this scene, on the stage where voyeurism implies power as well as fear of being seen. Perhaps at this point I have pushed the encounter with the image further than most readers will accept. So, as a gesture of academic goodwill, let me turn to the second issue, of historicality.

Is there any historical support for this reading, so that those who fear the anarchy of subjectivity can be reassured? The desire for such evidence is an academic habit and as such is as much entitled to acknowledgment as reading from left to right or voyeurism. To see if there is historical support, it makes sense to turn to the Dutch seventeenth century, the timeplace or chronotope (Bakhtin 1981) of this image's emergence. The Bible translation that was most authoritative at the time was the so-called Staten translation, the official one produced in the wake of Synod of Dordrecht in 1618–19, at the command of the Staten Generaal der Verenigde Nederlanden, the first document of national unity in the Netherlands. There the double status of the man within the closed space of the house is foregrounded. He insists that it is within the house that his power is no less than that of his master, and the woman is called *huisvrouw* (house-woman), still the normal Dutch indication for a woman without professional status.

There is no evidence that the historical person Rembrandt the painter possessed a copy of this particular translation, although this would be likely; nor even that he actually *read* the Bible actively before setting out to represent biblical stories—this would be unlikely. He may have been too busy painting, drawing, or etching. Even so, he would rely on his doxic knowledge of the stories as they went around, in the culture imbued with the wordings of the Staten translation and the Lutheran one that closely resembles it. Such were the words that thundered from the pulpit on Sundays in a culture of an antivisual Reformation that had newly discovered, and was busy promoting, the value of reading the text—literally. This diffuse knowledge is as likely to have had an effect on ordinary citizens as Kepplerian optics might have had, for which Svetlana Alpers makes a case (1983, 26–70). Both discourses were hovering in the cultural air. What Brian Stock calls a "textual community" would have been familiar with the Staten version of our story (1983).

If, in addition, we take into account the polemical background of these translations at a time of religious contestation where the grounding in the text was an issue, using and depicting the precise wording—close to the Hebrew—would be a political act, for a renewed religious fervor as much as for a unified Dutch national identity against the Spanish Catholic tradition—hence antitextual and exuberantly visual. The stark translation of the word *prison* as "closed house" and the insistence on the dangerous emptiness of the house are striking. There is even the suggestion that since the house is a prison, the prison was also inside the house, which concurs with Kugel's suggestion of this, although he qualifies it as ridiculous. All this tinkering with the word *house* can very well have translated into the looming, albeit symbolic, presence of Potiphar during the fantasy scene.

Unsubstantiated as these remarks may sound as historical evidence, they are neither more nor less tenuous than much other historical discourse. For my purposes, though, their importance lies not in their status of evidence but in the timing. The evocation of the Dutch republic of the past is informed by that other historical moment, the present—or slightly before the present, the 1990s—of feminist critique, without which this talk of voyeurism would barely have made sense. If I am sensitive to the possibility of historical substantiation—if, indeed, I desire to at least try—it is because the historical moment of feminism is itself so keenly felt whenever I use words such as *voyeurism*.

Nor does it make sense outside of the fact, emphasized so frequently in the criticism and preposterously made central in Mann's novel, of Yusuf's son position, enduring beyond its time. And it is Yusuf who reacts to the displayed body of the woman with repulsion as well as attraction. At the same time, he reacts to the phallic object and its significance. For an overripe son, the father position is the position of legal rights, of having-done-it. It is the position from where the rules are set, from where the woman is taken in possession. There is, perhaps even more speculatively, a possible theological indication that makes my interpretation less outrageous, if more preposterous in the double sense. The unnamability of the deity in Orthodox Judaism and Christianity alike makes a search for other ways of pointing at the invisible presence a meaningful thing to do. In an anti-iconic culture—and the post-iconoclastic Dutch culture of Reformation was just that—hidden icons can take the place of the unnamable, fulfilling the desire to see what cannot be beheld, say what cannot be mentioned, listen to what cannot be heard. This invisible, unnamable quality of the deity pertains quite precisely to fatherhood—that other invisible, unprovable, symbolic-only position of absolute power.[2]

According to Freud's "scientific myth," as he called it himself, the story, in his 1913 speculative text *Totem and Taboo*, of the primitive hordes of sons slaying and eating the father in their exasperation, the father imposes on the son the position from where the son is barred from sex. Mann's somewhat tenuously motivated jealous god casts his preposterous shadow over this etching. The father position, finally, is the position of a different time, of the older generation in which the son cannot have membership. What a witness to have inflicted upon one's tentative encounter with the female body! Yusuf is confronted with the witness to the scene, a witness as internalized law forbidding him to do what, as I will suggest shortly, he seems to be doing. At the very least he is looking at the female body, the naked body of the father's "house woman."

I am getting closer to my brother now. Yusuf is looking where he should not be looking while simultaneously, or alternatively, looking at the authority that forbids that look. But perhaps he is doing even more. My brother seemed to think so. This whole body—hands, eyes, head, feet—is ambiguous. The head is turned away, already reaching the door of escape, but the eyes turn back, looking at the woman and the father, alternating. And his hand? Tongue in cheek, I imagine, the visual artist chuckles at the freedom of ambiguity granted him by the mere fact that the image is a still one. The hand might be grabbing for the body as well as pushing it away. Still visual images do not determine. This is not their handicap but their special power. On the basis of this ambiguity my brother had his experience of visual shock, seeing something he was not supposed to see. I will try to represent his brief and rather mad act of seeing in words. The best way to do this is suggest that my reader take a pencil and trace the line of what appears to be the fold on Yusuf's garment, which the woman holds.

2. Cornelis den Hertog has proposed a brilliant Lacanian reading of the unnamable name of the deity in the story of Moses' calling. And Moses, symmetrical to Joseph who was sold into the foreign land, is the one who led the people out of Egypt (Hertog 2006).

Another ambiguity presents itself, like either Freud's face or the naked woman, either the rabbit or the duck. Is Yusuf dreaming, or was my brother?

Psychoanalyst Christopher Bollas claims that the dreamer is positioned in the dream, in relation to the stage, its director, and its actors, props, time-frame and what-have-you, in ways that make the term *aesthetic* operative without an excessive appeal to metaphor, at least in the traditional sense of that term. In his theatricalization of the dream, Bollas phrases his theory using all the terms that characterize mise-en-scène: "I regard the dream as a *fiction* constructed by a *unique aesthetic*: the *transformation* of the *subject* into his *thought*, specifically, the placing of the self *into* an allegory of desire and dread that is *fashioned* by the ego" (Bollas 1987, 64; emphasis added). His insistence that the ego, not the subject, "directs" the play has specific relevance in the context of a discussion on mise-en-scène as well as dreams. The ego is, indeed, "other" to the subject. This alone makes subjectivity theatrical. The subject cannot take hold of, grasp, or confine the ego. We can now see, in a somewhat literal sense, how and why the sleeper is both the subject of the dreams—the dreamer as well as the subject matter—and emphatically not the dream's subject: not its narrator, its director, or its writer/painter. This reworked theory, incidentally, offers strong support to the anti-intentionalist position as more adequate for the practice of, specifically, *cultural* analysis than the more common author-based frame of reference.[3]

As an artistic practice, mise-en-scène is one of many techniques that engage the viewer in an aesthetic experience. In this sense it is a specialised artistic field, requiring training, skills, and talent. As a concept, it refers to something more adequately indicated as a cultural practice. This practice involves us every day but especially acutely in confrontation with situations that frame-freeze, so to speak, the mise-en-scène itself, as a cultural moment in which routine is slowed down, self-awareness increased, and satisfaction gained from going outside ourselves. Theatricality, offering a fictional realm of experiment and dreaming precisely because of its artificiality, remains a productive frame for thinking of cultural

---

3. I have argued extensively for this position in chapter 7 of *Travelling Concepts* (2002).

practice as a social binding of subjects whose subjectivity remains unassaulted. It offers interactive images of that binding.

Using the terminology of theater, Bollas articulates the nature of the aesthetic involved by insisting that the ego, not the subject, directs the play. This makes sense as long as we understand that the ego is defined as being indeed "other" to the subject, out of the latter's grasp. Hence the sleeper who is "having" the dream is both the subject of the dream, metonymically bound to it, and the non-subject of it—having rather than "doing" it. The sleeper "speaks" the dream, but as its voice, performing it without controlling it, in an interdiscursivity rigorously distinct from intertextuality. For the quotation has no source, no writer. Instead, the viewer stands in as an understudy, to take over the role assigned to the subject by the dream's director. To describe the viewer's part, then, the full meaning of performance—as in theater—must be realized.

Here, one assumes, the director is not the ego (Bollas's term) of the sleeper but that of the maker of the artwork. The director-alias-dreamer is subsequently shaped, like the dreamer's ego, by individual disposition but also by the logic of cultural framing. The role of the viewer is not to be the sleeper but to stand on the stage where the dream images make their disturbing appearance. Looking in, inevitably looking-in as in reading-into, yet also looking into the scene of looking.

I have shown the Rembrandt image many times to people. Some immediately blushed or cried out; others just couldn't see it until I gave them the photograph and a pencil. One can, of course, always fall back on the hypothesis of artistic clumsiness—a position that I find defensive and pointless—but failing that, we remain confronted with the fact that the fold the woman supposedly grabs fiercely does not seem to be crumpled in her hand, as might be expected. No small folds under her hand, an absence that allows the rabbit to become a duck, or the head a woman. Without such smaller folds, the hand is holding an object that is hard, not soft—no less hard than the bedpost it rivals. According to the myth, all is simple, and we are requested to not see anything odd. According to Genesis, the woman is holding the garment that she will use to betray Yusuf. But if we "forget" Genesis, suspend this reassuring universality of the Lustful Stepmother and, especially, of the Chaste Youth, we can look at the etching at our leisure, in private, in the detail the medium encourages. We can then see the boy being tempted, fantasizing an event that, ambiguous in its turn, both frightens and tremendously excites him. Since she is the one grabbing him, he can have the sex and remain innocent, have his cake and eat it too.

I can safely assume that my reader imagines what my brother saw. This is not the end of the story of my encounter with this etching. I will return to it later. At this point, though, I feel compelled to establish a long-lost symmetry. After dwelling, that is, on a fantasy of men where the "me" of fantasizing contemplated her "me/other" on stage taking all the risks, I now revert to a case of a woman's fantasy. For this I return to Mann and his preposterous directions for how to read the Qur'an.

5

The Invention of Sympathy

I will not be the only one to have memories, good and bad, of the heyday of feminist consciousness raising. I remember the happiness in the process of discovery that our felt lone- liness was a deception, useful only for keeping "us" in our assigned place, and that in reality women had a lot in com- mon and would be better off sharing their experiences with one another. After the initial jubilant happiness, though, many disputes within feminism caused a great and deeply felt disappointment.[1]

Solidarity was a key term. This concept was so central be- cause it did *not* go without saying. Laws, rules, exhortations all emerge because their content is not self-evident. In this line of thinking, the idea of "natural law" is an oxymoron. Laws are reactions, not eternal processes. Neither regulari- ties nor seemingly chaotic outbursts of states of exception in nature are subject to such reactive laws. Just so, the call for solidarity pointed to a lack of it. Indeed, solidarity among women has been a challenge.

1. The difficulty of solidarity in feminism has been amply discussed at different moments of recent history. See, for example, Hirsch and Keller 1990; Bronfen and Kavka 2000.

I always assumed this was the case because women were trained—socialized we called it—to be rivals, not friends. They had been trained to compete for the favors of men. Men, by contrast, had learned to bond, whether they liked each other or not. Hostility to or fear of women supported that bonding. Fear might in fact be the primary motivation for said hostility, instead of the other way around. Yusuf's deference to Potiphar in the biblical text suggests as much. This perhaps simplistic view was, I remember, what informed my astonishment when I read a scene in Mann's novel that was in no way traceable to the biblical account of Joseph and Potiphar's wife. It is a scene of Yusuf and Mut.

Sympathy, solidarity, as the basis of the formation of sociocultural groups is this chapter's contribution to the intercultural semiotic I am elaborating in this book. Because it is such an extraordinary scene, I felt that Mann could not have invented it out of the blue. I started to search, and the closest I came to a possible antecedent was in the Qur'an. This, in turn, seemed meaningful as a choice of "source"—if it can be considered as such, which I cannot determine nor wish to dispute. The meaning of this choice of ante-text, to use a more open term, or pre-text, to use a slightly more tendentious one, has been an occasion for speculation to me ever since, and I will revert to it in chapter 9. Here I simply wish to present the scene to my readers. For as I read it, against the backdrop of solidarity as a social problem of our time, the scene has the kind of resonance that preoccupies me. It is a scene of pain and bloodshed, a parody of civil war, a drama of women. Nietzsche claimed that pain is the best incentive to memory, and memory (of pain) to morality. I am not sure I can see it that way, but for now, let's assume this is possible. In that case, the scene in the Qur'an and in Mann's novel deserves detailed attention.

In the middle of the turbulence caused by Mut's desperate love for Yusuf, the closed circle of the harrowing house of Genesis is broken. After the famous seduction scene in the bedroom, something else happens. In view of the ethical-artistic success Mann ascribes to himself in the preface, this scene is simply a masterpiece. I quote it here, first of all as an example of the novel's flowing, dreamy prose and dramatic mise-en-scène, so utterly different

THE INVENTION OF SYMPATHY

from the biblical sparseness of words. In addition to this general reason—to give a taste of the modernist (anti)versioning of the story—I wish to make strong claims about it, and therefore I feel the need to put it at the disposal of my readers.

In this talkative text, the character who is central in the episode cannot speak. Mut-em-enet is pressed by her women friends to tell them why she is as unhappy and sick as she appears to be, but she cannot speak about what ails her. The text proves Elaine Scarry's analysis right: pain cannot be shared (1985). Or, more precisely, Mann specifies pain cannot be shared in words. This difficulty brings us to the heart of art's social function and its limitations. Words fail Mut. The inadequacy of language must be compensated for by means of art. Note that the friends' deduction is based on appearance; clearly, faces are more telling than words. Unable to answer this request, she stages a scene instead—a scene that can be *seen* where words fail.

She invites her friends to a banquet. Toward the end of the merry meal, the following happens:

> Again Mut-em-enet had beckoned, and he who now appeared on the scene was the cup-bearer, the pourer of wine—it was Joseph. Yes, the lovesick woman had commanded him to this service, requesting, as his mistress, that he should himself serve the wine of Cyprus to her guests. She did not tell him of her other preparations, he did not know for what purpose of edification he was being used. It pained her, as we know, to deceive him and deliberately make such misuse of his appearance. But her heart was set on enlightening her friends and laying bare her feelings. So she said to him—just after he had once more, with all possible forbearance, refused to lie with her.
>
> "Will you then, Osarsiph, at least do me a favour, and pour out the famous Alashian wine at my ladies' party day after tomorrow? In token of its excelling goodness, also in token that you love me a little, and lastly to show that I am after all somebody in this house, since he at its head serves me and my guests?"
>
> "By all means, my mistress," he had answered. "That will I gladly do, and with the greatest pleasure, if it be one to you. For I am with body and soul at your command in every respect save that I sin with you."

So, then, Rachel's son, the young steward of Petepre, appeared
suddenly among the ladies as they sat peeling in the court; in a
fine white festal garment, with a colored Mycenaean jug in his
hands. He bowed, and began to move about, filling the cups. But
all the ladies, those who had chanced to see him before as well as
those who did not know him, forgot at the sight not only what
they were doing but themselves as well, being lost in gazing at
the cup-bearer. Then those wicked little knives accomplished
their purpose and the ladies, all and sundry, cut their fingers
frightfully—without even being aware at the time, for a cut from
such an exceedingly sharp blade is hardly perceptible, certainly not
in the distracted state of mind in which Eni's friends then were.

This oft-described scene has by some been thought to be
apocryphal, and not belonging to the story as it happened. But
they are wrong; for it is the truth, and all the probabilities speak
for it. We must remember, on the one hand, that this was the most
beautiful youth of his time and sphere; on the other, that those
were the sharpest little knives the world had ever seen—and we
shall understand that the thing could not happen otherwise—I
mean with less shedding of blood than it actually did. Eni's
dreamlike certainty of the event and its course was entirely
justified. She sat there with her suffering air, her brooding,
sinister, masklike face and sinuous mouth, and looked at the
mischief she had worked; the blood-bath, which at first no one
saw but herself, for all the ladies were gaping in self-forgotten
ardour after the youth as he slowly disappeared toward the pillared
hall, where, Mut knew, the scene would repeat itself. Only when
the beloved form had disappeared did she inquire of the ensuing
stillness, in a voice of malicious concern:

"My loves, whatever has happened to you all? What are you
doing? Your blood is flowing!"

It was a fearful sight. With some the nimble knife had gone an
inch deep in the flesh and the blood did not ooze, it spouted. The
little hands, the golden apples, were drenched with the red liquid,
it dyed the fresh whiteness of the linen garments and snaked
through into the women's laps, making pools which dripped down
on the floor and their little feet. What an outcry, what wails, what
shrieking arose when Mut's hypocritical concern made them aware
of what had happened! (802–3)

Some of the women are seriously wounded, and soon the court looks like a hospital ward. In its—postmodern?—excess, the scene has its moments of comedy. I will limit myself here to what I consider its most poignant event, the dream-like, half-unconscious collective production of collective suffering.

When I first read this, two things struck me most forcefully. First, I was in the middle of a study on the relations between words and images, linguistic and pictorial traditions that each in their own way struggled with the possibilities and limits, licenses and taboos, of representation. In that context, the scene's visual nature struck me immediately. This visuality is in accordance with modernist aesthetics. For example, Marcel Proust's *Remembrance of Things Past* is in many ways an exploration of literature's capacity to "paint," "photograph," and otherwise make visual the world it ostensively depicts (Bal 1997). In Mann's (or Mut's) scene this visuality is so stark that it cannot escape attention. I take this as meaningful and will speculate on its meaning in chapter 9. Second, the collective nature of the bloodbath and the subsequent pain immediately suggested to me the literal meaning of the word, with the prefix *sym-* (with) and the noun *pathy* (suffering): suffering-with. In view of theories of identification and its drawbacks, its different modes, and its alternatives, this aspect has a renewed actuality I would like to take up as well. These theories have recently been discussed widely in the context of art that grapples with the difficulties of representing suffering.[2]

Thus the two theoretical themes of the present book come to the fore: cultural memory and the social production of meaning, on the one hand, and modes of representation and their effects on the other. The position of Mann writing his novel during the advent of the Nazi power, the other producers of artifacts "on" Yusuf well before him, and my own position looking at these instances of cultural memory from after the great divide: in a

2. In this context, attention has been paid most prominently, but no longer exclusively, to art related to the Holocaust. In turn, the fiftieth anniversary of the latter disaster contributed to the interest in cultural memory, an interest made more urgent by the realization that survivors and eyewitnesses were disappearing. In particular, Marianne Hirsch (1992–93; 1999a; 1999b) has written sensitive essays about these delicate issues.

preposterous conception of history all these positions speak to each other—without merging.

Integrating the two aspects, then, I contend that the scene, versioning on an old cultural memory that sustains men's anxiety over women, literally sets the stage for a visual "theory" of solidarity. A theory that cannot be transhistorically reified but to which each moment, looking back and ahead, contributes its own reflections. The theoretical import of the scene—its status as a "theoretical object"—accounts for its stark visual appeal. Theory here is mise en scène. Like a dream we witness but in which we also participate.

The visual vividness of Mann's narrative prose is foregrounded, first, in the use of visual words, such as specifications of color and form, to describe visible things. Second, the terminology of the theater foregrounds this aspect as well. Third, a metadiscursive strand runs through the scene that draws attention to its own bias toward the visual. Hence—and in view also of the novel's repeated myth-critical commentary, to which I already drew attention—this self-reflection on the nature of the scene displays a strong push toward visuality's special contribution to the idea of the "version" and the interpretation of the story it promotes. How does this scene contribute to Mann's stated project to humanely vindicate Mut as a figure of a woman in love with a foreigner?

Visuality is a feature of a tradition in Western art and literature that, by contrast, counters such a vindication, because it depicts its objects as strange, reified, and essentialized. I am referring to the tradition of Orientalism, most prominently addressed critically by Edward Said (1978). The critique of Orientalism is by now almost commonplace in Western academic discourse. In spite of strong criticism of some of Said's notions, Orientalism as a tradition is still so common that it can be seen as a habitus in Pierre Bourdieu's sense (1984), invisible to those who practice it yet offensive to those subject to its generalizations. Traces of an Orientalist literary tradition are certainly not absent from the scene we are contemplating.[3]

---

3. Inge E. Boer has both criticized and continued Said's critique most subtly and effectively by drawing attention to its self-deconstructive aspects as well as to its stereotyping (2004a; 2004b). I find both Said's pathbreaking view and Boer's revision of it compellingly relevant for the case at hand.

The depiction of the court, the hall of pillars, the exuberant banquet, and the presence of servants fits the stereotypical imaginary of "the Orient." But overwriting this stereotype, indeed thickening its carpet, is a skilled literary form that refrains from or counterbalances the descriptive, exoticizing excess characteristic of Orientalism in literature. The passage shows a rather surprising lack of unmotivated wordiness, an economy of narrative that alternates and balances description with narration, motivation, and dialogue. There is no reveling in exoticism for its own sake. This is nothing wildly extraordinary; as Boer has argued, even the traditional Orientalists of the eighteenth century, such as Montesquieu, cannot be considered *simply* that, for their Orientalism overwrites a Western desire whose traces remain in the resulting palimpsest (2004b, 27–48).[4]

Color-wise, there is a predominance of white background, against which the red of the blood will be starkly visible. Yusuf appears "in a fine white festal garment" holding "a colored Mycenaean jug in his hands" so as to compose a memorable, "colorful" visual image. White as the color of a willfully constructed backdrop is also foregrounded in the description of the women's blood, the "red liquid" that "dyed the fresh whiteness of the linen garments." The shapes painted and lines drawn by the blood are also quite emphatic, most notably in "snaked through into the women's laps, making pools which dripped down on the floor and their little feet." The word *snaked* suggests line, the word *pools* implies shape—albeit the abstract form of blots of paint—and the term *dripping* evokes the trace of the brush. All this fits Orientalist description, except for the fact that excessive detail is lacking. The details that are there are all meaningful for the scene and its art-driven lesson.

The theatricality of the visual description is also remarkable. The scene just quoted is remarkable in this respect. The use of the very word *scene*, as in the beginning of the description, alerts us to this: "Again Mut-em-enet had beckoned, and he who now *appeared on the scene* was the cup-bearer, the pourer of wine—it was Joseph." What follows is a retrospective explanation of how

---

4. Orientalism in literature and its characteristic wordiness has been analyzed, for example, by Jan van Luxemburg in his study of Louis Couperus (1992).

he came to *appear* on the stage. The verb *to appear* must be taken in the strong sense. On the one hand it indicates the action of entering the stage. On the other it suggest a miraculous appearance of a supernatural order, pretty much in the way the women see him. The grace of Yusuf's way of moving amongst the woman appears to be rehearsed and in slow motion, as if he commences a dance: "He bowed, and began to move about, filling the cups." The women gazing at the cup-bearer are presented as both participants in the play and implied spectators, later turning into a chorus.[5]

Finally, the metacommentary with which the passage is interspersed, and which I can only read as slightly tongue-in-cheek proto-postmodernist, reminds us that this is indeed a scene. "This oft-described *scene*," begins the narrator after giving us the bare essentials, and he proceeds to claim its truthfulness. "We must remember," he says, turning cultural memorizing into an obligation. And then he comes up with a most rhetorical hyperbole, "on the one hand, that this was the most beautiful youth of his time and sphere; on the other, that those were the sharpest little knives the world had ever seen." Why must we remember this? Taking Yusuf out of his specific time and place, the narrator reiterates the absolute and metaphysical nature of his beauty—its necessity for the story to unfold through Mut's incapacity to resist her attraction to him, an attraction that serves as the basis for her vindication.

But Mann exaggerates just as strongly about the most menial of elements, the "sharpest little knives the world had ever seen." While the text thus recalls the theatrical function of the knives as props, as instruments that move the plot forward in a visible manner, it is also simply ludicrous to claim absoluteness for their sharpness. What can be the point of this latter hyperbole, which only casts the former in irony? To answer this question, we must first consider my second, seemingly unrelated response to the text: its "theorizing" of sympathy.

Sympathy, the act of suffering-with, in solidarity with someone who suffers, is an emotion we know from everyday social life as well as from aesthetic experience. Mann vividly and visually depicts a scene of suffering-with. We feel for, with, and on behalf

---

5. A study by William E. McDonald, entirely devoted to this aspect of the tetralogy, elaborates on this aspect (1999).

of others whose suffering saddens us. This emotion is not socially useful per se—only if it leads to actions that diminish the suffering. Usually when suffering is represented in fiction, we identify with the characters and weep with them, just as we feel fear when a serial killer stalks his victims in a mystery novel, even while we are safely ensconced in our armchair. But the point is not that since we are safe from grief or harm, our emotions are false, vicarious. The point is, those feelings have nowhere to go. On the contrary, spent in the aloneness of reading, they might make us more cynical or at least indifferent when suffering comes upon us in "real life." Mann counters this diffusion in this very vivid literalization. I find that move useful, because the diffuse quality of emotion is, for me, a political and ethical problem in the relation with artworks we call aesthetic experience. It is the problem of sentimentality, of an identification that either appropriates someone else's pain or exploits it to feel oneself feeling in a time when the overflow of visual representations of suffering tends to inure one to the confrontation—and thus feel good about oneself.

The visual emphasis in Mann's scene appears to be in agreement with the idea that visually represented suffering, hence, suffering that is *seen*, lends itself particularly well to an emotional appeal for sympathy. Just think of feeling that odd lump in the throat when watching a movie of great sentimental appeal. Seeing is not an automatic ticket to identification, but it lends itself to it. Then again, what is wrong with identification, why is it often not at all political but instead politically counterproductive, and what alternatives can be mobilized to shape an art that is truly political? This question emerges from Mann's passage, which represents identification without appealing to it. This is the meaning of his deflation of realism in the metanarrative reflections as well as the hyperbolic rhetoric embedded within it. The scene is emphatically not real—it is hyper-realistic. And that is what shocks us into reflection, because it denaturalizes realism as a dominant reading habitus resilient in the postrealist twentieth century. Thus the metanarrative passage draws attention to the problematic place of realism in the relationship between art and politics—the place of the political in art.

In a book on the subject of political art, Jill Bennett brilliantly explains the traps of sentimentality that seem inherent in identification when suffering is at stake (2005). Such a sentimental identification is based on an appropriation, a kind of "trauma-envy" that denies the uniqueness of the sufferer's plight. It also fails to compel the identifying subject to desire to change the situation that causes the ongoing suffering. And in the end, it fails to produce a productive empathy. Bennett's account is clear and convincing and leads her to a position on political art with which I will affiliate myself in this essay.

Bennett discusses primarily visual art, but I will generalize her points and include literature. She follows the trail of a long discussion that started with feminist and postcolonial protests against the "double exposure" of objectionable images. The traces of Orientalist fantasy in Mann's passage, counterbalanced as they are by self-reflexivity, exaggeration, and the functional use of details, concur with this caution. For the argument against "double exposure," it matters that the scene is so starkly visual. The argument in my book *Double Exposure* was that showing, unlike rendering in language, cannot avoid repeating that which the author wishes to critique and dismiss.[6]

Identification has a long history of theorizing usually considered to have begun with Aristotle's theory of catharsis. This term indicates the "purification" of emotions such as fear and pity by the vicarious experience of them when contemplating on-stage fictionalized adventures that trigger them. This discussion has been taken up also within the framework of psychoanalysis. If we keep in mind this debate on what is, indeed, best termed an ethics of vision, in my interpretation of the scene, the scene of such painful suffering-with takes on a new actuality. Loneliness is a political issue, and it can be cured by a politics of cosuffering.[7]

6. I have written about this problematic in the context of postcolonial critiques of colonialist imagery, where I found the indictment of colonial exploitation and racism was unwittingly reiterated when the offensive images were reproduced as "evidence" (Bal 1996, chap. 6). The discussion was further pursued in the 1990s, in the wake of studies of cultural memory, Holocaust studies, and trauma studies and at a time when Mann's mythical novel was a bit forgotten. Ernst van Alphen has contributed in the context of art related to the Holocaust (1997), as has Hirsch, whose work I just mentioned.

7. Lest I vulgarize this highly complex body of thought, I refrain from integrating it here but refer to Kaja Silverman's lucid and brilliant account of what she calls "an ethics of vision" in this context for an in-depth discussion indispensable for anyone interested in that field (1996). For a philosophical analysis of the politics of loneliness, see Vardoulakis 2004.

As the scene demonstrates, the politics of loneliness and the concomitant politics of cosuffering work by means of binding among the women. Therefore, I cannot dispense with some remarks on identification, since it is on this mechanism that the scene's lesson in suffering-with is based. Identification is a mostly unreflective process, a response to seeing something emotionally charged. This unreflective quality is crucial to the scene we are examining. The friends hurt themselves because of it: they see Yusuf and forget themselves, acting exactly as Mut had done before them. The term *identification* points to the act of putting oneself in the place of another emotionally, body-and-mind. It is not something one does but rather something that happens to one. This passivity is tied to or developed on the basis of earlier psychic formations and tendencies, or by socializing training under the pressure of ideological formations. This, I speculate, is the meaning of Mann's vivid description of the women's suffering as at first unaware, as an event of self-loss: "All the ladies, those who had chanced to see him before as well as those who did not know him, forgot *at the sight* not only what they were doing but themselves as well, being *lost in gazing* at the cup-bearer." The text carefully stipulates that novelty is not the cause of their loss of self, because that would have made the effect relative to time and memory. Instead it is *visuality*. It is the visual confrontation itself that makes them all vulnerable to the split of self I described earlier as the characteristic of fantasy. Sheer sight has this effect.

Mann insists that they forget both what they were doing as well as themselves. While Mut is pining away in lovesickness, her friends, quite suddenly, almost kill themselves. This is not a case of suicide, since the "self" of that term for self-killing is lost, but an involuntary movement out of Mut's friends' own subjectivity into that of Mut. Obviously, the scene is as excessive in its drama as it is implausible for someone with a realistic mindset. Mann's protestations of truthfulness, rather than making such a claim, point to the redundancy of the consideration of realism. The exaggeration itself rhetorically underscores the intellectual, "theoretical" nature of the scene as a representation not of any actual event but of the inevitability of sympathy.

Nevertheless, while such occurrences are useful reminders of the untenability of the mind-body split and the culture-nature divide, three ethical traps threaten. First, identification can occur in two ways. It takes place either on the terms of the self, who absorbs or "cannibalizes" the other, subsuming her and thus neutralizing her difference, or on the terms of the other, so that the self risks alienation in "becoming" the other. The former is appropriative, the latter potentially generous but also potentially dangerous. Silverman calls the former form idiopathic, the latter heteropathic identification, a term I have used above.[8]

For our passage, the emotional realm in which identification may occur is that of suffering caused by cutting, a literal and hyperbolic wounding. The word *cutting* is suggestive of a sudden and physical wounding. In turn, the word *wound* suggests that theoretical term that is derived from the Latin word for wound: *trauma*. The invocation of trauma, however, entails the second trap, frequently discussed within trauma studies. This is the appropriative move mentioned above, a kind of trauma-envy that cheapens other people's suffering and, in line with Scarry's point that suffering cannot be represented, de facto obscures the traumas of others.

This is a trap because, taken as a cannibalizing form of identification, the viewer identifying with other people's (represented) suffering appropriates the suffering, cancels out the difference between self and other, and in the process diminishes the suffering. Vicarious suffering, obviously, is an extremely lightened form, and if this lightening comes with the annulling of difference, in the end the other's suffering all but disappears from sight, eaten up by the commiserating viewer. Making the scene into a bloody one occurring at the other's house, Mann keeps this risk in check. To remedy this danger, historian Dominick LaCapra proposes a response he calls "empathic unsettlement." This term indicates something that Mann hyperbolically presents as "real" suffering through physical pain. Through this concept LaCapra attempts to articulate an aesthetic based on both *feeling for* another and, as Bennett phrases LaCapra's view, "becoming aware of a distinction between one's own perceptions and the experience of the other" (LaCapra 2001, 41; Bennett 2005, 8).

8. This distinction is a summary rendering of Silverman's psychoanalytic theorizing of identification, mentioned above.

The third, related trap concerns a predicament that lies at the heart of this passage and makes it suitable both for a reflection on contemporary aesthetics and for a theory of fantasy. On the one hand, suffering requires witnessing. This is why seeing Mut's suffering had to trigger this scene. This need made Theodor Adorno partly recant his indictment of art after Auschwitz. Without witness, the sufferer is irremediably alone, deprived of a social environment and hence all but dehumanized.[9]

In despair over such an asocial confinement, Mut calls the party. The women of the city are called in as fellow women "city-zens." This point joins Scarry's thesis on the loneliness of suffering due to the fact that pain cannot be expressed. What suffering requires, then, is what Van Alphen, in a study of art that mobilizes the experiences of the Holocaust, calls "testimony's performative quality as a humanizing transactive process" (1997, 153). On the other hand, the production of what Geoffrey Hartman and others have denigrated as "secondary traumatization" (2001, 119) poses the double danger of vicariousness and, conversely, of renewed hurt, of "trauma envy" and art-induced suffering (LaCapra 2001, 135–36). Graphic imagery of suffering is especially likely to produce such an effect. The belated witness can experience a smaller dose of trauma. This can even be dangerous to the well-being of the viewer, as the scene of collective bloodletting intimates so strangely.

On the basis of these three problems pertaining to identification as a nonreflective process to which the art of suffering exposes the viewer, Bennett attempts to articulate what she calls an *aesthetic of relation*. Her framework is Deleuzian, mostly derived from *Cinema II* and *Francis Bacon* but also from Deleuze's early *Proust*. From the first she derives the importance of *thought* in art, as a weapon against unproductive sentiment. This is the subject of a book by Van Alphen (2005) that is closely relevant for my argument, as is Bennett's (2005). Van Alphen develops the notion that art actively "thinks" or shapes thought, providing a useful antidote against the unreflective quality of identification. For one can be held responsible for thought, not quite so easily for near-automatic responses. This is important in view of Mann's

9. Adorno's writings on this problematic have been collected in one volume in English (2003).

insistent metareflections. While he allows his characters to lose themselves, he holds the writer to the ethical standard of accountability. The former embody what the latter proposes. They suffer-with, thereby blurring the delimitations of their subjectivity even more than Yusuf has done. Instead of a soft-focus image, we are seeing a collective drama verging on abstraction.

From the second Deleuzian source comes the importance of sense perception and sensation in our interaction with art, including Mann's storytelling. This idea helps understand the visceral nature of response and the resulting difficulty of neutralizing damaging responses, but also the possibility of diverting these and transforming them into more socially responsible responses. The women suffer-with Mut in order to break her loneliness and demonstrate the possibility of even half-unconscious unreflected identification. This is Mann's ad hoc solution to the particular problem of women's social isolation.

The third Deleuzian notion, the concept of "encountered sign," completes Bennett's picture, which she sums up as "feeling is a catalyst for critical inquiry or deep thought" (2005, 7). This matches Mann's scene and explains the otherwise odd juxtaposition of the drama of collective pain and the ironic myth-critical reflection on truthfulness. For Bennett's argument, there is an additional difficulty with identification, and this brings me closer to the problematic of our story. The art Bennett discusses is, if not abstract, at least avoiding of realism. One of her key cases, for example, is the art of Doris Salcedo, a Colombian sculptor who uses altered household furniture to relationally address the violence of civil war in her country. The furniture is "real" but the violence is nowhere in (realistic) sight. Of course, no more than photography, to which I have applied Bennett's theory elsewhere (Bal 2006b), the novel can no longer be held to the naive rhetoric of realism that characterized its heyday.

Mann is not exactly a realist but a modernist and, as I am suggesting, a proto-postmodernist. In a chapter titled "A Life in Quotation," Jan Assmann alludes to this postmodern tendency in his discussion of Mann's view of myth in the *Joseph* tetralogy. After stating, to my taste somewhat facilely, that the biblical background is at the opposite end of such a "life in quotation," he writes in parentheses, "(and in this respect it is comparable to the

thinking of postmodernism)" (2006a, 174). The opposition over-
states the power of the canon. It is clear, in particular from visual
versionings, that Genesis 39, even if blatantly misquoted, keeps
being quoted by rewriters who, quoting from memory, seem to
think they know what the text says literally. Assmann uses the
term *quotation* here as tacitly based on two concepts as if they
were interchangeable: intertextuality, where quotes can be traced
to a source, and interdiscursivity, where they cannot. But he does
point to a relevant issue, the acknowledgment in Mann's novel of
the impossibility of inventing, and instead the need to quote, rephrase, or flesh out what cultural memory has laid out for us. This
is a postmodern view indeed.

It is from within such disenchantment with invention that
Mann's metanarrative passage must be read, not as obedient to
but as critical of realistic rhetoric. Instead of privileging "real"
witnessing, his scene promotes the importance of fantasy. This
is how he reinvents sympathy. Given the narrative passages and
the convincing visual descriptions, I find myself compelled to remain attentive to that rhetoric, whose power still holds sway over
the everyday discourse of photography, as well as the novel, and
is inevitably entangled with the ways we process the stories we
are being told. Mann invokes that rhetoric when he writes: "It is
the truth, and all the *probabilities* speak for it," and "We shall
understand that the thing could not happen otherwise." Probability is, in fact, the primary standard of realism—not factual truth
but plausibility. The logic of inevitability underscores the pseudo-
rational discourse deployed to foreground a point of emotion.

In a later chapter I will return to the rhetoric of realism as a
form of truthspeak. Here I take up the other side of Mann's metacommentary, irony and all. As Assmann insists in the chapter of
his book on religion and cultural memory aptly titled "Thomas
Mann: A Life in Quotation," Mann sinks his entire novel into
the mythical discourse that he allegedly quotes. The verb quoting seems a bit too precise, suggesting a specific source for all elements of the novel's story. This is, on the one hand, a useful
reminder that stories can be developed in language in all sorts of
ways, creating a prose that is both unique and still anchored in
sources that the stories quote. On the other hand, though, the
verb suggests that the case of Thomas Mann is somehow distinct,

more citational, than other cultural artifacts. Such an interpretation would take away some of the most important lessons of Mann's recycling acts.[10]

Mann's scene, to be true, is anchored in the Qur'an, at least if I favor (as I do, for reasons inherent in cultural analysis) the canonical, widely known, and interreligious source over possible exegetical sources within Judaism. This decision will be more extensively justified in chapter 9; here, suffice it to say that the better known a tradition is, the more likely it is that someone coming from outside its culture will find it. I consider Mann's choice to consult the Qur'an an important act that already folds the quotation or reiteration within a genuine act of invention. This act is the invention of sym-pathy, and I name this chapter after it. The impressive implications of this act are best understood against the background of a theoretical discussion of invention *as* reiteration, but with a difference, offered in Derek Attridge's discussion with Sartre and Derrida on creation, innovation, and invention (1999).

Attridge mounts an argument, ethical in nature, which distinguishes creation as individual from invention that harbors a relationship to otherness. For this reason, what distinguishes the two activities also makes them dependent on each other: "To be creative, in the limited sense I mean, the mind needs only the materials it happens to have, whether shared or not, but invention—which is the only way in which creativity can be registered—requires a close engagement with the circumambient cultural matrix" (1999, 23). The act of invention Mann performs in his scene, then, is an act of creativity registered in as well as derived from the encounter with the "other" text. Later I will argue that this is his *invention* of sympathy as not merely created. Instead, sympathy is articulated in the historical situation where otherness was being exasperated into radical monstrosity by the ideology of Nazism. Mann's character indeed harbors the alterities that history keeps projecting on her: as a woman, as an exoticized Egyptian, as mad (e.g., madly in love), as confined and driven to acts of insanity by her own assigned role. If we can call this scene a quotation, it is an invention in this sense.

10. Assmann's recent book on Mann's Joseph cycle examines this point in much more detail (2006b).

In this respect one element of Bennett's discussion points to the scene of bloody sympathy. Bennett makes a distinction between characters, which she understands as fully formed, preprogrammed roles, and the interaction or relation that she values in the encounter with art (2005, 17). Characters, she argues, promote a naturalized and naturalizing effect. This objection is understandable. Characters are anthropomorphic and individualized. Relations, by contrast, do not even need anthropomorphic figures. Characters are one of two elements in art that hamper rather than help an affective response capable of avoiding the traps of identification. The second element is the autobiographical posture, where the artist claims, or the viewer assumes, that the artwork transcribes personal experience. Mann's frequent interventions undermine this character effect, as they also, especially in our scene, counter the tendency to facile identification in a scene that dramatizes sympathy. Instead of these two modes of soliciting identification, politically effective art triggers a "direct engagement with sensation as it is registered in the work" (Bennett 2005, 7).

Not, that Mann left himself out of the story—not at all. But character, not biography, is the site of identification, and this saves his novel from the vicarious identifications Bennett critiques. As George Rosenwald argues in an in-depth psychoanalytic study of the writer in relation to the *Joseph* novels, "Throughout his life, Mann's ethical relationship to his society was and remained that of exile" (1978, 524). Whether he was living the life of an exile long before he actually went into exile, under the influence of his mother's Creole background and his difficult relationship with his brother, or only at the time of his later escape from the Nazis to California, is of no concern to me. If an argument can be made for Mann's autobiographical involvement in the *Joseph* novels, it is not only with the character of Yusuf that he may have identified. Mut, too, in the relationship the narrator has to her, which may or may not have been (unconsciously) modeled on the writer's relationship with his mother, benefits from a sympathy of which the scene discussed here is the most powerful but not the only example. As for Joseph, the exilic alienation of his life between "refugee and citizen of the world" (Rosenwald 1978, 533) opened his character up to a potential of ethical concern, rather than foreclosing it, as Bennett suggests that characters do.

The argument against identification and vicarious suffering, and for a sense-based close encounter, leads to a conception of affect-based art as *political*. Only when we remain on the hither side of the individual, the private, and the particular does it become possible to engage with the suffering of others in all its singularity. Only then can we avoid trumpeting the moral line of indignation, falling back into the simplistic binary opposition between victim and perpetrator, and taking up the appropriative and diffuse gestures of sentimentality. Importantly, this reluctance to endorse individualism brings into my reading one feature listed earlier for fundamentalism—its anti-individualism. This, first of all, goes to show that fundamentalism is not entirely alien to any reader. It also requires a further qualification of the definition of fundamentalism. *Anti-* does leave open the question of the alternative, that to which the fundamentalist adheres instead. For fundamentalism, this is the group and the deity in whose wake or name the group is constituted. For affect-based art, the alternative is what I call here "porous subjectivity." The individual remains validated but is communal, not autonomous. This makes it possible to stay on the side of literalism without falling back into individualism.

Mann is not giving us an identification trap but showing its dangers while also demonstrating its social function. This is, I contend, the primary function of his (self-)irony. In exemplary fashion, the narrator explicitly cautions his readers against doxic belief, voiced in the metacommentaries that claim the truth of the story—its nature as quotation: "Before it could be told, it happened, it sprang from the source from which all history springs, and tells itself as it goes. Since that time it exists in the world, everybody knows it or thinks he does—for often enough the knowledge is unreal, casual, or disjointed" (180). Rosenwald, who quotes this passage, comments: "Subtly and ingeniously, Mann confuses the reader as to the narrator's position with respect to the events and thereby, at one further remove, as to the relationship between author and audience" (1978, 544). Mann manages this remove from fundamentalism because "character," I contend, need not be considered the naturalization of moral roles that Bennett, in the wake of Nietzsche (1974 [1882]), attributes to it.

As literary theory has been arguing practically from its inception, characters can be evolving, complex representational tools, figurations and "discussions" of ideas, resting points on which the reader can hang a host of emotional and intellectual responses. To put it in the framework of the terms of this essay, characters are porous. And so is the relationship between author, narrator, and character, because characters' subjectivity, at least in Mann's conception of it as expounded in his little scene, is itself porous. The problem is not in character but in the forceful domination of the realistic tradition within which it, as much as photography, is caught. Instead, for my purposes I consider character a concept that facilitates the transition from the Deleuzian sensate, relational aesthetic that does not need figuration to the subject of that art form most powerfully caught in realistic rhetoric, the novel, our contemporary form of narrative.

Mut planned this event explicitly and consciously to lead her social world into an understanding of her plight. She wanted her friends to understand her love not intellectually but experientially, on the level of sensation. Or rather, their intellectual understanding had to happen simultaneously with their bodily experience. The difference between the two can be mitigated, negotiated, precisely, by means of identification through affect, a sym-pathy that is not vicarious, not an exploitative sentiment, but a passage, painful as it is, from lonely subjectivity to social intersubjectivity, from inexpressible pain to sharable meaning. Thus, to put it simply, the split created by discourse is cured by sight. This, then, is where the seemingly theoretical theme of word-image interaction joins the one that pertains to cultural dealings with prejudice. There is no longer a "third person," an object of gossip radically isolated. This fits well with Mann's attempt to humanize the character by generalizing not her transgression but her self-transgression, not her crime but her feelings. As a result, he makes her transgress the denial of female subjectivity, of the right to love outside of the narrowly defined realm of property and propriety. Instead, he imaginatively stages the right to love in the domain of the cultural, where otherness is a space of negotiation, represented as the stage—the right, in other words, to love "Yusuf."

What is the point, then of the vivid visual descriptions, the colorful evocation of a long-obsolete Orientalist aesthetics overwritten by a starker visual beauty, in the staging of bloodshed, self-inflicted violence, and loss of self? Here the theorizing of social solidarity as a need and capacity of women joins, at the most profound level of artistic writing, the three elements mentioned above that foreground visuality in a linguistic artwork. *Theatricality* is ostensibly subjectivity's other. Yet Mann suggests—and this makes him most forcefully postmodernist, and our contemporary—this is where contemporary culture has an opportunity to celebrate subjectivity as an authenticity of a different kind, where difference is neither ignored, for the erasure of otherness, nor hypostasised, for a boxing-in of people in categories that confine them. I have suggested that Mann's scene deploys his art to "argue" that those whom we overlook and isolate can derive support from sym-pathy. The image of collective pain is now present as historical translation, mise en scène, framed and performed. This artificial, contrived performativity that compels participation in the performance is the source of a renewed authenticity, put forward as beautiful in a culture replete with false claims to an authenticity based on myths of origin and tired of "beauty."

This contemporariness of Mann's scene of sympathy offered the bond I was seeking to establish between my contradictory memories of rejection (in primary school) and a sad longing for solidarity among women (of my later feminist awareness). Might they be connected—in other words, might my diffusely motivated contempt for a Mut I didn't understand have fueled my sensitivity to the poverty of women's sociality later on? The two memory topics seem unrelated but share an emotional investment that I can explain only by connecting them. It is as if the disconnection itself hurts. So to seek to understand it, I wonder how Mann, a man and an artist writing at that heaviest of historical times, in exile in the United States, was able to draw out such an impressive scene of pain and the need to share it among women, long before my own memory of that need took shape.

Where did he find the inspiration for this scene with these millennia-old characters at its heart, in his "life in quotation" (Assmann 2006a)? I will suspend the question and resist the temptation to dig up sources. But it must be meaningful that for this moment in the story he switched from one canonical tradition (of Genesis) to another, its brother and rival (the Qur'an). I will speculate later on the historical meaning of that choice. First, I seek to counter both fundamentalist tendencies in reading the Bible, the Qur'an, and other sources—tendencies shared by all those who attribute what Mann elsewhere called "false authority" to texts, as if too lazy or uncertain to sustain their values otherwise—and I turn to the Muslim text itself in the next chapter. But I will not, or not yet, claim it as Mann's "source." Instead I pull the old Muslim document into the present. From the preposterous vantage point of this contemporary sensibility—that positions authenticity in artifice—Mut's story as it is embedded in the cultural memory of many contemporary subjects can be most profitably reread.

6

Sign Language

Let me take the reader to the present, a time of worldwide tensions between the legacies of the mythical brothers Ishmael and Isaac. The temporal discrepancies between the brothers' life stories and the religious traditions they embody suit me fine: Ishmael the older brother, Isaac's religion the older of the two. The mirror images of fundamentalists of all three sides of the monotheisms, revering the same God, distract from the obvious affiliations among them, as well as from the majority's more moderate and peaceful desires. A time when loving Yusuf—sym-pathy across the artificially constructed divides of "ethnicity" and of home and exile—is again, half a century later, construed as treason. I cannot help coming from one of these three traditions, yet I feel ashamed of what allegedly democratically elected officials, representing me, are promoting in my name. In the Netherlands in 2006, the minister of immigration and assimilation ferociously expelled whomever she could and refused to honor the wish of the democratically elected parliament to grant legal residency to those who had been waiting for years in the jaws of a hostile bureaucracy. In this, European nations emulate a discourse of retreat into outdated and deceptive notions of authenticity and autochthony that flourishes in the United

States. Inventing a clash of civilizations, they have embarked together on a medieval crusade, using that term shamelessly.[1]

But like most people, I know little or nothing beyond the ho-
rizons of the world I was born into. Dissatisfaction, sometimes
horror, concerning what is happening between cultures, and ignorance beyond the limited horizon of my own—how can I come
to terms with these twin limitations? At first I sought aid among
those who, from within the tradition I am a stranger to (Islam),
endorse one I consider my own tradition (feminism). Many Islamic feminists have argued for a reading of the Qur'an as non-
patriarchal or even antipatriarchal. Leila Ahmed's well-known
argument bases such a view on the pluralization of Islam (1992).
Others have written passionate pleas for a reconsideration of the
Qur'an from the vantage point of believers. For example, Amina
Wadud has argued for a flexible reading of the canonical texts,
so as to make them adaptable to the exigencies of modern life, in
line with the principles of justice that inhabited them from the
beginning. She maintains that the text has a built-in flexibility
that encourages adaptation. The continued relevance of the text
depends on such a reinterpretation and reevaluation by each new
generation of Muslims (Wadud 1999, 17). To be a good Muslim,
according to this argument, one needs to read the Qur'an as a
literalist, not a fundamentalist.

In contrast, Asma Barlas argues for a return to the source texts,
which, she contends, have been covered by layers of the dust of
commentaries mistaken for the law. She focuses on the holistic
vision of the Qur'an. For her, a return to the text is the liberating move (Barlas 2002, 15). Both scholars, and many others who
argue along either of these lines, manage to provide new readings
that, to my mind, are authoritative enough to compete with the
most culturally ingrained patriarchal ones.

I have learned much from these writings but feel unable to engage the Qur'an on such terms. For me such an indirect engagement would lack the "critical intimacy" necessary for a productive

---

1. French presidential candidate Nicolas Sarkozy adopted the term *crusade* to
further his campaign—successfully, as it turned out. Until she was forced to resign
in fall 2006, the Dutch minister Rita Verdonk made great efforts to expel whom
she could, sometimes with remarks in their identity papers that were dangerous to
them, and shamelessly lied about such "details."

sense of self-implication and as a result would feel disingenuous (Spivak 1999; Bal 2002). My "ignorance" is, therefore, an indispensable element for my analysis. It helps me to avoid what has been called "feminist Orientalism and Orientalist Marxism." The discussion between the papers of Wadud and Barlas is indicative of a debate that informs my argument but in which I do not feel equipped to intervene.[2]

The flaws in any attempt to characterize Islam, or the reading of the Qur'an, that I have encountered make it difficult for me to write this chapter, not unlike my earlier hesitation to write on the Hebrew Bible, and for similar reasons—a hesitation I have felt compelled to overcome. These flaws—the assumption of a monolithic Islam, an Orientalist conception of that religion, the selective use of passages, the simplification or absence of class as an analytical category, and, as a result, a simplified and bourgeois notion of feminism—can't simply be passed over (Hammami and Rieker 1988, 1).

How then to approach the Qur'an's story of Yusuf and Mut from a position of outsidership and ignorance? This is a problem of the ethics of reading from the perspective of cultural analysis. Reading the Qur'an from my partial subject position addresses possibilities of intercultural literary study, of the bonds and tensions between the knowledge that academics aim to produce and the cultural contexts that frame our work and are the settings of the texts we read. It raised issues that, I submit, are central to the intercultural study of literature in a postcolonial perspective (for a slightly different but compatible view, see Rajan 1993). If we are to get acquainted with texts from contexts we don't (yet) know, we read the book unprepared, untrained, and unknowing of the "context" that responsible readers are alleged to bring to their acts of reading. Making explicit who the "we" is in the preceding sentences is imperative—say Western academics—even if this collectivity feels uneasy as it is crossed over and out by others, such as Europeans, women, those worried about the current state of the world, and many more. In this chapter, the issue of knowledge or the lack of it, ignorance, must be a subtext. Without defensiveness

2. These terms come from Hammami and Rieker 1988, responding to an article by Mai Ghoussoub, 1987.

but in need of endorsing responsibility, I aim to turn ignorance into a tool, useful if acknowledged, devastating if repressed.

I read: "And he who bought him—an Egyptian—said to his wife: 'Treat him hospitably; haply he may be useful to us, or we may adopt him as a son'" (12:21). The passage presents an ethnic or national indicator, neutral but vaguely reminiscent of the ethnic slur in Genesis; the status of Yusuf as an object bought and sold, is utterly revolting for anyone today, I'd hope; then the urging to hospitality, known to and admired by many, including me from superficial tourist visits and slight acquaintance with "Middle Eastern culture." And then that element from the myth: the idea of the stepson or adopted son. The double shadow it casts on the story: abuse of hospitality and a kind of incest, perhaps even child abuse. All these associations are preposterous, subjective, impertinent, and probably irrelevant. They offer a stark counterpoint to the possibility that, nevertheless, the woman is portrayed, in both Mann and the Qur'an, as deserving of a self-construed sympathy. In many ways, reading this text that I cannot ignore, I cross the border that European canon formation had silently drawn around my field. A border that coincides, also, with the line between professional competence and personal curiosity. Lines between legitimate and illegitimate, between proper and improper: in some sense, these lines are exactly the kinds of borders I find most problematic about the contemporary world, in which religious differences and similarities produce a bloody mess.

Being a beginner, I paid attention to some guidelines in the work of others. When I was doing research for this book, a friendly colleague sent me an unpublished series of very helpful remarks titled "Can Christians Believe in the Prophecy of Muhammad?" (Heck 2005). Along with that text, I came upon a few others, variously titled *The Bible and the Qur'an* (Jomier 1964), *Ishmael Instructs Isaac: An Introduction to the Qur'an for Bible Readers* (Kaltner 1999), and *Islam: A Guide for Jews and Christians* (Peters 2003). All these books, and others, were very useful, and Heck's few unpublished pages were more than that. Precisely because of their introductory nature, these pages addressed so many points of great interest that I will have to return to them frequently in this chapter. From these and other texts I learned a great deal about the composition of the Muslim holy book—of the suras that are its units, their

relative autonomy, and their meaning as a visible sign of a transcendental reality, rather than confabulated stories. I learned also
of some elements I cannot access: the rhymed prose, the rhythmic
diction, the sophisticated phonetic structures (Sells 1991).

The studies also made me feel ambivalent. On the one hand,
they helped me not so much to understand the Qur'an as to understand what for Christians and other Bible readers required attention, unpacking, and explaining. For example, it is crucial for
any reading across the canonical divide to realize that the familiar
chronology of the Bible does not regulate the order of things in
the Qur'an. On the other hand, I did not partake in their starting point, which was to bridge the gap from one side of the abyss,
that is, from the Western mainstream of Judaism or Christianity
or both. In narratological terms, their focalization was consistently
religious-Western, and as such inevitably "othering." This is not to
criticize these sincere attempts to make the Qur'an less strange to
those for whom it initially seemed to embody the cultural-religious
"other." Such attempts are helpful to this intended audience. For
me they were a bit less useful, simply because I had long ago ceased
to belong to the communities they addressed. Yet I do come from
there; my memories of the story of Yusuf and Mut attest to that.[3]

Heck's unpublished lecture notes had a different starting point.
Like these books, they were addressed to Christians. But instead
of explaining the Qur'an, they sought to understand Christianity.
The initial question, whether Christians can "believe in the prophecy of Muhammad," already quite provocative for Christian believers, is further sharpened into "Is there something about Islam
that Christianity *needs* in order to understand *itself*?" Again,
there is ambivalence here. On the one hand, the question is more
radical than just seeking to promote understanding for the "other"
religion—problematic "tolerance." Here the understanding is
necessary—which goes well beyond the well-meaning but often
condescending liberal, voluntaristic bridging. It is also needed for
Christianity itself. In other words, the position from which the
author writes is self-critical, and the teaching expected from the

---

3. The word *sincere* carries an enormously relevant baggage that I cannot address here. See, however, the collective volume *The Rhetoric of Sincerity* (Alphen,
Bal, and Smith 2008).

"other" religion is indispensable for the self-understanding of the writer and his audience. And although the text ends on a question mark, its final sentence sounds pretty radical to me: "Should Christians, out of fidelity to their own message, not also affirm the prophecy of Muhammad?" On the other hand, it could be regarded as even more self-serving, as it offers Islam as a tool for self-understanding, an effort born of a need for self-preservation. This latter goal is of little interest to me.

Yet my own interest is just as obvious, inevitable, and hard to accept. "And she in whose house he was conceived a passion for him, and she shut the doors and said, come hither" (12:23). That house again. Now the doors are mentioned, turning the house into a closed-house. Those doors are ominous. A shadowy version of them shows up in Rembrandt's etching. They will return, activating the plot. A bit later: "And they both made for the door, and she rent his shirt behind; and at the door they met her lord" (12:25). The door locked Yusuf in. It is also the border with the outside. Just as for children abused at home, the house offers no safety; the outside might. The race makes the scene more theatrical than it is in Genesis, and in that sense served as an aesthetic inspiration for Mann the theatrical author. But the two characters are halted by a temporal coincidence absent in Genesis: just when the slave is about to escape, the master comes home. Farcical like a nineteenth-century boulevard play, this is a narrative ploy that produces suspense. Is such a preposterous association legitimate? The tearing of the shirt and the detail "behind" also further the plot. They will determine the judgment. In Genesis, Joseph simply left his garment behind, but we don't know how naked this left him.

I can go on like this, but it doesn't seem to lead anywhere. Differences between versions are commonplace. And although the differences so far enhance rather than diminish the narrativity of the episode in sura 12 (contra Kaltner), there is not much point to them for my interest in the projected roles of the woman who has the courage (Mut) to love Yusuf. Only one element resonates with my memories. That is the slightly different phrasing of the initial passion. In my memory, my interest in Islam has to do with faces, and the act of facing. In this sense, if taken at its word, the phrase of Genesis 39:7, "his master's woman lifted her eyes upon Joseph," resonates with an initiatory act of casting eyes of my own. As I suppose to be the case for many, my interest in Islam coincided more or less with getting neighbors who were Islamic and seeing their faces—looking them in the face.

This facing happened literally. One day in the late 1970s, I was giving a breakfast party in a townhouse flush with the street. While we were having fun, three children's faces suddenly appeared at the other side of the window, as if stuck to the glass. My daughter said she knew those children; they lived across the street, and she had played with them. She knew their names too. We invited them in and talked to their parents to ask their permission, and so my first real contact with immigrants from the Middle East occurred. Enjoying their company, I thought I should learn a bit about their beliefs, read what they read. In my ignorance, the first surprise was how close the Bible and the Qur'an are in terms of myth: how many stories overlap. The second, how their rules of behavior are similar. The two are, of course, related.

It seems safe to assume that the general moral lesson to be drawn from, or projected on, sura 12:20–35 largely overlaps with that of Genesis 39:3–20, at least in my schoolmistress's version. The Qur'an version sets Mut up as even more wicked, as her forms of hospitality and mothering are quite outrageous. Because the possibility of adopting the lad as a son is explicitly mentioned here, she transgresses two social contracts, of hospitality and of parenting, that count among the most binding. How different are the versions anyway, how can we grasp the differences, and what can we do with them? Both tales are of the same length, and a structural analysis of the plot would show them to be identical: the master's favoring of Yusuf, the woman's passion, the trap, the lie, and the prison. Yet although it is not really longer, we have already seen that the Qur'an has elements Genesis lacks, and vice versa. Most remarkably, the astounding scene we have read in Mann's novel is right there (12:30–32). Equally remarkably, the woman does not cast her eyes upon the young man and doesn't get to speak to him. She just "conceived a passion" for him and acts upon it.

Other differences are striking and have been pointed out (esp. Kaltner 1999, 28–34): Potiphar doesn't speak in Genesis but speaks, takes counsel, and judges in the Qur'an; Joseph refrains from defending himself in Genesis but refutes the accusation in the Qur'an; and God's input as director of the play is absent or ambiguous in Genesis while being prominent in the Qur'an. Thus the latter version is much more explicitly theological than the former, as is the case with most stories the two books have in common. Kugel traced some of these differences in traditions of biblical commentaries. The ambiguity of the phrase "his master" in Genesis—God or Potiphar?—is resolved in favor of God in the Qur'an text. What can we make of these differences?

The books mentioned above offer two different perspectives, although both lie within Bible readers' focalization. In the introduction to his book, Peters foregrounds similarities but historicizes these when he writes, "Jews, Christians, and Muslims not only worshipped the same God; they also shared many, though by no means identical, ideals and aspirations, operated often in the same social and economic environment, and at certain times and in certain places lived side by side within the same culture, indistinguishable in language, costume, and manners" (2003, xii). Part of the motivation for his book might well be the desire to turn this past tense into a present one, but the author doesn't make that transformation. Indeed, his approach emphasizes similarities, but these remain embedded in a historical view that, for all the useful information it offers, doesn't really build the bridge needed today.

By contrast, after pointing out similarities, Kaltner draws attention to differences. For my quest to see "versions" as "versionings" in the sense outlined above with reference to Peeren, this is more helpful, even though the differences I am interested in are stylistic and narratological more than ideological. But style *is* thought, and ideology emerges from or is attributed to narratological features as much as to words. Kaltner describes the difference as follows: "[The Qur'an] conveys only the information essential to make that point [rather than tell a story], is usually less detailed than the Bible in its presentation, and will often abruptly shift gears to discuss a seemingly unrelated point" (1999, 17). From this passage I retain the notion of "point." "Seemingly unrelated" is on the order of the "why?" question, like Kugel's apparently unnecessary repetitions. What I glean from this view is that details matter. It also makes me even more puzzled about the insertion of Mann's scene. Clearly this scene has a point, if

Kaltner is to be believed—a point that may be relatively unrelated to the main point, the one about the danger of women, sex,
and other worldly interests that distract from a tight relationship
with God. From the preposterous vantage point that Mann's text
offers, the absence of Mut's gaze cast upon Yusuf as the trigger
of her passion, as well as of the visual nature of the women-of-
the-city's collective trigger, cast doubt on Kaltner's stylistic view
of succinctness. Unless, that is, the scene is essential, and its point
crucial. In order to make sense of the scene within the stylistic
feature of succinctness, I will assume it is and try to find a reason
for its importance.

As I mentioned before, Kugel attempts, perhaps a bit too des-
perately, to argue for the Bible's position as the source even for
this scene (28–68). Through his argument runs the undercurrent
of the meaning of house as lineage, the reign of men. He makes
his case through a forced interpretation of "the men of her house"
as a general "people of her house." But if we suspend the idea
of lineage, the people of the house are domestic staff, likely, he
assumes, to be predominantly women. He then even turns the
"us" into ladies, who, along with Mut, complain to their collective husbands. But if this domestic staff includes only one man,
the pronoun would be masculine. In my view this is a case of in-
reading if ever there was one—of dismissing the words in favor
of a preset idea (Kugel 1990, 28–68). Kugel even writes explicitly
that the text must be taken "a bit more loosely" for this gender-
bending to be plausible (49). This idea appears to make the Bible
stand out, and over, the gap-filling activities of later Talmudic,
Midrashic, and Qur'anic rewritings. As Brenner and Van Henten
have pointed out, gap filling is a rigorously readerly activity, always liable to change (1998). The Qur'anic claim to truth is obviously not based on historical priority but on improvement, a
process that has artificially been halted by canonization but that
unofficially continues with every reading.

The desire to claim source status and temporal priority for the
Bible echoes the age-old claim that in the creation story of Genesis the woman was created after the man and therefore lesser.
Both claims are dubious at the very least, as I have argued in an
interpretation of the creation story (Bal 1987). To summarize my
argument: First, the clay creature prior to sex differentiation was

simply an unfinished, because undifferentiated, creature, so it can be argued that both man and woman, as such, were created at the same time, in the same act of further perfecting. For this reason alone, second and more relevant for the comparative perspective of the current discussion, temporal priority is not qualitative primacy, rather the opposite: Eve, as she comes to be called, a name resembling the nonname of the deity, is closer to the latter, for she too can (pro)create life.

The logic of the ongoing labor to make the texts more "perfect," hence, more worthy of being heard as God's words, explains the continuous exegetical efforts that characterize Jewish culture. Talmudic and later commentaries, folk versions and strict religious ones alike, continue to fill in what subsequent generations have felt to be gaps—elaborating on succinctness. What one group considers self-evident raises "why?" questions in another. Each social environment construes its own gaps; this is how the old stories remain alive. The Qur'an is no exception. What becomes paradoxical is the way all three Abrahamic monotheistic religions diverge in handling the fundamental tensions inherent in scripture-based cultures. On the one hand, the scripture must be fixed, canonized. Yet, or rather because of that fixation, it continues to require exegetical work. The signifiers fly, and the literalist reader follows their flight.

In this, religion is no different from worldly law. On the one hand, the laws must be fixed, written down, to form a universal standard. But words, and the norms they are meant to fix, change with time. On the other hand, then, subsequent judges keep performing exegetical labor, not least to adapt laws to different social norms that have developed in spite of them. The judge tries to interpret the law according to the spirit of the legislator. The reasoning that underlies jurisprudence is that the legislator, if only the circumstances now relevant had existed at the time of writing, would certainly have taken them into account (Vlies 1993; also Smart 1989; Smith 2008). This is why the fundamentalism that has often plagued all three religions is *fundamentally* mistaken. For example, the issue of rape is still contested; the evidence of crying out is still invoked, even if cultural environments where lack of evidence of self-defense leads to the death penalty are rare (alas, not extinct) in all three. The signs—crying out loud or not, being audible or not—are relevant; the meting out of punishment can change, because the meaning of the transgression changes. This is where literalism and fundamentalism part ways.

So far, I have pleaded for respect for the words as signifiers. This chapter attempts to deal with words as signs, without leaping from signs to signifiers and splitting the signs too easily. In what way, then, can the Qur'an sura be seen as "improving" the biblical version, versioning it from a mythical tale that warns against the danger of women into a text with points to make about, for example, women's solidarity? I find it difficult to reconcile the concepts of danger and solidarity, ideologically so far apart. This is where knowledge meets ignorance.

This, I contend, is not an exception but an instantiation of the will. Interpretation is an issue of knowledge meeting ignorance. Knowledge, like stories, and like the law, is also subject to the tension between literalism and fundamentalism. Even in the most general terms, knowledge is also subject to the probing of the way it erects boundaries in the thrust of globalisation. I'll even bracket the obvious inequalities in the access to knowledge that remain bound to economic and national limitations. Obviously, we need only to think of the ongoing "brain drain" from everywhere in the world to the U.S. academy, where the system's expert absorption of political trends that oppose its power remains irresistible. This is just a symptom of the deeper problem, which, as Arjun Appadurai formulated it, is much more serious: "Globalization as an uneven economic process creates a fragmented and uneven distribution of just those resources for learning, teaching, and cultural criticism that are most vital for the formation of democratic research communities that could produce a global view of globalization" (2000, 4). The systemic consequence of this situation is what he calls "a growing disjuncture between the globalisation of knowledge and the knowledge of globalization" (4). Such statements draw our attention to the need to keep the two elements bound tightly together. The conditions and objects of knowledge should be tied into a knot. This is indispensable if we are to understand changes in the world behind which, temporally speaking, knowledge-producers inevitably lag. Knowledge is a focus that, prior to any knowledge construction, tells us what is worth knowing and what can be known. Borders, here, can never be taken for granted.

In the face of the developments in literary theory from new criticism through structuralism to poststructuralism and beyond, all developments that countered the temptation of referential reading, the question is: what reflection theory of representation underlies the search for "points"? In order to avoid presuming the obvious about points, in other words, the mythical "lesson" instilled in me so early in life, I will shift my focus to a different—perhaps related, perhaps unrelated—point, which has been brought up many times but not so clearly a propos of Yusuf's misadventure. This point is the *face*, or rather, the act of facing as what kindles love. An act present or at least hinted at in Genesis, avoided in the Qur'an.

The face raises the twin issues of individualism and representation. The taboo on the graven image inflects passion based on the face. The Qur'an is just as opposed to graven images as the Bible is. This taboo on "semblances" has always intrigued, indeed revolted me. For me, as a Westerner of Catholic background, it seemed utterly bizarre as well as oppressive. Why censor art, why forbid what people enjoy? Plato, that other inventor of censorship, offered a reason for it—the indirection, hence the false, illusionary nature of images as well as of all representation. But the biblical and Qur'anic opposition targeted visual images specifically. For someone whose interest in vision has been a lifelong searchlight, this was incomprehensible. Until I came to understand realism.

It became clear to me that it is not the image itself but its seduction that acts as the moral and theological danger. A wonderfully illuminating book by Françoise Meltzer (1987) has helped me understand the nuances of this cultural complex, which I have to simplify here. The stake of the taboo on images is not the image per se but the danger of mistaking it for the real thing and acting upon that error. I have looked at issues of pornography, sex crimes, hate speech, images of abuse from the Abu Ghraib prison in Iraq, biased narratives and rape victims whose experiences are denied, narratives focalized from mainstream vantage points at the detriment of marginal characters. Even though I still don't want to defend it in its generality, the interdiction of images no longer strikes me as so bizarre. I don't like attempts to control people's minds, but if the issue is mistaking image for reality and, most importantly, *acting upon* that mistake, I can see how politicians and other well- or less well-meaning leaders such as priests, rabbis, and imams would like to come up with rules that spare people serious, in their view dangerous, mistakes. Just imagine those early cinema spectators who seriously worried that the people shown in close-up really had lost their bodies (Buck-Morss 1994), or the Australian aborigines or Native Americans who wanted to shoot back at the screen (e.g., Jane Campion's *The Piano*, 1993).

The word screen has come up before in this book, as a metaphor for the emptiness of myths on which readers can project their fantasies. I wish to recall that metaphor here to articulate an issue few critics have paid attention to, namely the seduction of Joseph's face *as image*. This idea invokes the taboo of the image as well as alternative ways of meaning-making that the Qur'an and the Bible might favor. What I seek to approximate is a view of the text, including its relationship to visuality and acts of seeing, in particular facing, that is not bound to a reflection theory of representation.

The central act of facing here is the moment that Mut's friends suffer-with—cut themselves—when they "see" Yusuf's irresistible appeal. They truly see, without projecting the already-known from recognition: "And when they *saw* him, they were *amazed* at him" (12:31). As in the text as a whole, the presentation of the issue is primarily theological: "God keep us! This is no man! This is no other than a noble angel!" (12:31). God is invoked to protect the women, and at the same time Yusuf is made godlike, or god-sent. Paradoxically, it is through an act of seeing that the not-quite-human nature, hence the invisibility, of Yusuf is brought up. Rather than with representation, the text aligns Yusuf with signification. This I consider a particular "Qur'anic" semiotics. I propose that such a semiotic reading can help to make reading with ignorance a bit more ethical. I don't mean to suggest it is particular to the Qur'an, as if unsuitable for the reading of other texts. On the contrary, as a particular but not exclusive inflection on seeing signs, it could be considered a contribution offered by the Qur'an to the theory of reading in general.

A major source for this perspective has been an article by Hamid Dabashi titled "In the Absence of the Face" (2000), mainly based on the Joseph sura. According to Dabashi, the struggle acted out in the Qur'an concerns the invisibility of the face of God—from sight to sign (140). Dabashi attempts to theorize this Islamic semiotic from within the idea of the Qur'an as recitation—citation where "sightation" is forbidden (128). Hearing replaces seeing, and I think of Mut's limited access to the word, only partly counterbalanced to her self-assertive appropriation of the possibility of seeing. The interdiction of seeing the face—not, or not yet, bound to the interdiction of images in general—is generative of narration. "There is a story," Dabashi writes, "inevitably in Signed Language, waiting, inevitably, to be told" (129).

This interdiction against seeing God's face doesn't mean God doesn't have a face—on the contrary. "Everything will perish save His Face" is Dabashi's epigraph. But because the face cannot be seen, it is subject to mass amnesia. The author offers an interpretation of this amnesia that can help us get closer to Yusuf's appeal and hence to an understanding of Mut's passion: "The amnesia is made possible not by political *imposition* but by biological *implication*. We are *implicated* in the collective act of amnesia because the absence of the Face of the Unseen is *replicated* in our own inability to see our own Faces—mirrors not-with-standing. The thing in the mirror is not the Face. It is always-already a Signifier, mutated by the *identity* of the person we recognize, and never the sign we behold" (2000, 133–34; emphasis his). The reference to the mirror in this passage resonates with two contemporary texts. One is Lacan's short essay on the mirror stage. No matter how often I read it, this text remains illuminating. The strangeness of my own face comes across every time anew. The face in the mirror is, indeed, other to the self and as such a primary example, or allegory, of the sign status of all images. The face has no face value; the visible surface becomes a *sur*face, like a surname, apposite, derivative, and inherited. The deceptive quality of the mirror image lies in the misrecognition, that is, the illusion which in the very act of seeing makes us unable to see. The use of *recognition* as opposed to *seeing* strikes a chord when we remember Mann's insistence on the absence of recognition in the women's bloody act of seeing. "But all the ladies, those who had chanced to see him before as well as those who did not know him, forgot at the sight not only what they were doing but themselves as well, being lost in gazing at the cup-bearer." Would he have found the idea in the single word *amazed* in Sura 12:31?

The second association is related in that it too points to the deceptive nature of seeing-as-recognition, the false illusion in which we risk believing. It is an association with Frantz Fanon's encounter, in a Parisian movie theater, with his own face as alien because imposed on him by others, who looked at him as black, hence, in a sense, faceless.[4] This little primal scene of racist othering as experienced by the one subjected to it is the starting point for Silverman's ethics of vision (1996). The Qur'an in general derives a rule, an interdiction, a taboo from the danger posed by seeing the face, a law that is obviously called for in the face of the difficulty of upholding it. One may find the strictness of that taboo confining; I certainly do. It is one of the common elements in the three monotheistic religions. Within Christianity, Catholicism, as well as the iconoclasm it has triggered, goes to prove the difficulty. More humanely, to recall Mann's project, the Yusuf story probes the two sides of the coin—or the face.

In the women's act of seeing, Yusuf is seen as nonhuman. This makes his countenance and face areas of danger, for if he is not a man, he must be closer to God. Mann certainly presents him in that proximity to divinity and both critiques his megalomania and affirms its mythical justification. But Yusuf, too, is in danger, in a way that Genesis did not suggest. And for him, too, the danger is in the act of seeing. "But unless thou turn away their snares from me, I shall play the youth with them, and become one of the unwise" (12:33). The issue of the veiling of the faces of women lurks in the wings of this verse. The plural of the objects seen makes plain that Yusuf needs God's help to stay on his course of righteousness and wisdom. The seduction attempt by one woman yields to a general acknowledgment of his irresistibility, which goes some way toward absolving Mut. That is, clearly, the point of the scene with the knives. If we take it that the episode with Mut as a whole makes the point that sexuality, passion, and love—I refrain from making a distinction among these—are dangerous,

4. See Fanon 1986, 14; for a highly relevant commentary, Silverman 1996, 27–31.

perhaps taboo similarly to seeing the face (of God), then Yusuf's prayer acknowledges that, notwithstanding the women's view, he is human after all.

Not only that: his humanity is also emphatically bound up with seeing. He asks God to remove the temptation ("snares") from him, and by implication from his sight. The answer shifts from sighting to citing: "And his Lord heard him and turned aside their snares from him; for he is the Hearer, the Knower" (12:34). *Hearing* is used in the strong sense, as granting the wish; and God's epithets, Hearer and Knower, bind the act of perception with that of insight in exactly the same way as seeing in the biblical sense equals understanding. Yusuf, on the other hand, continues to see, and this in a strong sense, again intricately linked with understanding. Yet his seeing is not unproblematic either. His departure from home into exile was motivated by a dream of grandeur, a vision of himself as the object of veneration—as godlike. This was "just" a dream, made to come true because, against his father's explicit warning, he could not refrain from telling his brothers about it, thus triggering the envy that sent him into slavery and exile, so that he could rise up from his base position and become almost the most powerful man on earth (because the smartest economist). As Dabashi phrases it, calling on the title of Stanley Kubrick's last film to explain this form of seeing: "Joseph sees with his eyes closed what others cannot see with their eyes wide open. Joseph's eyes are wide shut" (2000, 142).

The dreamer and boaster will later become a master interpreter of dreams, hence an indirect seer, seeing (with his eyes even more wide even more shut) what others see. Thus he comes to stand for what I call here the Qur'anic semiotic, anchored in the paradox of seeing invisibility and the subsequent danger of mistaking signs for reality. In a slightly different sense he becomes somewhat of a fantast, but one who sees the fantasies of others or who is other to his fantasies. Both features explain why the Qur'an, pace Kugel, can rightly be considered the "original" of the story in its function of allegory of semiotics. It is original, that is, *as* derivative.[5]

_____

5. I mean this view of fantasy in the way suggested by both Borch-Jacobson (1988) and Weber (2000, see chap. 3).

This derivative, hence original, status is the consequence of its insight in semiotics. Yusuf's adventure stages the almost-successful eradication of seeing to which the Qur'an devotes so much effort, but one whose repressed returns. Dabashi phrases it significantly in terms reminiscent both of psychoanalysis and of cultural memory: "Interpretation . . . is the architectonic edifice of hermeneutically burying the repression of the absence of the Sign in the Qur'anic memory" (2000, 143).

Memory here is defined as the double negative of repression and absence. A burial leaves traces. So does Yusuf's face, as well as his act of seeing. "And he would have desired her had he not *seen* a token from his Lord" (12:24, emphasis added). Seeing the sign overrules seeing the woman. This second seeing makes him race for the door. But as Dabashi keeps reminding us, seeing the sign requires refraining from collapsing the sign into the signifier. For that collapse violates the sign's "invisibility." I take this to mean its untranslatability into the (Platonic) indirectness that breeds the illusion of realism and destroys singularity.[6]

Jacob, when confronted with Yusuf's coat of many colors, is taken in by that illusion, compelled by his sons' truthspeak of indexicality. The evidence of Joseph's death they present to him—the coat smeared with blood—foreshadows the blood shed in Mut's courtyard. But it is false, having been abducted from index to symbol. As a belated result of his error, being tricked by Yusuf's own deceptive plot of evidence, Jacob loses his sight. "And his eyes were whitened with grief, for he bore a silent sorrow" (12:84). Silent: in a text where hearing equals and replaces seeing, silence can only mean repression. But white is a color, as visible as blood-red, although it makes Jacob unseeing. It is, in fact, the merging of all colors.

Many of the "details" that differentiate the Qur'an from Genesis have turned out to be capital differences. Seeing them as any less would be a violation of the text that, from my perspective, belongs to the other. At the same time, excessive differentiation goes against the acknowledgment of the interculturality *within* the respective religious traditions. And I use *within* here in the

---

6. Translation, that is, must retain traces or remainders of the foreign within the domestic, so that appropriation is hampered (Venuti 1996; Laplanche 1996).

sense of deconstruction, as pointing to differences-within. In that context, the preposition indicates the impossibility of the illusion of wholeness or purity. There is always a differentiation within ideas, states, or situations. This is a useful reminder in the face of current attempts to represent the Islamic world as unified, as an excuse to unify a Western world we know to be riddled with differences and conflicts. This difference-within can be preserved only if, unlike Yusuf, we do not turn away from what we see: the words, the images of the text.[7]

Let me reiterate that I am not alleging a special knowledge of what I am calling a "Qur'anic semiotic." On the contrary, I am trying to argue for a cautious deployment of ignorance as a road to knowledge. For this idea I call on Shoshana Felman. As she has argued in the context of psychoanalysis—a discipline within which ignorance is the precondition to achieve knowledge—ignorance is a necessary prerequisite for access to knowledge (1982). Reading the Joseph sura with ignorance offers innumerable opportunities to address the critical questions of the positioned comparative cultural analysis I am exploring here, and to turn reflection on them into a productive, constructive activity. To take advantage of these opportunities, I would like to look at knowledge *as* ignorance, therefore requiring a practice conceived of according to Appadurai's concept of "the research imagination." For him, this term points to the ways we imagine "good-enough" research, according to often "taken-for-granted" standards on which our research ethics are based. When he writes that "replicability" is the "hidden moral force" (2000, 11), I am inclined to juxtapose this, somewhat irreverently, to the Qur'an's status as Recitation, *hence* original. Here, too, a paradox lies at the heart of the matter. Whereas traditionally this force sustained the idea of "value-free" research, for Appadurai replicability foregrounds the nonindividual. Replicability demonstrates the profoundly social, nature of research, even if individuals experience and imagine their work as individual. In other words, in the social nature

---

7. Most convincingly Barbara Johnson has been a proponent of this vision, from her first book in 1980 to her more recent one in 1998. The unified image of the Islamic and Western worlds I am at pains to counter has been (in)famously promoted by Samuel Huntington (2001).

lies the recitability, so to speak, that appears to counter originality but that in a different way constitutes it. Today this social character of knowledge production raises two questions at the same time. The first is that of plausible protocols, theories, and models that enable transnational, transcultural, and truly global knowledge production. This question calls for a research imagination that accommodates cross-cultural and inter-social diversity, as well as for comparison and distribution of attention.[8]

Once ignorance is mobilized to supplement the failure of a truly transnational and transcultural production of knowledge, the aspect most needing acknowledgment is the performative nature of knowledge production. And here, of course, the work of Judith Butler is indispensable. Yet in all its groundbreaking brilliance, Butler's work underilluminates two aspects of performativity that I believe deserve a more prominent place: memory and narrative. The two join forces in the tale that is allegedly a pre-text meant to make a point. "Memory" as a hub where the individual and the collective, the personal and the social spin around each other; "narrative" as the process that mediates through these whirling forces between past and present, as the mode in which memory takes place. Both explain how performativity works in cultural practice. There is performativity in reading or not reading any of the versionings that judge the interethnic, interclass love between Mut and Yusuf and imprint those judgments into the memory of young children. In other words, the readings I am doing here—just one instance of working through cultural legacies of fear, hostility, and desire—*matter*. They matter specifically qua narrative-through-memory. For the performativity of cultural as well as intercultural reading continues the building of cultural memory, slightly shifting it perhaps, this way or that way.

One practice in that complex of memory and narrative is the resulting construction of knowledge. I imagine replicability not

8. For me, the notion of replicability resonates with Derrida's famous critique (1988) of J. L. Austin's speech-act theory, which set the tone for the contemporary politicized version of that theory made famous through Judith Butler's work in queer theory (1993; 1997). This version of the theory of performativity, masterfully followed in its tracks by Jonathan Culler (2000) superposes poststructuralist skepticism onto structuralist models of commensurability.

as a prescriptive but a heuristic standard. As such it can help us assess the deployment of research protocols, not as a search for what we already know (a re-search) but as a search for what, in the unknown, can be meaningfully connected to what we thought we knew but wish to reenvision. This view of knowledge, then, can in turn become a guideline for reading the Qur'an's versioning of Yusuf, understanding its specific and anxiously contained semiotic theory without either appropriating or othering it.

This view of knowledge makes me want to find points of entry into texts that remain all strange to me, whether I have been informed by them in my early life or later. All the texts under discussion here are embedded in cultures and languages I don't know, so that I must shed my protective shield of expertise in favor of the object itself as the source of knowledge. My task in this endeavor is, in part, procedural: it is to theorize and justify the model of knowledge that makes it possible for the research imagination to establish a heuristically productive affiliation with the literary or artistic imagination. The artifact, then, becomes a "theoretical object." Bringing narrative theory, my field of specialization of old, to bear on this case, then, is not a priori a Eurocentric domestication of difference but rather a search for ways to expand the questions this theory helps us to ask through the resistance this object—Yusuf's encounter with love—mounts against it.

Replicability, then, is the tool not for iteration, nor for comparison mobilized to distinguish between "good" and "bad" or "original" and "derivative" versions, including the scholarship about them, but for shifting the boundary between commensurable and incommensurable objects. As a result of the affiliation between the research imagination and the literary, artistic, or, as the case may be, religious imagination can suspend insidious normative standards. These standards are inevitably implied in comparison, even in a judgment of incommensurability, and posit, in the words of Edouard Glissant, "equivalences that do not unify" (1981, 466). This shifting, which Natalie Melas sees as the task of comparative literature, forces me to transgress and shift boundaries of all kinds.[9]

9. See Melas 1995, 275. Melas's 2007 book came too late to be fully taken into account.

In this, the performativity I claim for my readings is a form of travel. As Jonathan Culler wrote regarding the concept of performativity, the point of arrival when one is speaking of a performative concept of gender is very different from the point of departure, Austin's conception of performative utterances. "But to make your fortune, as the genre of the picaresque has long shown us, you have to leave home and, often, travel a long way" (2000, 48). Culler considers such "travels" between philosophy and literary or cultural studies. I am engaged here similarly with the boundaries between "Western" and other, not-quite-non-Western texts, as much as with literary and visual studies and the replicable protocols that can facilitate responsible border-crossings there. In both cases, what is at stake is what Homi Bhabha has felicitously phrased the "politics of the theoretical statement" and the ways such politics can shift the "horizon of the true" (1994, 22). The blinding effect false testimony exerts on Jacob forecasts the eyes wide shut with which Yusuf experimentally devises seeing as insight and as hearing.

The face of Yusuf, replicating that of God in the way Dabashi claims that "the absence of the Face of the Unseen is *replicated* in our own inability to see our own Faces," is most clearly, albeit symbolically, made (in)visible in a crucial detail (if such a thing can be envisioned) that the Qur'an offers while Genesis does not. This is the evidence, mocking the false evidence of Joseph's colored coat in its many misuses. In Genesis, the "men of her house" were set against Joseph by means of ethnic anti-Hebraism combined with class envy. Supposedly they went along with the plot; at least, nothing indicates they did not. In the Qur'an, the men of her house are not solicited. Since the master is at the door at the moment Yusuf tries to leave, there will not have been time for such a plot. Instead, one of those men steps forward as a witness—"a witness out of her own house." Rather than making false claims of indexicality, this witness uses specifying, materialist logic. "If his shirt be rent in front she speaks truth, and he is a liar; but if his shirt be rent behind, she lies and he is true" (12:26–27). This is an instructive instance of the always dubious shift from material object to sign. And so it happened that Mut is caught red-handed in a lie. For the master, this is supposedly a moment of insight, for he grandly extends his blame to the entire

female sex, saying: "This is one of your [plural] devices! Verily
your devices are great!" (12:28). And he orders Mut to apologize
to Yusuf.

On the (sur)face of it, this is the moment of truth. It is indeed,
not only the truth concerning what "really" happened but also
the social truth of woman's claim to the right to desire, which
must be denied. Immediately after this, the episode of the woman
in the city begins with the rumors about Mut's passion. Their
first response is that they "clearly *see* her *manifest* error" (12:30).
While the sentence binds seeing-as-insight with seeing physically
(manifest), it leaves the question whether they see (know) the
trap and the lie suspended. But they are in error themselves, as
will soon become apparent when they fall in love with Yusuf collectively. A third truth that transpires from the moment of truth
is that of Yusuf's face. His face cannot be seen; being righteous,
chaste, and honest, he turns his face away, refraining from looking at the woman's face in the bargain. Here his eyes have truly
gone wide shut. The witness's logic thus also has symbolic meaning. Rent from behind, the shirt is evidence of Yusuf's invisible
face—his refusal to face. By averting his gaze from the sexual
attraction, he saves his greater seeing as insight.

Such very special eyes have been depicted by Rembrandt. The
tiny blot that left some of Yusuf's eye white in the etching has a
counterpart in the figure's downcast eyes in a painting. I imagine
painting as work with all the elements—color, line, shape, composition, perspective—that are deceptive as well as evidentiary,
indexical, because they can keep the collapse between sign and
signifier at bay. Evidence, that is, not of the image-as-real but of
the act of making it, including responsibility for its versioning.
Far from necessarily dangerous, hence liable to being tabooed, I
consider even this most classical of paintings an example of the
paradox put forward by the Qur'an text. That is, on the condition
that we take it at its word, line, or blot. In a further versioning,
then, I propose another (re)turn to visuality.

7

Eyes Wide Shut

If words can be signs and signs can be faces shown or withheld, so can elements of paintings. Reading a sura is processing and responding to a "visible sign of a transcendental
reality" (Neuwirth n.d.). Visibility and the sign go hand
in hand. A sura that tells the story of Yusuf from point to
point shows rather than tells: it is a sign rather than a tale.
According to one of the founders of contemporary semiotics, Charles S. Peirce, signs can do their work of signification without having to be split in signifier and signified, as
continental semiotics tends to have it. The sign's elements
are unstable only temporally. In this chapter I will argue for
the temporality of semiosis and for the actuality of its anchoring in philosophy. I will bring Peirce, Rembrandt, and
Spinoza together to further elaborate my argument for a
literalism that counters fundamentalism. The central issue
in this discussion is the elusive referent.

On Peirce's view, semiosis as a process of signification
is more important than semiotics, the (logical) system he
devised to explain how semiosis works. This process is a
temporal as well as a social phenomenon. It requires both
sequentiality—one step after the other—and people who
do the processing of signs put before them. In all semiotic

theories, the tenacious problem is the place of the referent. The longing for realism in theory makes many scholars anxious when the referent seems to be bracketed. Yet the referent needs to be suspended—neither canceled out nor forgotten—if we are to account for changing interpretations in a meaningful and responsible way. That is, if we are to be responsive to the text or image as well as to the social constituencies processing these.

The sign can retain a trace of the bond between signifier and signified as long as it is not reified, not fixed. It moves, and that mobility is essential to the life of signs; but the trace of the bond must be clung to so that the signified cannot slip away from under the signified, cannot take on a life of its own, parading as the referent it is not. The fear of this slipperiness is what informs iconophobia. It is also the ground on which the textual fundamentalism I am addressing here manages to appear convincing. But fear rarely furthers insight. As Derrida has explained clearly in a debate about the ethics of theory in the face of politics, the *indeterminacy* of signification does not imply *undecidability*. On the contrary, it is because signs cannot answer our anxious questions, our search for authoritative certitude, that we must have the courage to take decisions.[1]

Instead, the sign is an element—or should I say, episode—in a process that is fundamentally social in nature. The sign can remain endowed with traces of the signified, hence function in an ever-changing kind of "wholeness" because the reader "makes" the meaning. She does so on the ground of relations fleetingly established between signs and something that, for that reader, becomes the meaning. The reader can and frequently does attach such meanings to referents; this is the sign user's decision on how to use meaning, it is not inherent in meaning itself. This process is essentially mobile yet also anchored in historical awareness. Not fundamentalism, then, but literalism.

These grounds are not codes operating automatically and mechanically. They overlap, collaborate, shift and change with the

---

1. Derrida came to this most useful formulation in a performative confrontation with student protests at Cornell University against the university's investments in South Africa, at that time still under the spell of apartheid (1985; reworked in 1988).

times. A twice-used index already slides toward becoming a symbol, for example. One of these grounds is called "iconic." It incites the act of meaning making because the reader "sees"—let's take that word as I have so far—a similarity or analogy between the sign and a potential meaning.

A second ground is called "indexical." Here the production of meaning is a response to a perceived existential contiguity between the sign and that meaning. Where there is smoke, there is fire; where there is blood, there is violence (or was virginity); where a shirt is torn, somebody has been assaulted. That is, the sign user assumes this to be so. The referential reality of these meanings remains to be decided. A virgin can fail to bleed; smoke can lead us to a house on fire but also to a desolate, totally harmless site where the flames of a fire have all but disappeared. The shirt torn proves nothing about who assaulted whom, unless additional signification is practiced and the side on which the shirt is torn becomes an index in itself. These decisions are not inherent in the signs but in the use made of them.

The third ground is social-cultural habit. If English uses the word love interchangeably for sexual passion, parental attachment, and polite but informal friendliness to strangers, this leads English speakers into interpretive directions that may be utterly strange, even dangerous or immoral, to speakers of languages where such notions are attached to different words.

These grounds mingle; hardly any sign works "purely" and this, too, comes from the view of the sign as both whole and unmoored. What happens, then, when media take over each other's preferred signs? As we have seen, speech acts are central in the texts of Genesis, the Qur'an, and Mann's novel, although in different degrees and modes. This seems obvious, since texts consist of words. But this is overdetermined by the reported speeches, more numerous in Genesis during the seduction scene than in the Qur'an, more numerous in the latter during the aftermath, the scene of the banquet that makes the second point. When representing speech, visual works of art might have a hard time. Common (albeit erroneous) lore has it that paintings work with icons and texts with symbols. But when paintings represent words—the words that are the story—the media change places in relation to signs.

Two aspects are often said to distinguish reading texts from reading images. Both distinctions can be challenged, with the help of sura 12. First, processing words takes time. That time is involved in processing literature is a given. But according to Peirce, the reader who does the work of reading still builds up images as the new signs that emerge from the processing. Peirce called these *interpretants*. The sign user "sees" these new signs, sometimes as concept-images. Similarly, although less obviously, we must contend with the fact that looking takes time as well. The famous glance cast upon an image can only lead to quick (mis)recognition, not to new insights, to "seeing." Seeing narrative painting obviously requires going over the visual field, moment after moment to construct the story, or point after point to construct the sign. We have seen this already in chapter 4, and differently in chapter 5. In visual art, such a viewing attitude is promoted by the accumulation of different moments within one image, not unlike comic strips.

Second, reading words may only appear to be grounded in symbolicity rather than in iconicity. This common view is challenged when we realize that reading reported speech (also called direct discourse) is a case of iconic reading in literature. The speeches supposedly are similar to what was said by the characters. That is why we call Mut a liar. Her speeches conjure up interpretants that are dissimilar to those we "saw" before, based on the signs of the narrator's utterances. On the other hand, representing speech in painting requires conventional signs, such as hand gestures—"speaking hands"—and compositional devices. These require symbolic—and to an extent indexical—activity on the part of the viewer. Rembrandt used this device frequently. There is no reason to understand pointing and other forms of gesturing as speech, other than through convention helped by indexicality.

Taken together, these two challenges to conventional views of the reified difference between text and image mobilize the interaction between sura 12 and Rembrandt's versionings of the tale. In this chapter, I allege that Spinoza turned Rembrandt into a star of popular culture. The best case for the popular-culture aspect of the images is to be made through the history paintings. For these address popular stories and myths, including the ideologies such stories embody in their various popular manifestations. The recurrence of well-rehearsed stories in culture would today be associated with Hollywood cinema, for example, or soap operas on television. In earlier times, the theater would be a place of such recurrence. This is why I will make my case here through our well-worn story of misogyny, of Joseph/Yusuf and his seduction and betrayal by Potiphar's wife, Mut.

Rembrandt painted the scene of Yusuf and Mut twice. The repetition is generally explained in terms of the theater play after which he painted them, Joost van de Vondel's *Joseph in Egypt* (1640). Halfway during the successful performance of this play in Amsterdam in 1655, a new actress began to play the role of the main character. For the viewer today, this historical information is falsely reassuring rather than relevant. It can give rise to the illusion that we understand the two paintings. Especially the very different look of the woman in each is simply explained with reference to the actual different woman playing the part. Thus a "difference that might be a *visible* sign of a transcendental reality" is explained away and turned invisible.

Instead, on the basis of convention or symbolicity, I propose to read these two paintings according to the three modes of visual storytelling common in Rembrandt's time: the symbolic sequentiality of episodes represented from left to right on a single picture plane; the theatrical mode of gesturing, wherein hand gestures indexically represent speech; and the condensation of iconically represented episodes or moments within a single expressive visual unit, usually a figure. These are only accents, not essences. In these two paintings, I propose to read what we see in the first place as a comic strip, hence as a sequence, as if they were subsequent moments or scenes in the episode of the accusation. The first painting, now in Washington, DC (fig. 3), is the first phase. Here the accusation itself is acted out. The second painting, now in Berlin (fig. 4), represents Joseph's protestations. This is the gap-filling painting; in the Bible Joseph does not protest; in the Qur'an he does, and in Vondel's play he does too.[2]

A third mode of encouraging narrative reading of paintings is the concentration of several moments, as if in a doubly exposed

2. It would be pointless to claim that Rembrandt had read the Qur'an. The coincidence merely points to a certain story logic.

Figure 3. Rembrandt van Rijn, *Joseph and Potiphar's Wife*, oil on canvas,
106 × 98 cm, 1655; National Gallery of Art, Washington, DC.

photograph. Rembrandt used all three—the comic strip, the gesturing hands, and concentration—to version his Mut-and-Yusuf
story. We will see that he contributed to a vindication close to
Mann's, or the Qur'an's, even if no little knives wreck bloody
havoc in his paintings. In this chapter, I will simply propose my
own reading of these two paintings. They occurred to me—or better, I performed them—after I read Mann's novel and after I read
the Qur'anic version. In order to connect this moment to a memory that, I think, had great impact on my life, I have to briefly tell
how I came to this engagement with Rembrandt.

The first stage of that itinerary I already recounted in chapter 4. The second stage occurred not long after. I spent the year
after that conference in Jerusalem in the United States, and I had

Figure 4. Rembrandt van Rijn, *Joseph and Potiphar's Wife*, oil on canvas,
113.5 × 90 cm, 1655; Gemäldegalerie, Berlin.

Figure 5. Detail of figure 4 (Joseph's head).

Figure 6. Rembrandt van Rijn, *Lucretia* (detail), oil on canvas, National Gallery of Art, Washington, DC.

opportunity to visit the National Gallery in Washington, DC. There I had the thrill of being taken down to the restoration workshop to see a painting I had inquired about, Rembrandt's *Lucretia*. That encounter determined my shift from texts to painting just as strongly as had the earlier encounter with the etching. I have told the story elsewhere and am loath to repeat it (Bal 1991, 60–93). Suffice it to say that I had the brief but strong sensation, when the protective veil was suddenly removed from the painting, of seeing Lucretia move her head. Later I was able to rationalize that sensation by noting the earring that hangs obliquely, as if moved by the swing of the figure's head (fig. 6). This feature of the painting worked together with the sudden unveiling (that is, anecdotal) to produce a sensation that I was ready to accept as an instance of informal knowledge. It was the beginning of the development of a mode of narrative reading that I have been developing ever since.

I saw the *Joseph* painting during that same visit, after having seen Lucretia move her head. Hence I was "into" seeing narrativity as "seeing" in the biblical sense: as insight, based on reason and sensation alike. The Berlin painting I saw later. Perhaps for that reason I found it less compelling, less "beautiful," than the one I considered earlier (at least in the narrative sense). Both paintings offer a gap-filling and indirect versioning of Genesis—if we assume that Rembrandt was familiar with the biblical story if not necessarily with the text, and most likely saw the play at least twice, but is unlikely to have read the Qur'an. There are a lot of assumptions here. I offer them only to make what follows a bit less outrageous than it might otherwise be. I am not making any historical claims about the paintings. On the contrary, as with my other readings in this book, my point is preposterous: it is contemporary and constructing the past as part of the present.

To clarify this updating, I introduce a new figure in the discussion at this point; the figure of a philosopher. It may seem strange to base an updated view of Rembrandt's relevance for today on his possible encounter with a contemporary who was, like the painter, recalcitrant, a social oddity, and in trouble with the church and the synagogue respectively. I am alluding to Baruch Spinoza. For a while Rembrandt and Spinoza were neighbors, living in the Jewish quarter in Amsterdam. Whether they ever met is unknown. They had one acquaintance in common, Rabbi Manasseh ben Israel (Rembrandt's friend and Spinoza's teacher). I am not interested in such biographical facts but in the question why both are so in vogue *today*, the one simply because of an anniversary (2006 was Rembrandt's four-hundredth birth year), the other due to the urgent relevance of his ideas, developed in critical intimacy with those long-influential ideas of his contemporary Descartes. An introduction of Spinoza through Rembrandt and vice versa helps lay the groundwork for the analysis of two Yusuf paintings in this chapter.

To begin with the most obvious points of communality between Spinoza and Rembrandt, traditional scholarship has mentioned the following elements. All these connections cast light on
the relevance of the paintings, illuminated by the philosopher's
ideas, for an actualized understanding of the story.

- Spinoza's materialism has been likened to Rembrandt's
  realism. In this view, the individuality of his figures would
  demonstrate the innumerable modifications of the one
  substance of matter.
- Spinoza's synthetic unity might be substantiated in
  Rembrandt's vision of human beings' unity of body and
  soul, expressed in the psychological depth of the figures'
  appearances.
- The two men shared an interest in actions and passions.
- Spinoza's dynamic conception of affects is embodied in
  Rembrandt's depiction of continuity and change within figures,
  which he depicted as in a present moment replete with a past
  and ready to step into the future.
- Even Rembrandt's interest in the lower classes might recall
  Spinoza's democratic tendencies.
- Both men shared a keen desire for freedom, neither traveled
  abroad, and both had an inclination for objectivism over
  religious dogma. (Valentiner 1957)

For me the Spinozist inspiration is bound up with ways of connecting—the vision of signs as social glue. This connective function
I address here through the preposition *inter-*, as in *intercultural*,
intertemporal, and *interdisciplinary*.[3]

   In the wake of a recent anti-Cartesianism and a turn to Spinoza, the concept of "second-personhood" means not only that
we cannot exist without others—in the eye of the other as much
as in sustenance of others—but also that it is from the interaction
with others that we derive most fulfillment. That is where I would
start any attempt to develop an idea of the aesthetic, returning

---

3. An extensive version of this Rembrandt-Spinoza encounter is to appear
separately (Bal and Vardoulakis, in prep.).

with "critical intimacy" (Spivak 1999) to moments of the past, such as the dawn of rationalism in the seventeenth century.

How does Spinoza help clarify Rembrandt's Peircean semiosis? According to Genesis, Potiphar is told about Joseph's alleged attempted assault only after the event and in Joseph's absence. Therefore, in terms of Genesis the presence of Yusuf in the paintings suggests a condensation. The scene, then, presents the seduction attempt for which the husband has to be absent together with the later accusation for which Joseph had to be absent. In the Washington painting, Yusuf's position toward the back, on the far left of the picture plane and at the far side of the bed, suggests not only his subordinate position in the house and his subdued position as the accused but also the temporal anteriority of his presence.

Although in order to avoid burdening the text with references, I will refrain from alleging specialized Rembrandt scholarship, one example of the reasoning in this scholarship might help understand the difference between the kind of speculation I perform in this essay and the equally speculative reasoning common in art history. The great Rembrandt scholar Otto Benesch claims that in both paintings Joseph was originally kneeling (1970, 93–94). This is quite plausible and makes the final decision to depict him standing more meaningful. Yet I find Benesch's argument that in the Washington painting this must have been so because the woman's hand is gesturing toward the bedpost an utterly unconvincing instance of in-reading. First of all, she is pointing to the red cloth, supposedly Yusuf's coat, the evidence of his assault for Potiphar, of her desire for us. Not to speak of other possible associations with the bedpost that I brought up in chapter 4.

While the Washington painting condenses two moments, the Berlin one takes the aftermath further by expressing Joseph's desperate protestations of innocence. Here we have the seduction attempt, the accusation, and the refutation. Both images position Joseph at the far side of the bed as the earlier moment. In Berlin he becomes the spokesman in the third episode. Potiphar, at the other side of the bed and closer to the woman, embodies, as listener, the second moment of the accusation but is drawn into the third by Yusuf's reply. Thus time is represented by means of space. This I consider a narrativization of the scene. Its move of condensation takes the story further qua narrative. While the text had to present the events successively, thereby avoiding the meeting of the men, the painting is capable of drawing the three moments together so that this meeting must occur. What the text had to separate, the painting—and the theater—can integrate: two men, one woman.

In the painting from Berlin, the third narrative device, the representation of speech through speaking hands, is integrated more explicitly. This makes the painting more theatrical. The woman points more explicitly to Joseph than in the other work. In both images her left hand covers her breast, as if to protect herself from the assault while also protesting that she is telling the truth. In terms of the representation of speech, this hand indicates that she is telling about Joseph's physical assault on her, and the lively, theatrical manner in which she tells it strengthens the readability of her speech. Moreover, legally she confirms what Genesis assumes and the Qur'an questions. Potiphar's right hand is resting on the chair, slightly behind the woman, thus creating a sense of intimacy between the two that excludes the accused. Now we have a structure of man-and-wife versus the other man. The Berlin painting is adequate to the mission of telling the story as the doxa knows it.

The other painting does more. The same semiotic devices are used: sequentiality to symbolically represent narrative time, condensation, and "speaking hands." But the same devices of narrativization are much more ambivalent here as signs. For example, the hand with which the woman supposedly accuses Joseph does point, but not at him. The index is misdirected. It points perhaps to the red garment, the false token—evidence, index—of Yusuf's misbehavior: the object that lies. But even that direction is not so clear. And instead of gesticulating theatrically in despair, Yusuf here is standing still with downcast eyes. His left hand, which is just a little bit above his arm, suggests that he was about to say something but has hesitated.

The device of speaking hands is deployed more subtly here. Yusuf's hand goes up as if about to protest, but such a protest would not be compatible with his face. Hence, the image inscribes the short duration of the still. Potiphar's hand is on its way to Mut's breast, which she covers, then, to protect herself from him, not from Yusuf. This painting is much more enigmatic than the one in Berlin. For this reason alone, I would like to experiment with a reversal of reading. In the Western tradition, where reading goes from left to right, images tend to be structured in the same way. Moreover, Rembrandt frequently plays with the tension between compositions on the flat surface of the canvas and the structure of linear perspective. This is, at least, how I have proposed to read two of his major paintings, *Danae* (St. Peterburg, Hermitage) and *The Blinding of Samson* (Frankfurt, Städel). Here, in his first Yusuf painting, a reading from the left side of the bed, guided by the returned look in the etching, versions the story in terms quite different from those of Genesis. Now, in the image seen as flat and from left to right, Potiphar's hand is not so clearly behind the woman but slightly in front of her, as if on its way to grabbing her. The woman protects her breast again, but in combination with the lesser distance between her and Potiphar, his grabbing hand, and his determined facial expression, it seems as if, ignoring the biblical story, it is he who is approaching her (sexually?) against her will. Joseph, meanwhile, is just standing there. His passivity, downcast eyes, and darker shape make him now less likely an accused. Rather, he could be seen as the more desirable, younger, more handsome love object—Mut's fantasy. Yes, this is a preposterous interpretation. Several indications for it, however, can be construed—with the help of a semiotics that holds on to the sign as whole.

First, there is the work of light—one of Rembrandt's signature signs. The light is much more subtle in this painting than in the Berlin one. It falls on the bed and the woman in both paintings, but in the Washington one Joseph is also very subtly illuminated while Potiphar, by contrast, is almost ghostly. The light produces a pattern in which the young man and the woman are illuminated to the exclusion of the older man. As a ghostly figure, the latter comes to evoke the dead father of Freud's "scientific myth" *Totem and Taboo*, who threatens both son and woman. Joseph's face has an intense yet unclear expression. It is hard to decide whether he is anxious, desirous, or admiring. This intense ambiguity points to dreaming, to fantasy. Moreover, Yusuf seems here sexually ambiguous. His gender wavers. The curtain, much more clearly indicated in the Berlin picture as a (realistic) representation of a bed curtain, is here so vaguely indicated that its only function seems to be to set off Yusuf as standing in a space, lighter and farther away, *at the other side*. Finally, the allegiance between Mut and the younger man is further enhanced by the color scheme. Her dress is pink, the mantle on the bedpost is red, and so is the belt that offsets Yusuf's golden robe.

The most intriguing detail is the eyes of each of the three protagonists. Each figure looks intensely but inwardly. No figure looks at a clearly defined object. The woman does not look at her husband. Rather, she seems to stare at an inner vision—the vision where her desire is staged. The older man does not look at the woman. He, too, may be concentrating on his desire, or, from another perspective, he may not be looking at anything at all; he may already be dead (in the desire of the woman, or the dispossessed son of Freud's text). Yusuf's look, not directed anywhere either, is even more inward than those of the two others, while also almost directed at the viewer.

Australian philosophers Moira Gatens and Genevieve Lloyd (1999) have offered a preposterous reading of Spinoza that I wish to bring to bear on these two paintings. Their versioning of the philosopher's ideas has led to important and productive revisionings of the image, perception, and feeling that lie at the heart of my interpretation of the paintings. Their book helps connect this interpretation to the previously advocated reading of the Qur'an versioning on the basis of a specific semiotic congenial with Peirce's. Before returning to the Washington painting and its key difference from the Berlin one, let me briefly present these ideas.

First, the Australian philosophers invoke the relevance of Spinoza's work for a reasoned position in relation to aboriginal Australians' claim to the land that had been taken from them by European settlers. These claimants' claims, based on a culturally specific conception of subjecthood and ownership, make an excellent case for the collective and historical responsibility the authors put forward with the help of Spinoza's vision of the bond between past, present, and future. And this entails responsibility.

That this *"intercultural ethics"* should be based on a seventeenth-century thinker who never met such claimants—although he can be considered a second-generation migratory subject—makes, second, a case for the kind of historiography I have termed *preposterous*. In alignment with intercultural relationality, we could call it *intertemporal*. Such a term reminds us of the thick mutuality of relation, as opposed to a lean linearity of progress.

Third, the authors make their case on the basis of the integration, an actual merging, of Spinoza's ontological, ethical, and political writings, three philosophical disciplines traditionally considered one by one. This, of course, exemplifies interdisciplinarity.

These three connective uses of *inter-* provide Peirce's account of the process of semiosis with ethical, temporal, and academic dimensions. The difference in Joseph's look in the Washington painting reinforces the radical separation between Yusuf on the one hand and the couple on the other. How can he be connected again? When viewed from the other side of the bed, his image is almost detached, as if it were a portrait on the wall. The lower seam of his garment is the end of him. No legs are attached to his image. Of course, the resulting floating impression of his image will probably have increased over time. Time darkens paint, and thus the dark underside of the embedded image of Yusuf has turned more abstract over the centuries. For today's viewer, this material effect is immaterial—it increases the immateriality effect of the man the Qur'an women call "not a man" but "an angel." Visuality, in this way, is pluralized by the different modes of looking, so that the figures do not have the same visual status. Yusuf is and remains a sign, both for the viewers and for the viewers in the image, the couple. He remains a dream image, the result of a fantasy. Like a portrait on the wall—a projection on a screen—the floating figure of Yusuf is itself the inner vision, the object of preoccupation of the two others. When viewed in isolation, Yusuf seems full of feeling yet not involved in any event.

Between these three still and intense-looking figures there is an object that attracts attention, if not from the figures then at least from the viewer. This is the moment when the viewer turns indeterminacy into a responsible form of decidability. That object is, of course, the red cloth, the garment lying over the bedpost, thus standing erect between the woman and the youth. The color points to the blood that, as we have seen, testifies in the Qur'an and in Mann's novel to the desire of all the women—the plural *you* as in "your wiles" of Potiphar's contemptuous generalization. Should the red garment testify here, by the color it shares with blood, of the event the woman is supposed to evoke with indignation as the one that really happened? Or does it represent her desire, her hallucination that it happened? Between the

grounds of iconicity, of which, for Peirce, color is the quintes-
sential example, and that of indexicality, where it can point to
prior events or desired futures with equal plausibility, the sign,
Qur'an-wise, should not be split.

Fantasy here becomes the social glue that helps make sense of
the figure's apparent isolation. This fantasy, for Spinoza, would
be the result of the imagination. And this, importantly, is social. It
is also a kind of emotional battleground. Invoking Spinoza's version of the imaginary as undeniably social in nature, Gatens and
Lloyd write: "Intersubjectivity here rests on connections between
minds which are grounded in the impinging of bodies which are
both alike and different, giving rise to affects of joy and sadness,
love and hate, and hope" (1999, 39). They recall that Spinoza's
conception of affect is explicit in its intertemporality:

> The awareness of actual bodily modification—the awareness of
> things as present—is fundamental to the affects; and this is what
> makes the definition of affect overlap with that of imagination.
> All this gives special priority to the present. But there are two
> ways in which the present is involved in imagination and affect:
> first, the awareness of the immediate state of bodily modification,
> which applies, by definition, to all affects and to all imaginings;
> and, second, the special relation to the present which arises where
> not only the bodily modification but its causes are present—that
> is, where the affect relates to something here and now, rather than
> past or future. (52)

This passage captures quite precisely where for me the Spinozist
inspiration comes in. Such images possess a temporal density that is
inhabited by the past and the future, while affect remains an event
in the present—an event of, to use a typical Spinozian-Deleuzian
phrase, *becoming*. The intertemporality of aesthetics, then, is
a privileged aspect of art to situate its contribution to social life.
This concerns the presence of the past. "Spinozistic responsibility" is derived from the philosopher's concept of the self as social;
it consists of projecting presently felt responsibilities "back into a
past which itself becomes determinate only from the perspective
of what lies in the future of that past—in our present" (81). Taking seriously the "temporal dimensions of human consciousness"

includes endorsing the "multiple forming and reforming of identities over time and within the deliverances of memory and imagination at any one time" (81). This "preposterous" responsibility based on memory and imagination makes selfhood both stable and instable (82). This instability is a form of empowerment, of agency within a collectivity-based individual consciousness. In Deleuze's work, this becomes the key concept of *becoming*.

In the Washington painting, the imagination can thus connect—*inter*—a semiotic of process with that semiotic I have dubbed for the sake of my argument here particularly "Qur'anic," so that it can be involved in this reading without being appropriated. As I mentioned, all the elements that set the Yusuf figure apart point in the direction of fantasy. But they have led us rather far from Genesis, unless we reprocess Genesis in light of the painting. These are the details that differentiate this painting from its successor in Berlin more radically, say, than they differentiate the painting from the Qur'an or Mann's novel—neither of which we can presume to have been Rembrandt's "source." With Mann's pictorial scene it shares the hallucinatory quality. With the Qur'an it shares the tenderness with which it attends to the woman's desire. The point is one of the two seemingly divergent points of the Qur'an story, the theological testing of Yusuf and the vindication of the woman's desire. Or, we may now say, in this painting the two points are joint, condensed. Not, we can see, as two episodes but as two arguments—a staged debate between the painter and the philosopher.

Interdisciplinary thought is needed to make the connection, in the present and across the cultural divide, between a number of discourses and activities routinely either treated separately or—equally problematic—unwarrantedly merged. These twin traps are caused, I contend, by the focus on *intention* inherited from the cogito's first-person discourse—a focus I have discussed at some length elsewhere (Bal 2002). Considering Rembrandt as popular culture can help out in attempts to appropriate the artistic images for present-day culture without giving the artist's alleged intentions a central place. The details, or rather, the detailed looking that allows the narrative potential of the picture to unfold, lead to the idea of fantasy. Fantasy, as the uniquely staged projection of a dreamer temporarily split between the roles of director and actor, is itself held together, albeit tenuously and provisionally, by the intensity of the committed viewer. The latter takes part in the play. This is why fantasy in culture takes on a function that distinguishes it from myth. If myth is the open structure, the screen onto which the cultural doxa can make us unreflectively project preconceived opinions about our "others," fantasy, also a projection, engages each of us personally and commits us to looking-with, as in suffering-with: with a commitment to integrate the thrill of sensate vision with intellectual, critical reflection.

At this point let me bring back Mann's scene, its succinct version in the Qur'an, and Rembrandt's etching to meet the paintings. Like the detached, ontologically separate figure of Yusuf in the Washington painting, Mann's attempt to vindicate the woman by making her desire understandable, even justified, is orchestrated by means of the dreamy, unreal status of Yusuf. Early in the novel when he is first introduced, this is the Yusuf we get to see: "A youth famed for his charm and charming especially by right from his mother, who has been sweet and lovely like the moon when it is full and like Ishtar's star when it swims mildly in the clear sky" (4). His beauty is not described in detail, but his unreality is. Just like Rembrandt's floating figure, this youth is an object of generalized attraction. In line with this, the bloody scene generalizes not Mut's lie, trap, or misdemeanor but her feelings. Like the Washington painting, the scene has the same aspects of intersubjectivity, of lack of limits between subjects, that I have called earlier a "porous" subjectivity. The cutting scene, perhaps also a defloration scene, at least reminiscent of the requirements of evidence of virginity in Deuteronomy 22, enhances and explains the accusation. Here I would like to reiterate two elements of this discussion. First, the Derridian response to the suspension of the referent in (semiotic) theory: indeterminacy enhances responsibility for decision making. Second, the Spinozist view of porous subjectivity as an affect-based existence: "Intersubjectivity here rests on connections between minds which are grounded in the impinging of bodies which are both alike and different, giving rise to affects of joy and sadness, love and hate, and hope" (Gatens and Lloyd 1999, 39).

In the Qur'an, we remember, Potiphar commended Yusuf to his wife's care through the invocation of two obligations, hospitality and parenting. In Genesis, Yusuf is said to be seventeen years old when he leaves home. This seems a bit old for a child-minding set-up. The Qur'an doesn't specify his age in numbers but in stages. Again, there is no gap but a narrative need. In order for the privileged position he will acquire in the house to be possible, he needs to be hosted like a member of the family. And for this he must be assumed to be young. All this is story-logic, a sequence of signs for us to process—offered for affective response but indeterminate in affective content, leaving us a choice among "joy and sadness, love and hate, and hope." This youthfulness is also required for the story of Yusuf's temptation. God leads him through the risks of youthful folly. Before any of the mishaps began, God has already done this. "And when he had reached the age of strength we bestowed on him judgment and knowledge; for thus do we recompense the well doers" (12:22).

Transitional age is often symbolized as liminal, from *limen*, threshold. Thresholds and doors represent passages of the life stages. Thus the race of the two characters to the door puts Yusuf and Mut in the same situation, perhaps at the same transitional phase. In the Rembrandts, including the Washington painting, the older man's presence on the hither side of the bed suggests that the door is on the right. In the etching it is on the left. There Yusuf still has a choice, but he looks back instead of fleeing. And whereas in the painting the figure of Yusuf has the aura of a fantasmatic projection, in the etching the woman's distorted body looks less than real. Does this justify the speculation that Rembrandt used the different media of painting and etching to explore two radically divergent versionings? In painting, the medium of commissions and sales, he explored the official version that the doxa of his culture prescribed, so that within the margins of socially acceptable behavior he could tamper with the scene of the crime only enough to turn the accused into a fantasized image.

In the etching, by contrast, we can imagine—according to Spinoza's conception of the imagination—that he is exploring different possibilities. Now Yusuf is the one hallucinating. What he sees with that weird back-looking eye is a distorted, fat belly. He might see in that belly a future in which the woman would bear him children, or the chubby belly of a child that could be his sibling. Nothing is too crazy for hallucination. Nor does anyone have to see what this imaginary Yusuf sees-in. That he does do precisely that, seeing-in, seeing more than is there, is what makes him the great visionary, the dream specialist to which the Qur'an devotes an entire sura, exceptionally.

"A man shall not take his father's wife, nor discover his father's shirt," said the end of Deuteronomy 22. There appears to be a link between adultery and transgenerational offense, as there is between the father's shirt and the son's, from the drunken Noah to the tempted Joseph. "Can Christians believe in the prophecy of Muhammad?" asked the title of the unpublished text I mentioned at the beginning of chapter 6 (Heck 2005). Although it strongly suggests a positive answer, the text ends on a question mark. That is fine with me, for belief is not the issue here. Not because I don't respect other people's beliefs but because I am looking at belief's underside. Fantasy, desire, hallucination, and projection are the stuff that makes belief possible. Clearly, Rembrandt suggests, if only through the quietness of his Washington picture of hallucination, there is no harm in thought or feelings. It is when you begin to believe in what you see that you get in trouble. Yusuf in the etching sees things that attract and frighten him. No harm done. Mut in the painting sees a youthful, handsome beauty. No harm done. The (absence of) harm is in the eyes of the beholder. Yusuf does not look up. His downcast eyes make him the famous visionary, like the blind Homer of old.

Rembrandt's means of storytelling condenses, as we have seen, the two and three key events respectively that compose the episode: the attempted seduction—against which Yusuf has already been protected beforehand—the accusation, and his refutation. In that sense he also acts as a prophet, for he predicts what is to happen later. But according to both biblical and Qur'anic logic—and differently from the contemporary Western desire for origins—later is better. The perfectionism implied in the further refinement of creation as well as the relevant exegetical choices retained to make the two points is the perfection of prophecy: to guide humans in the right direction by means of re-citing what will happen. This is the paradoxical performance of prophecy on which we can now begin to imagine a cross-cultural perspective (see Overholt 1985).

If we cast the Washington painting as a preposterous response to Mann's scene with the little knives, moreover, the self-enclosed image of Yusuf also stands out as a form of absorption. The women who see in him a noble angel respond to this absorption. But, the Qur'an version told us—and Mann took it at its words, and images—the women are contaminated by this mode of looking. The self-enclosed Yusuf solicits a total absorption on the part of the woman who gaze, who stare at him. This idea of absorption is one of the outcomes of the process of recycling the Qur'an version occasioned in the Islamic tradition (Wagtendonk 1985, 137). For the lover, the feeling of pain disappears into the emotion of love. Kees Wagtendonk concludes that the development (his term) of the story in the Islamic tradition has the advantage over the tradition of biblical exegesis in that it avoids the moralizing exemplum of the chaste and patient Joseph. Instead it shifts attention to the woman—he calls her Zoelaicha—who achieves truth and peace through struggle and redemption. Wagtendonk ends his article by suggesting—but not elaborating—that this conception is not as far removed from the Bible as it might appear. He too, it seems, is seeking to read the earlier tradition through the later one instead of establishing origin as priority.

How does this logic of ongoing perfection and its temporal version, prophecy, leave Yusuf whole, including the face that cannot engage in the face-to-face? Yusuf's face can be seen because he is not God. What is more, it must be seen for the temptation to be possible, and to be so generalized that it becomes—let's face it, with God behind it so explicitly—sacred. But he cannot see, he must keep his eyes downcast, so that he can "see." Again, he is like Homer, and all those blind sages and prophets who, as suggested by the material Derrida has brought together in an exhibition composed out of the archives of the Louvre, are the true seers (1990b). The paradoxical connection between blindness and insight that sustains the biblical story and becomes radicalized in the semiotic program of the "perfectioned" version of the Qur'an is in turn conventional. The stakes of this paradox bring us back to the lures and the (im)possibilities of intercultural knowledge.

To start off a discussion on claims of knowledge and discourses of truth, I end this chapter with another memory of Yusuf. It is a memory of seeing-again, of reencountering the other painting—the one I never managed to like as much as the Washington one. Perhaps because the phantom Yusuf allowed me my own fantasies, the dramatically gesticulating one in Berlin seemed to dictate my emotions. I hate that, for the same reason that I hate exclamation marks. The Berlin painting also seemed to dictate the truth claim—the lie that the Qur'an version so cleverly undercuts by the logic of the (in)visible face. Here Mut points, simply and unambiguously, to Yusuf. The three figures seem to speak with their hands, all three simultaneously, thus orchestrating the intertwinement of the three episodes. I imagine the speeches, heard from right to left this time.

"Whatever happened to you, darling?" asks Potiphar, and I hear the echo of Mut's words to her wounded friends. "Oh, don't ask me . . . This horrible man assaulted me." "Who?" "Yusuf. He left his coat in my hand when he fled. He wanted to take it but I held fast to it, and here it is, torn." "No! She is lying! My God, how can she be so mean!" The phrase "my God," both banal and literal, I imagine as spoken through the uplifted hand, both banal, as a gesture of exasperation, and in its vertical movement literally appealing to God. I always thought the Washington painting was enigmatic and ambiguous, potentially sympathetic, doing to the viewers what Mut did to her friends, while this one appears melodramatic and accusatory. But now the gestures of drama themselves seem to leave room for ambiguity. As if warning me that the sign can be slippery but cannot be divided.

Space intervened. From a distance my eyes fell on the rather small painting, and I was taken aback that Yusuf appeared to be smiling, as if mocking Mut. But how could he, since the joke was on him? Then, closer up, the facial expression changed to despair. I stepped back in astonishment; he smiled again. Coming closer, the smile faded. I repeated the exercise; then I tried it out with the black-and-white photograph I had of it. Then with some other people. The same transformation occurred with spatial distance. Seeing is liable to distancing. When you are too far, you can't see; when you are too close, you also can't see. What is the "right" distance then? The distance that makes him smile or the one that turns comedy into tragedy? Two different stories versioned within the same picture. This is the "truth in painting." A "truth" based on theatricality, where "theater" is a "critical vision machine" (Bleeker 2006).

From afar, I thought, he laughs at the panic his presence has created in the bedroom. But right here, under my hands, the stories proliferate. You may change the order of the words in this sentence to produce a number of different stories. His presence in the house has caused the older husband ("pro forma" or not) to panic. His presence in the bedroom has caused the woman to panic. He panicked himself when he found himself not alone in the bedroom, and he laughs about it retrospectively. She panicked when he emerged in the bedroom, or when he wanted to leave it. In this whirlwind of versioning the figure of Yusuf stands apart from the couple. He is not only at the other side of the bed but, helped by that spatial position, also separated from the event. The interaction between husband and wife "happens," and his smile comments on it, from the outside. His raised hand enhances the mockery. Or is he straining his ear to better overhear the bedroom talk?

Close up, the situation is entirely different. The figure suddenly steps into the story and becomes one of its actors. The woman's pointing hand aims at him like a gun; his raised hand now speaks of protest. The story turns back to its doxic meaning. The panic is his alone. A distance of a few feet makes the difference between two different traditions: the misogynistic one that represents Mut as perverse, lusting after her social son whom she betrays out of spite when he spurns her, and the other, almost forgotten one, casting Yusuf as ambivalent, attracted but too fearful. That version is the one the Qur'an enfolds, so that the two topics can be connected. Yusuf needs his trial-by-desire; Mut needs her friends' support, their sympathy. Two needs, utterly compatible. This is what Mann picked up and developed. I had written about the painting long before my reencounter with the Berlin painting. I had never seen how this painting, which I liked least, enabled me to "see."

This suspension of preferences was an important lesson to me—a lesson of knowledge and ignorance. Not only could I see both traditions emerge one after another, like a rabbit/duck ambiguity, but I realized that it depended on me—on my bodily position in relation to the physical object, the painting—which story I was able to see; which story the painting was able to show me, if only I let it. This experience has shaken the last remnants of my belief in the visibility of truth.

So Yusuf's face is not exactly visible. It can be seen only provisionally, under the condition of my bodily participation, my position in space that is a literalizing metaphor of my position in my culture and its doxa. There is no way Yusuf's face can become a floating signifier only, for as soon as I try to split it that way and come up with a single, potentially fixed meaning, my legs grow tired of standing still and I move forward or backward. Preposterously, then, this face Rembrandt painted is a live sign, participating in a porous subjectivity today, one that keeps shifting much in the way Peirce theorized sign processing. Should I say, then, that this face is "Qur'anic"?

8

Truth Speak

We have learned from the Qur'anic perspective, in chapter 6, that the sign must remain "whole"—that is, it must retain the traces of its past meanings even if the mobility leads to a counter-meaning. In chapter 7, Rembrandt's paintings explained why this is important. Spinoza's vision of subjectivity as porous and the imagination as social fleshed out this semiotic principle. To recapitulate: the sign must not be split into signifier and signified that each goes its own way, for if this split is radical the former without the latter is empty, form only, and the latter risks escaping from underneath the signifier and becoming myth, doxa, prejudice, falsity. Literalism protects the sign from such splitting, while fundamentalism neglects the sign as alive and kills it into the status of empty shell for a rigidified meaning. Derrida called it "logos," and the belief in it "logocentrism" (1976).

To counter these two sterile tendencies, the sign must remain "whole" without being reified, changing but retaining its past—allowing, as a result, for ambiguity. Only then can the reader be free to deploy indeterminacy for decision, decide what and whom to believe, and thus willfully do the right thing. That is, she can willfully—according to the great paradox of religion—submit (Muslim) to "the truth."

Truth and signs thus appear to be, but are not really, in tension. Such a tension occurs only within a fundamentalist belief; literalism can accommodate truth and the sign's history, hence to an extent "wholeness," together. This chapter explores the adventures of truth as a discursive claim, in preparation for the subsequent, related issues of authority.

But adherence to any religion is not the only result of such a conception of the sign. More in general, this qualified, transformative wholeness of the sign provides the space for a freedom à la Spinoza. Such a freedom is "critical," as philosopher James Tully says (1995). Critical freedom is the practice of seeing the specificity of one's own world as one among others, and intertemporally, this freedom sees the present as fully engaged with the past that, insofar as it is part of the present, we can freely rewrite. Remaining as I do outside of religion—even if culturally I am more "critically intimate" with one—I feel strongly about the need for this consequence of critical freedom; that need to rewrite the past is, so to speak, my truth.

The relationship to truth as it manifests itself in the discursive versionings of Yusuf's and Mut's story is the subject of this chapter. I call this relationship *truth speak*. This phrase draws attention to the speech-act nature of the truth as that to which the believer submits. I seek to understand what it is that compels that submission. This larger question implies smaller ones, concerning the subject of truth speak, the authority of that speaker, and the circumstances in which the speaker is able to claim to speak the truth. This truth speak might be what at first most repels the nonbeliever, or the "other"-believer. In the name of which truth, always out of grasp, can anyone, any group or authority, tell me what is true and what is not? The question is relevant for my case study because Mut's outrageous, primary transgression of loving Yusuf may be assessed in different ways according to different moral frameworks, but the nasty hard core of the story in any version is her lie. And lies are thinkable only as transgressions of an established truth.

True, truth speak is a speech act that allows one to lie, and it thus sets semiosis in motion. For the sign's primary property is that it can be used to lie. This, according to Umberto Eco, defines the realm of signs and the study of it, semiotics. Signs are those things, or phenomena, that can be used in order to lie (Eco 1976, 10). And as we have seen, and will consider more in this chapter, truth speak is the best frame for lying. I can even go further. If truth speak is so central in these artifacts, and lying is what is done through it, then this story may well be primarily "about" semiotics. The Qur'an version, with its indexical scenes of testimony and suffering-with, suggests as much.

Truth speak is a constative speech act—one that informs—and in this function it can be held to the standard that discriminates between true and false. But it is also performative. First, it is an act through which the speaker affirms, confirms, or simply claims the authority of knowledge to speak the truth. Second, it is an act that solicits belief, thus turning the listener into a (non)believer. Third, and simultaneously, this act appeals to the listener to judge for himself. This becomes clear in the different reactions of Potiphar to the lie proffered by his wife.

But there is more than a constative and a performative aspect to truth speak. Each literary tradition has its own truth. This truth is embodied in the very structure of the artifact, such as the Book, that holds the tradition together. This interpretation of the structure of the Bible and the Qur'an respectively—as the form taken by the truth—is indispensable for anyone who wishes to understand the truth claim of these traditions without, or without necessarily, adhering to that claim. It also explains why scholars who claim priority in terms of temporal precedence to confer higher status on one particular version—as superior because "original"— where such prioritizing is not relevant, not only are mistaken (intellectually) but also show their adherence to that tradition and for that reason alone risk positioning themselves less convincingly as scholars in the modern, nonreligious sense of the word.

The Bible, especially Genesis, is ordered genealogically. Genealogies are not as fixed as believers in it might wish, and surely different versions of it are possible. From Adam to Abr(ah)am to David to Jesus for Christians; from Adam to Abr(ah)am to David for Jews; from Eve to Sarah (with Hagar) to Naomi to Mary for some feminists. For still others, these two genealogies—of the father-son succession on the one hand and the mothers doing the birth-giving on the other—are polemically mixed: the former struggle to achieve predominance, the latter throw sand in

the machinery. To sum it up somewhat tendentiously: the story
of Genesis at least treats the difficult, slow, and conflicted establishment of patriarchy and monotheism together, as conceptual
twins, with the pain points of genealogy and chronology elaborated to provide the story's "flesh."

This story requires a structure of chronology and the concomitant truth claim of historical evolution—of history *as* evolution.
The tradition of biblical scholarship has adopted this perspective,
thus showing its allegiance to the Book it considers the heart, or
the hard core, of that tradition. But the pain points of that chronological story intimate the potential of other stories, on the condition that one allows, and is willing to see, another structure.
Those other stories are what many have attempted to read-in.
This is exegetical work. My reading of Kugel's attempt to read the
Qur'anic "addition" of the banquet scene—he calls it "The Assembly of Ladies" (1990, 28–65)—as potentially "in" the Bible,
in the shape of Mut's appeal to the men of the household, fits this
description of allegiance. The Qur'an reader wouldn't mind, for
the Qur'an does not have the struggle for, and belief in, evolution
at its heart. Nevertheless, Kugel's detailed account of the exegetical tradition had to evolve, by necessity, toward the "core" of that
episode in the Bible, however hard-won that (for me, unconvincing) triumph is.

The pain points, this exegetical work goes to show, are sub-
stantial. They turn the chronological structure into a painfully
won, tenuous, perhaps illusory victory, rather than a self-evident
truth. These other stories and their traces of other structures need
to be taken into account if we are to understand the full potential of the book, but then this threatens the truth speak of the
chronology. The problems are many. If we take up only the most
crucial ones that threaten the main story from within, the following issues come up. There is the problem of sterility—usually
though not always women's, which also goes to demonstrate how
indispensable women are. Then the doubt cast on primogeniture
and the wavering attitude toward exogamy further complicate the
truth of chronology.

The first issue, sterility, the topical narrativization of the "scientific" question of procreation, has been patiently, masterfully,
and relentlessly unpacked by Carol Delaney (1989; 1991; 1998).

Delaney's lifework puts forward the claim that the genealogical litany of begettings in Genesis harbors a theory of procreation as monistic, erasing women's share in genetic creation. This theory, which conceives of men as providing fully formed cellular babies that the women host in their bodies, leaves to women the role of the nurturer only—the soil for men's seed. The word *seed*, so readily used for the male contribution to procreation even today, is a misnomer, for the word systematically obliterates the part of women in the formation of seed itself. It is a metaphor for which there is no "literal" alternative, so that its metaphorical character is forgotten.

Delaney's analysis indicts the way even contemporary culture colludes in this lie, which gives men both the prestige of (pro-) creation in the name of God and the authority to require great sacrifices of their children, or subjects, to hold up the family or nation. The (near-)sacrifice of Isaac is the core of that lie. Who or what, Delaney asks, moved Abraham to think the child was his to give up in the first place? Perhaps only a word, used frequently as if to drive home its false meaning: *seed*.

Derrida (1995, 85–114) sees the usurpation of omnipotent power by the father, emblematized by the sacrifice story, as the site where ethics struggles to emerge. For him, the situation between father and son is a basic site of the conflict between ethics and sacrifice in the Jewish tradition. But if in this sense the story of Genesis 22 is foundational as Delaney keeps reiterating, other problems concur to "found" patriarchy in its biblical incarnation.

A second issue is just as ethically inflected and just as pervasive in the Bible. Even within the male-only culture that results from the lie of seed, there is a pain point that keeps staging ever-new problems. This is the nonobviousness of the rights of primogeniture versus preference and of the resulting brothers' strife. This issue casts an important light on Yusuf's adventures.

The many cases of deception concerning which sibling came first thinly hide the favoritism that the great fathers practiced against the custom or rule of primogeniture. Abraham sent away his firstborn son Ishmael, along with Hagar his mother, at the instigation of Sarah, who used class superiority much as Mut will do. The son of the lower-status Hagar, a mere servant, should not inherit. And Abraham, the great patriarch, cowardly complies.

Isaac mistakenly gives his blessing to Jacob, tricked again by his
wife Rebecca. Incidentally, this also happens to women. Leah, Laban's oldest but less beautiful daughter, was married off to Jacob
by an act of deception, a material lie. Laban was culturally justified because Leah was the oldest, and Jacob's favoritism in select-
ing the younger Rachel—later repeated with his sons—reiterates
the favoritism that had put him above his older brother Esau.

Jacob, Joseph's father, favors his two youngest sons, because
they were born of his favorite wife Rachel. But really for no
particular reason—which is what favoritism is about—he loves
Joseph most of all. Here the structure of the text foregrounds the
breach in chronology and the tenuousness of that thread. Genesis
37 tells one of two episodes of Joseph—the one of his brothers'
envy, amply provoked by both Jacob's favoritism and Joseph's
boasting. Genesis 39 tells the second one, of Joseph in Egypt. In
between sits an extremely interesting episode of Joseph's older
brother Judah. This episode, structurally an "aside," tells a story
of straying—another kind of aside—which harbors a story of the
difficulty of primogeniture. Narrative structure—the paralepsis
or aside—is iconic of the narrative content: straying told in straying form. This is as good a case as any of the impossibility of radically splitting the sign.

The reason for Jacob's privileging Joseph is also clearly an
opposition against the rule of primogeniture. This is one of the
thematic elements that bind the structurally "deviant" chapter 38 to the two that frame it. "Now Israel [Jacob's nickname]
loved Joseph more than all his children because he was the son
of his old age" (37:3). The reason for the brothers' exasperated
envy is a dream of Joseph's. His telling this dream to his brothers makes their envy murderous. But as if the structure of the
book were making a point of reading nonchronologically, Genesis
38 interrupts the story of Joseph with another one which singles
out Judah. This story tells of his sexual hypocrisy resulting in
a murderous unfairness toward the woman who carries his—or
rather, their—children. A material token—an index of the stature
of Joseph's twice-alleged garments—demonstrates the truth. Not
coincidentally, Judah's two sons are, yet again, reversed at birth.

Third, there is the issue of exogamy and the resulting uncertainty of how and where to live. This problem, most dramatically

elaborated in Judges 19–21, shimmers through the story of the wooing of Rebecca, given away by her brother with her consent. The decision to leave her father's house and live among Abraham's people was hers to take, and clearly it could have turned out otherwise. In that case the father line would have been interrupted. In *Death and Dissymmetry* (Bal 1988a) I have argued that this decision implied moving from one societal organization to another, from the woman's father's house to the man's father's house. I have called this the transition from a patrilocal to a "virilocal" kinship structure. Leah and Rachel, similarly, had to be tricked away from their father's house, and this was a difficult and dangerous endeavor. It was also a phase in the long and difficult transition from polytheism to monotheism. In all these stories that flesh out the tale with rocks—stumbling blocks or "scandals"—on the path toward monotheism and patriarchy, women stubbornly demonstrate their importance by means of either being or making problems, and specifically by being the object or the subject of lies (Bal 1988b).

The story of Genesis has solicited much feminist commentary because of this struggle to establish the dominance of fathers, the definition of fatherhood, and the faith in the one God defined as obedience, all at the expense of women. In relation to this power structure, Esther Fuchs develops a whole typology of women characters in the Bible, so-called gynotypes (2000). But few have made the connection between these problematic stories of the near-erasure of women and the sheer need of chronology itself. Savina J. Teubal, to name one example among many scholars who have come near, alleges the story of Hagar, who was literally sent away with her son, as a key to the erasure of a tradition of matriarchal kinship relations (1990). The possibility of a matriarchal structure is an always-alluring feminist utopia of which I am a bit skeptical. Nevertheless, the idea that other than the patriarchal kinship structures we know today—not easily and symmetrically matriarchal—have been prevalent and became the target of violent erasure can be demonstrated even within the corpus of the Hebrew Bible alone.

The relationship between the difficult establishment of patriarchy, chronology, and the erasure of women comes across at its clearest in the stories of sons that fit uneasily in the chronology of the father line. Our Yusuf is one of those. This structure is required to firmly establish a connection between *forms* of storytelling suitable to streamline and maintain cultural memory and ideological *content*. This discourse of begettings, of the order in which the father line is established and maintained against all odds, is easy to mistake for a simple development narrative. This makes sense on the surface, simply because, especially as of Abraham, the line itself seems to be the topic. The structure that punctuates the narrative with temporal indications on the order of "and it came to pass at that time" solicits a chronological reading. But to turn this into a mono-reading is as mistaken, I contend, as the monogenetic theory of procreation—that is, to assume that procreation is a matter of fathers and their seed.

We learn from the Qur'an that other organizations of narrative are meaningful, and I see here a cause for preposterous learning through ignorance. For readers raised in chronological reading, the organization of the Qur'an according to length—ordered according to decreasing length of the units, or suras—is at first sight very disorienting. What is the point of such an order, which seems automatic and arbitrary? Now that we can see how motivated the apparently self-evident chronological structure is, I would like to see a similar point—to use a key term—in this seemingly random structure. If the biblical chronology has such a tenuous status and must be held up with such keen interest, then the "other" structure will most likely also have a point, beyond the official one of Muhammad's "blind" writing down what God dictated.

Point, as the poetics of the Qur'an, and line, as the poetics of the Bible—the characteristics of the forms of the books suggest that they both possess a visual poetics, at least metaphorically. Point and line are the visual-conceptual metaphors of how to read these texts. Yet while the Bible contends with a linearity it struggles to maintain and ultimately must give up, the Qur'an's points need a certain degree of narrative chrono-logic to be made. Hence the differences between the two are at the same time radical and relative. This suits my purposes well, since I am not interested in giving primacy or priority to either one nor in presenting cultural differences as absolute, incommensurable otherness.

First and foremost, as a process of unlearning the alleged self-evidence of chronology with its ideological connotations of development and historical truth, a contraction of meaning is a very useful exercise. Soon, and second, the Qur'an's stories begin to make sense according to a very different logic, that of "points to make" or topicality. Even within the most narrative parts, that is, the bits that are internally chronological, such as the Yusuf sura, the different episodes may be chronologically tied together without that chronology being important at all. And if we then take Mann's metacritical commentary as it is woven into the scene of Mut's sympathetic friends, topicality itself as a different kind of truth can be taken as a first point. This point entails the preference for scenes—slowdowns, close-ups—that enhance the point that is being made. This is how narrative structure intervenes in a different way from that of sequence. Duration is the issue.

Indeed, reading the other artifacts through Mann's metacritical lens—in other words, reading-with the Qur'anic organization—makes sense of all our versions. According to the norms of the mode of storytelling where points are to be made and the story need not be coherent for its own sake—the Qur'anic mode—the Rembrandt paintings do, perhaps unexpectedly, quite well. Both paintings do their work by means of Yusuf's face as an unbroken albeit slippery sign. The one does well for allowing the face of Yusuf to be a sign and remain so. Here, in that point of the Qur'an that Mann adopted, we see the visible sign of the transcendental reality made available, by Mut's courageous bet, to all the women in the city.

This sign is generated by the woman who points to him and looks at him, or rather at the sign of him—his portrait. The other painting manages its point for the implication of the viewer who must step into the story, literally and bodily, in order to "see" the two versions of the truth in his face—laughter and despair. Rigorously, the point is being made that the viewer must put her body on the line. The truth of these paintings is not the truth of history, of development, of fact—nor of the doxa that indicts the woman for loving Yusuf. The truth is the instability of truth. This instability is the logical consequence of porous subjectivity à la Spinoza. No visual sign makes this clearer than the close-up, the face that, according to Deleuze, defeats linearity.

Indeed, this is where the affection-image Deleuze theorized as emblematically situated in the close-up comes in with its typical temporality. Close-ups subvert linear time. They endure and thus inscribe the present into the image. Between narrative images and close-ups, then, a particular kind of intermediality emerges, one that stages a struggle between fast narrative and stillness. The particular, Spinozist intertemporality at stake here takes its starting point from the present—the present of reading and, in reading unsplittable signs, "seeing." As will become clear shortly, in the biblical version but more strongly in the Qur'an, seeing plays a dramatic role bound up with truth speak. As we have seen in chapter 5, Mann has already insisted on the difficulty of truth speak, its rhetoric, deception, and indeterminacy. Mann moves with ease among three different versions of truth speak, thus adopting the Qur'an's insistence of the difficulty of assigning truth as logos or signified. First, Mann takes on the rhetoric of realism, with the argument of probability. Then, conversely, he takes on the realism of rhetoric, the irresistible appeal of truth claims. The second truth claim is that of textual authority. The test of this truth claim— of which canon is right and which one is wrong—is the scene of suffering-with where the story slows down.

Right before the hyperbolic passage quoted earlier, Mann introduces the debate in the following words: "This oft-described scene has by some been thought to be *apocryphal*, and *not belonging* to the story as it happened. But they are wrong; for it is the truth, and all the probabilities speak for it" (802, emphasis added). The use of the word *apocryphal* harks back to the struggle of canonization, on which more in the next chapter. Which stories belong, which don't? Belonging, in this sense, is a feature of particular religions. Each of the three monotheistic Abrahamic religions has its own canon, a canon on which it falls back to stake its truth claims. But Mann appears to refuse this discourse. Instead, his text lightly shifts from belonging to the story—the issue of textual canon—to the third truth claim, "as it happened," the historical, factual truth claim.

All three forms of truth speak are based on a paradox. The rhetoric of realism informs us of what we already know. Only because we recognize the norms according to which an event is plausible can we learn it anew. Recognition as the condition of information is a paradox. This is how doxa works, and how cultural memory risks working if we fail to critically examine its claims.

In other words, the first truth claim concerns what readers tend to believe because it fits their expectations. This is plausibility, the basis of realism as it came to be theorized in Western classicism. This realism concerned norms of propriety as much as logical plausibility, and thus showed its ideological hand. The second truth claim is based on authority. It stipulates the authority of (a certain version of) the text as the (only) true one. The belief in this claim lies at the heart of Kugel's definition of exegesis already quoted: "Such narrative expansions are, by definition, *exegetical* because they are ultimately based on something that *is* in the text" (1990, 4, emphasis in text). This claim invokes another paradox. On the one hand, the text is open, full of gaps and silences that solicit the reader's active participation. This readerly activity leads to ongoing exegesis, without which biblical scholars, rabbis, imams, pastors, and priests would be out of work. It leads to the paradox of ongoing improvement—which is why Muslims can claim, rightly from their perspective, that the Qur'an is the original in the sense of the only true one, *because* the perfected version.

The canonization of the perfected version is, in turn, paradoxical again. Even if Muhammad was the last of the prophets, stopping the process seems an artificial, indeed contradictory move. It falls back from one sense of originality—the perfected version—to another, the first one. If taken literally, moreover, it would halt the reader's freedom to willfully submit. If the Qur'an derives superiority from its later state, halting that continuous perfecting poses problems, the central one of which is the freedom of the believer to believe. Similarly, the canonization of the biblical text—without the scene of suffering-with—is another way of stopping the reader's activity. Specifically, it stops this process before readers are enabled to consider sympathy with the woman, making it easier to reject and condemn her without the uneasy remainders of emotion that would have made the text more powerful and encompassing. In that case, the claim to the original in the temporal sense of priority would forbid the exegetical activity that has in fact never stopped. Canonizing the story without the scene of bloodletting is an attempt to erase the woman who, on the other hand, is burdened with the lie that is the story's point.

The third truth claim is that of facticity. Mann sets it over against the other side of the truth claim, that of plausibility. In his metacritical irony he shifts a bit too smoothly from the one to the other. It must have happened because it seems so plausible. In other words, there is no reason why it should *not* have happened. This is, of course, a stretch; the scene is as hyperbolic as is the argument for its plausibility. The likelihood of its having factually happened is based on the outrageousness that made it famous, hence its *im*plausibility. The point is not to *make* the realistic claim but to unpack its logic. And for this unpacking Mann needs the magnifying glass of hyperbole—which goes against the grain of plausibility.

And then, while the reader is still steaming over this hyperbole, Mann throws in the third kind of truth claim, the factual one of historical veracity. "And we shall understand that the thing could not happen otherwise—I mean with less shedding of blood—than as it *actually* did. Eni's dreamlike certainty of the event and its course was entirely justified" (802–3, emphasis added). The claim of factual truth is put forward, again hyperbolically, as if the exact amount of blood could have been measured and verified. But wait a minute. The truth claim is here stopped in its tracks. The certainty is thrown back onto the subjectivity of the character. Eni (one of the many other versions of Mut's name) is justified, not here in her infatuation or her decision to trick the women into suffering-with, but in the certainty about what just happened, orchestrated as it was by herself. The serpent of truth speak bites itself in the tail, or tale.

The point Mann is making about truth in its three forms of truth speak is, I contend, double. On the one hand, it is made in earnest, philosophically so to speak, addressing human life. There is no single truth but many—here three—and the subject must imagine (dream up) the truth that is best for him or her. But this judgment must be justified by a community of sympathetic others. In terms of storytelling, achieving this communal justification is a cultural activity of great importance, as it carries cultural memory through time and communities. This dreaminess of the truth fits the modernist aesthetic and ethics of Mann's time. It also honors the porous subjectivity discussed earlier by attributing to it a porous truthfulness.

The second point about truth is metacritical, an instance of Mann's myth-critical position. This point addresses the truth claims that are possible or impossible, untenable, within each of the discourses of truth. This claim is more specific. Here, by weaving a "discussion" of truth through the scene of cosuffering, Mann stakes out a claim about the truthfulness of a particular tradition *on its own terms*. This argument is far-reaching in what I see as Mann's political position in this novel, to which I will return below. To take a shortcut at this point: the metacritical passages make points about the point-making tradition of storytelling.

This leads us to a major difference between the Genesis version and the one in the Qur'an. Whereas the former presents Joseph's adventures as a sequence in the difficult establishment of the father line, the latter puts a very different slant on it, which in my view concerns, among other points, the nature of truth, truth speak, and subjectivity. In Genesis, Joseph's father is the first to love him. Pretty arrogant at the outset, he tells his brothers about his dream of grandeur against his father's warning. As a consequence, he is led astray, literally into exile; then, privileged as he is by God, he is reunited with his father, albeit on foreign soil. Remarkably, Joseph the favored son of Jacob never becomes a patriarch himself and never returns to Canaan. The father line skips a generation, after the by now well-known trick of the "wrong" blessing, and two tribes come out of his two sons. The "point" of Joseph, thinly disguised, is a disturbance of the development narrative. While the story of Abr(ah)am was a story of father-and-son issues, Joseph's story concerns the relationship among brothers. But in order to make sense of it we must read it also as a narrative of "points." In this sense we must take the Qur'an as a poetics for Genesis, as Genesis's "original." This, then, is the truth of the truth speak that Mann weaves through the different points. We must read the Qur'an story as a direction for how to read the Genesis version.

To be sure, considering the Qur'an as a source for Genesis is preposterous. The case I seek to make, however, is indispensable for an intercultural understanding. I pursue, that is, a mode of reading that does not need to claim (qualitative) primacy or truth status as the result of temporal priority, a mode of reading that does not conflate origin with value. Nor, I hasten to add, can origin be claimed so easily; temporal priority is often deceptive, a consequence of in-reading from a later position. Hence the very claim of origin is a preposterous act. For Mann, fantasy returns where truth falls short. Spinoza's view of the imagination as social helps to counter the tendency to dismiss fantasy as individual subjectivism.

Instead, at the heart of truth speak is the issue of dreams. As we have seen, in both Genesis and the Yusuf sura of the Qur'an, Yusuf is a dreamer as well as a dream specialist. Through his dreams God tells of his own favoritism, which turns God and Abraham into twin fathers. The dream of Joseph's power inflames the brothers' hatred beyond endurance, and thus triggers the story of debasement and exile that is needed for Joseph's later triumph. Mann elaborates on this, suggesting that Joseph is himself responsible for triggering his brothers' hatred, not, as in Genesis, because he reveals to them his dream of grandeur but because of a feminine vanity. But in Genesis, the story—its surface structure of chronology—tells the story and makes the point. In the Qur'an the point is made differently, since the structure does not establish lineage. The dreamlike quality that Mann attributes to Mut and Yusuf alike, and that Rembrandt deploys to set Yusuf apart from the other characters, is used in the Qur'an to offset truth speak. Indeed, in this allegedly perfected text the story proper begins with the truth speak of dreaming: "When Yusuf said to his father, 'O my father! Verily I beheld eleven stars and the sun and the moon—beheld them make obeisance to me'" (12:4).

The first episode is thus the one not of Jacob's favoritism but of God's, and of dreaming—a form of fantasy—as a non–seed-based form of procreation. This episode is protracted compared to its counterpart in Genesis. Yet it contains not only less detail—only one dream—but also more. The father warns Yusuf not to tell his brothers of the dream and also says that the dream means that God will choose Yusuf. The form this election will take is that God will teach him "the interpretation of dark sayings." The second episode, of the brothers' plot to get rid of Yusuf, is riddled with truth speak. This discourse is embedded in the dialogue between the brothers and the father. In a mere seven verses, words of truth occur no fewer than eight times, nine if we count "false."

Not coincidentally, the episode of truth speak is an ascending gradation of acts of lying. Thus it posits the Qur'anic semiotics that requires the sign to remain unsplit or, at the very least, to retain the traces of its splittings, as well as Western semiotics that stipulates signs can only be, hence, be "whole," if they can be used in order to lie. The more the brothers lie, the more they claim the truth: "*Indeed* we mean him well" (12:11). "We will *surely* keep him safely" (12:12). "*Verily*, your taking him away will grieve me" (12:13). "*Surely*, if the wolf devour him, and we so many, we must in that case be weak *indeed*" (12:14). The series reaches its climax when the lie is at its worst and belief is put on the line: "O our Father! *Of a truth*, we went to run races . . . but thou wilt not believe us even though we speak the *truth* (12:17)." "And they brought his shirt with *false* blood upon it" (12:18). The final element of truth speak is physical and speaks indexically. They bring the shirt—forecasting Mut's lie later on—with blood on it, forecasting Mut's friends' blood on their white robes, as evidence. This form of truth speak, evidence based on indexicality, is the fourth kind, not mentioned in Mann's commentary because it is already so central in the scene upon which Mann comments.

The second episode ends with the beginning of Yusuf's exile, his departure from the fatherland. It ends, that is, with the sale of Yusuf "for a paltry price." Debased literally when he is cast into the well, he is now debased figuratively by the cheap price fetched for him. Later he will be debased again, when he is cast in prison. The third episode of the sura's story is the beginning of his sojourn in the Egyptian household. The terms are auspicious: "And he who bought him—an Egyptian—said to his wife, 'Treat him hospitably; haply he may be useful to us, or we may adopt him as a son'" (12:21). No truth speak here but a discourse of ethnicity, hospitality, and kinship. I consider this a key moment in the Qur'an where it contradicts its own investment in father lineage, such as it is, as well as the investment therein that Genesis foregrounds so strongly. This, if any, is a point the text makes. All the elements of a new, complex, and crucial point are present. The fact that the buyer is Egyptian posits Yusuf's exile, his position as stranger. Yet the immigrant in the land of the Nile is treated hospitably, as guests ought to be. This, I cannot help thinking in light of the present, is how guests ought to be treated: they should be adopted, as it were. Sonship, the key form of kinship, is a matter of hospitality rather than "seed."[1]

1. Judith Butler's study on kinship (2000) resonates here in full force.

I don't think this business of sonship is a way of bringing up incest or Yusuf's allegedly tender age. Rather, it indicates the extreme favor Yusuf is to enjoy; again, the father figure—he who becomes a father through loving Yusuf—practices favoritism, here even without any reference to a bloodline. Kinship is not a matter of blood. The text here inserts a verse in the first person, stipulating how God favors Yusuf according to his purpose. "And when he had reached his age of strength we bestowed on him judgment and knowledge; for thus do we recompense the well doers" (12:22). Judgment and knowledge: these two nouns, these two gifts from God, sum up what the true truth speak amounts to, so to speak.

The point has now been made that hospitality deserves its name only if it is unconditioned, which is the only genuine form of hospitality (Derrida 2000, esp. 106–55). In a narrative of symmetry and point-making, this makes the point of arrival, the new house of hospitality, equal to the point of origin, Yusuf's home base in his father's house. The favorite son there is again the favorite son here. In the home base there was a great temptation toward arrogance and preempting God's plan. This led to a great act of lying. Here another great temptation presents itself. And again, truth and lie are confronted. They are set over and against each other in the terms of the intermediate verse: knowledge and judgment. Details are again omitted, others added. There is a point in the making, and it has to do with doors. And the entire confrontation takes place in a single verse, 23.

This is how it goes. "She in whose house he was," says the text, reiterating the discourse of hospitality as well as connoting possible confinement, "conceived a passion for him"—she fell in love with the stranger, with Yusuf the other-man. He is other in two ways, other than her husband, and a stranger. ". . . And she shut the doors and said 'Come hither.'" The shutting of the doors has a narrative function as well as, without doubt, a symbolic one. As Delaney argues, doors, thresholds, and other liminal places symbolically represent the female genitalia (1998). Whether or not one wishes to underwrite such a psycho-symbolic interpretation, the narrative function of the doors is to lock Yusuf in within the closed space that forecasts the prison, as well as the next episode.

Yusuf's words of refusal reinstall the issue of truth within the frame of hospitality. "He said: 'God keep me! *Verily*, my lord hath given me a good home: and the injurious shall not prosper.' " One may guess who the "lord" is who is mentioned here. Like Jacob and God, Potiphar and God cannot be distinguished. The ambiguity only goes to emphasize the dependence of the figure on masters above him. But later developments favor God as the lord.

While prosperity—Yusuf's materialist self-interest—does not go unmentioned here, the primary issue is decent behavior toward one's host. This grounds Yusuf's refusal in morality more than in a lust for power and money. The injury implied would be abuse of the unconditional hospitality that he is enjoying. The index of the earlier episode, the shirt, will return in due course, but the discourse of the sign within which that of evidence is embedded is broached by means of semiotic terminology, when the text says: "And she desired him, and he would have desired her had he not seen a *token* from his Lord" (12:24, emphasis added). The Qur'an does not indicate what token this might be, only that it is visible, at least in Yusuf's (mind's?) eye. Mann, along with some exegetical traditions, turns this token into the face of the father. An interdiction is borne on the father's face against the appeal of the face of the other—the other sex, the other woman. The commentary in the Qur'an—God's voice—specifies: "Thus we averted evil and defilement from him, for he was one of our sincere servants" (12:24).[2]

Evil and defilement. The former, I assume, stands for the transgression of taking what belongs to the host. *Defilement* suddenly harks back to my primary school memory. Yes, that was the word I did not understand. Dirty, for me, meant getting stains on my clothes or grit in the scrape wounds that decorated my knees regularly for some ten years. "Better dead than dirty" was the lesson from the story. Why was dirt such a big deal? I never got it. But here it is: defilement. Yet when I read this verse, it strikes me as unfair, the way some novels appear unfair when they reveal things to one character about the other but not the other way around.

This is an unfairness of information. Such unfairness must have informed my interest in focalization. It played a great part in my analysis of French novelist Colette's *La chatte*, the novel through which I developed my theory of focalization. There the

2. For this use of the phrase "the other woman," see Beal 1997.

narratorial focalization from the outside is equally distributed between the two newlywed protagonists, but only one party—the husband—has access to internal focalization. As a result, the reader shares his criticism of his wife, while she is unable to realize the damage. Here Yusuf is taken by the hand, given a token that saves him from a double transgression he is tempted to commit, while the woman must fend for herself. Both, the Qur'an says, are tempted. Both are subject to longing, to attraction. Only one gets the protection against it. The other one just serves the purpose of the lord—or of the story. *Defilement* is the word attributed to God. "Better dead than dirty" will be translated, a bit later, as "better imprisoned than defiled."

At this point, the door returns to its narrative function. In a vivid narrative style, the episode takes the drama to a new phase. "And they both made for the door," in a race between capture and escape (12:25). "She rent his shirt behind": the logic is clear. If he tries to run away, she would have to grab his shirt from behind. Why specify it in a text that avoids redundancy? For the sake of story logic. Because the indexical function of evidence is set up here. In a coincidence worthy of a Shakespeare comedy, "at the door they met her lord." This is a very different narrative style from that of Genesis. There the house had to remain empty for the woman to pretend to have cried out and remain unheard. The narrative in Genesis serves the purpose of connecting the events to the law. The emptiness of the house is not mentioned in the Qur'an, nor is the class-based appeal to the household staff and their sense of hierarchy, or the ethnic slur. Here the story is reduced to the bare essentials of *this* story—which has different points to make.

The vividness of the telling makes the scene visually strong. We see the race, and then the sudden halt when the master of the house—who remains unnamed—is on the other side of the door, claiming it and its symbolic counterpart as his. Confounded, I imagine, Mut stammers her question about how someone so abusive should be punished. But here, again in contrast to Genesis, Yusuf answers the accusation. "She solicited me to evil" (12:26). Not defilement—that is between him and his (other) lord; here, in relation to his host, evil is the issue: the abuse of hospitality. Then something utterly unexpected, at least unexpected by me, happens. The household staff does come forward, but not to accuse.

"And a witness out of her own family witnessed" (12:26). The truth claims are shifted to a higher gear. The term *witness*, reiterated as noun, then verb, brings the discourse into the sphere of legal contestation—as the crying out in Genesis had only implicitly done. The detail "behind" of the shirt-tearing is not redundant. Thanks to the witness, the story's cohesion is tightened and the index will be restored to its indispensable truth-value, but only if interpreted rightly. The logic cannot be blind but needs more specification than just "belonging." Truth speak at its highest, in its legal function, is the issue. "If his shirt be rent in front she speaks the truth, and he is a liar: but if his shirt be rent behind, she lies and he is true" (12:26–27). Clearly, in addition to the needs of the story of Yusuf's favor with the two lords, there is a legal point to be made here about truth finding, as well as one of the difficulty of turning material objects into signs. But before we get carried away in admiration for the rationality of this scene, we must realize that another point is in the making as well. Instead of just getting furious, the lord of the house listens to the member of the household. But his wisdom in doing so is short lived. For without any reason whatsoever he turns his loyalties where, according to the story, they belong.

"This is one of your [plural] devices! Verily your [plural] devices are great! Joseph! Leave this affair. And thou, O wife, ask pardon for thy crime, for thou has sinned" (12:28–29). Fair enough. He asks his wife to apologize, and that is indeed the least she can do. But the second-person feminine pronoun *your*, twice uttered as a qualifier of *devices*, turns Mut into a synecdoche. In both cases, the pronoun is used in the plural feminine. Why, in the midst of this trial of fair justice, need he address her in the plural? It could not be stated more clearly: this story has a point to make pretty close to the one of my schoolmistress: against women, plural. Not in terms of "dirty" but in terms of truth speak—of "devices," plots, as lies. Again, this is both story logic and ideo-logic. Story logic: without this extension to all women, the next episode, of the banquet, the knives, and the recognition of Yusuf's irresistible beauty, would come out of the blue. Ideo-logic: already forecasting the events to come, Yusuf's lord translates attraction into a snare. In the bargain he turns Yusuf's exceptional and story-motivated appeal into just the kind of thing all women would fall for. Banality replaces God-created beauty. From a creation, Yusuf becomes an invention. An invention of the kind Rembrandt invented in both his paintings: the invention of fantasy, in the Washington painting, and the invention of ambiguous storytelling, in the Berlin painting.

Thus at the moment of utter truth—of rationality against traps, of justice against lying, of witnessing against slander, of evidence against jumping to conclusions—the story ushers in a new point that reexamines truth speak on different premises. Over against this seemingly high moment of justice, suffering-with will come to spoil the party. "And in the city, the women said . . ." (12:30). The conjunction *and* shifts the story to the next episode, introduced not through temporal sequentiality—and then this happened, then that—but through spatial disjunction: here this happened, there that. From the single house of confinement to the urban world at large. A different mode of storytelling is in place here.

The various strands of the status of truth speak are now coming to a conclusion. The women in the city at first jump to conclusions. They have heard a fact and judge Mut on the basis of it. "The wife of the Prince hath solicited her servant; he hath fired her with his love: but we clearly see her manifest error" (12:30). Although in all likelihood, they have only heard, not seen the events, the truth speak they use takes a decidedly visual turn. The judgment is emphatic: clearly, see, manifest. After Mann, I would even call it hyperbolic. Hyperbolically visual, hyperbolically truth-claiming. What matters is the visuality of this discourse that, after all, only reports rumors heard. The notion of seeing is abducted to serve the purpose of social ostracizing on the basis of gossip. The act of seeing is one of recognition—to see what you (think you) already know. Soon, a mere verse later, they will see again, now on the basis of evidence, and this act of seeing will exonerate Mut.

The evidence of Yusuf's face, his irresistible charm, ordained by the lord —no mention of his real beauty here, as it was mentioned doubly in Genesis—decides in favor of Mut. The resulting suffering-with, the porous subjectivity where collective love becomes a possibility, was in fact set up by the master's pluralization of the possessive pronoun: you women's devices—you women's snares. He too pronounces what he already (thought he) knew. But instead of snaring Yusuf, in the next episode the women are snared by him. And the episode ends with Mut announcing Yusuf's renewed debasing. Again he will go down in order to go up. And again the lord must come to his rescue. Not because he risks being victimized by women's lies, but because he himself is tempted to commit the act of defilement. "Unless thou turn away their snares from me, I shall play the youth with them, and become one of the unwise" (12:33). Our Yusuf is not much of an autonomous character.

So far we have seen at work a number of discourses of truth, each organized around "points." They all have their own rules to comply with. Story logic, ideo-logic, psycho-logic, socio-logic. Each point is relatively independent of the others. This is how the Qur'an makes its points. The point is—and Mann had already demonstrated this—that each logic holds, provided we frame it properly. If Yusuf is bound to a rule of decent conduct, not otherwise stipulated, he must do what he does to avoid "evil and defilement." But no such rule applies to Mut. Only story logic, that is, until she is vindicated by that same logic. Mann wasn't the first to undertake this ethical task. He did so at an important moment, but the Qur'an showed him the way. In his turn, Mann guided me to the Qur'an.

Each logic follows a set of rules, none of which necessarily intersect or overlap. This brings me back to the paradoxes of canonization mentioned at the beginning of this chapter. For when we talk about rules, the meaning of the word *canon* resonates. From measuring stick to law and rule, the Greek word *kanon* speaks to the desire to regulate social living-together, a desire that institutes the political domain. Speaking about canon, then, implies a recognition that the cultural domain of reading and literacy, on the one hand, and of reading and following religious texts, on the other, is a political one, and that studying, or rather analyzing, elements of that domain is an activity that is by definition of a political nature, at least in part. The entire notion that "canon" is an object of study, as it has been brought under scrutiny during the last decades, presupposes a *political* grounding for what we read as "canonical"—not party politics but a movement against partisanship. That political concern can only be critical—aiming at real interventions—because it is from that side that the canon has been made to shed its innocent self-evidence. Canons may be and work differently in the various cultural domains, but some of their features, especially, tenacity, exclusion, and lack of reflection, are common to most. In this respect, critiques of the canon in the history of art and literature are just as instructive as strictly literary and religious contestations.[3]

Bringing up canonicity as a form of truth speak is all the more necessary as the preservers or curators of the canon don't even think about "canon," at least not as a term of analysis. They simply "do" canon: they teach, analyze, and frame the canonical texts "canonically" without questioning their choices and the self-serving methods of reading that leave the selection unquestioned. This unreflective self-evident repetition is the defining feature of canonicity. This is not to say that such lack of reflection is "innocent." Nor is it harmless. As Karen R. Lawrence wrote in her introduction to a volume of essays on the "British" literary canon: "The formation and revision of literary tradition and the canon reflect ideological struggle rather than a natural aesthetic order." She articulates her volume's thrust in the following words: "Perhaps it is more accurate to say that these essays explore the way literary canons disguise their own histories of violence" (1992, 2).

The project of revisiting the canon, as I am doing in this essay, must be revisionist, therefore, because the point of discussing the canon as a politically conservative force is to change its status, from a self-evident power to a phenomenon to analyze, and thereby by definition to transform. This form of collective, cultural truth speak is the subject of the next chapter.

---

3. Nanette Salomon (1991) has offered an astute critique of the art historical canon that acutely articulates the "sins of omission" perpetrated by that canon. What she calls sins of omission others might call gaps or silences (see also Pollock 1999).

9

Loose Canons: Facing Authority

The magical word *identity*, pointing to a feminist, queer, and/or multiculturalist perspective and connoting on its own a politically inflected perspective, relates the need to subvert the exclusionist and oppressive power, in the recognition that this power is wielded by a narrow group of people of an identical identity. The word *identity* indicates that it is precisely that social-political dominance of certain *kinds* of people over all "others" that the formation and maintenance of a canon facilitates. This is, of course, primarily an issue of authority. But authority is never entirely "out there." It is given, conceded, or withheld. It is struggled over and won or lost. Authority is what produces wars, and wars need authority to happen. This is Delaney's ultimate point and the motivating force behind her passionate attempt to understand both Abraham's authority over the life and death of his son and God's parallel authority over Abraham.

If the concern with identity and its politics is a bit tired today, one of the reasons is that it is too easily co-opted by an individualism that invokes freedom as the highest value, forgetting that the freedom to think, to be, and to express one's thoughts stops where that freedom hurts the freedom of others. This limit on freedom underlies the riots about the Danish cartoons that ridiculed Muhammad. True, the rioters were "bad" readers in two respects. They read the cartoons in a fundamentalist way, declaring the meaning fixed, immutable from the signifier's transformative flight. They also confused meaning with referent, thereby depriving their own minds of the freedom that sign use entails. Nevertheless, the cartoons also demonstrated the limits of freedom. Freedom ceases to be freedom where expression becomes insult, truth speak, and semiotic violence, and where authority becomes coercion.

Hence such a critique and revision of the canon that is "given" to us, that binds a number of people into a group that believes the book, must go hand in hand with a critique and revision of the ways "we"—each person, each group—read the canon, including the need to pluralize and read the canons. This other side of the double move is indispensable if we are to *understand* the power of canons. This is not only a political necessity but also, let's say primarily, an intellectual, academic one. For understanding is the "official," "canonical" task of the intellectual endeavor. Foucault called it power/knowledge: the bond between knowledge and power, the impossibility of achieving knowledge if we remain blind to the power that sustains its possibility.

This is also the reason to undertake a comparative analysis of artifacts from different *kinds* of canons. While Genesis and the Qur'an belong to religious canons, the episode I have been focusing on is among the less explicated ones. Similarly, Mann's novel is a less celebrated literary work by a writer of great canonical status, and Rembrandt's representations belong to the art historical canon but the images of Yusuf are, among the artist's works, not the most famous ones. I would suggest that these episodes, this novel, and these images sneak into the canon something that the highlights of the canons do not possess. For this reason alone, this analysis of the work that literary, artistic, and religious canons do, including shaping cultural memories and cultural identity, is quite plausible. For this work has a long history. One only need think of one of the canonical examples of an indisputably canonical text, Milton's *Paradise Lost*, to see this work as a valid principle to be critically analyzed.

The major thrust of *Paradise Lost* is a Christian revision of Hebrew Scriptures that was fit for Milton's time and place and that, precisely because it is such an artistic masterpiece, would help streamline the social environment in its ongoing Christianization. Its artistic success is never in doubt. Its religious content is obvious. But it has no status in a *religious* canon. Interestingly, Charles Altieri's famous article on the universal values of literary canons alleges this example in his larger argument that canon formation is *not* political—or religious, for that matter (Altieri 1983).

Indeed, there are good reasons to insist on the differences between religious and literary processes of canon formation. The former are fixed forever, the latter are in flux. The former constitute the basis for thought and behavior in a congregation whose membership has official status; the latter are primarily conveyors of aesthetic and formal value, and the group formation they promote is repressed, sometimes fiercely denied. In view of my analysis of truth speak, however, denials such as Altieri's call for a counter-move. There is a tight bond between artistic and religious canonicity, and the undisputable literary canonicity of an indisputably religious text like *Paradise Lost* proves it. This bond serves an interest that I want to put on the table before proceeding further. It is even more obvious in visual culture: the interest in *representation* as a social-political tool. And whereas I urge my reader to think of literature as close to visual art in its cultural "work," in spite of the fact that its medium is more acceptable for religions holding a taboo against visual representation, I have for this chapter limited myself to the written text.

In this analysis where Mann and the Qur'an respond to each other, a *social agency* is claimed for literature. What we read transforms us, or confirms us, specifically our identity, including, where applicable, religious identity. The project of analyzing both texts' questioning of truth speak is my attempt at transforming the canon of what the Western world sees as great literature in order to liberate and include forms of religious identity that are not captured by the mainstream institutionalized religious systems predominant there. If Milton's work was able to further promote a religious identity that included social divisions according to lines of gender—and on a different level, as we have seen, of socioeconomical stratification or "class"—then all those groups that feel not valorized, inspired, and confirmed in their religious identity by such texts may benefit from the work of opening up the canon. One need not be religious or feel affiliated to any religious denomination to feel the need for such opening up.

The need for this rethinking has become urgent by the social phenomenon of worldwide migration, which has made the near-exclusive predominance in the Western world of Christian and Judaic traditions less obvious and has imposed the participation in the social organization of, most visibly, Islamic traditions. The reality of migration has, more generally and vaguely, but also more incisively, made even the most self-evidently devout Christians as well as religiously indifferent people aware that religious identity, precisely, is not self-evidently Christian or anything in particular. That process of denaturalization of religious identity requires that we discuss the subliminal and therefore perhaps sometimes insidious contribution to the false and exclusionary stabilization of religious identities of that seemingly frivolous or lay instruction called "literature." I underwrite the logic that allows this to be a worthy intellectual project.

Literature assists exclusion and mainstreaming by means of its own canon and canonization, which are by no means identical—neither in content nor in process—to the canons of established religions, and which may therefore appear relatively innocent of imposing religious identity. Precisely because religious canons are established once and for all, the more fluctuating literary canons may have a greater power to shape social life. Therefore, I feel the need to revisit the artifacts discussed so far from the double perspective of canonization or "ruling" and the difficulty of monotheism. This discussion brings us back to the enigmatic appeal of Yusuf, its relation to vision, and the ethics of facing—of sighting the signs as facing the face.

The logic underlying the critique of identity politics is tenable precisely because of a deeper, even more invisible and therefore insidious power game that consists of binding the outcome of the process, the religious identity based on canon, to a less visible because less institutionally defined *form of identity* which is, strictly speaking, literary or aesthetic. This "literary identity," still to be defined, infuses the religious canon in many different ways.

Representation plays a central role in it, although not the only one. And as I will argue, the promotion of, and through, literary identity is connected to representation as forms of *incarnation* or embodiment. I mean this much in Richard Dyer's sense of promoting a particular way of considering the body as site of spirit, not defined by spirit qua body. Acting against the tradition that dismisses the body as a site of temptation and a transitory form of facing—an act of encountering beyond recognition—is the critical act par excellence. It counters the doxa, the repetition of what we (think we) already know, and it turns the very pronoun *we* on its head. "We" the group whose identity one shares becomes you-and-me, whoever the "you" may be. Identity, in this sense, is performative, an occurrence resulting from an act.

As Dyer has brilliantly observed in a critique of the unspoken self-evidence of a predominant "white" perception, this tradition insists on that curious notion that is so central to Christianity: *incarnation.* This includes representing the body in suffering and sacrifice, while qua visual representation it counters its own iconophobic or iconoclastic other-within, the Protestant tradition, as well as the two other monotheistic traditions that resist visual representation of the body. Christianity of the Catholic variety has a stake in this, one that goes beyond just wishing to be liberal about art. Dyer claims as the primary stake the attempt at putting forward a specific sense of *embodiment of spirit.* This is a specifically "white" endeavor to the extent that, if it is to be *self-evidently* predominant, the white body must be put forward but not foregrounded. Hence these representations are about something that, in Dyer's words, is "in but not of the body" (1997, 14).

Partly with such a claim in mind, I am interested in how Alice Bach, among others, has taken up the case of Mut and confronted the story with other versions of it, in a gesture that had as one as its goals to decanonize the religious canon (1997, 34–127). She also demonstrates how each of subsequent versionings takes on aspects of the story it recycles, addressing it in a sometimes polemical, sometimes reassuring attempt to answer fears and obsessions in the other (earlier or geographically remote) culture. This dialogical analysis makes a case against any fixation of canons. In fact, Bach's view of the texts as talking to each other goes against the grain of the idea of canonicity.

The confrontation with this revisionist work on canons is further informed by the by now classical, let's say canonical, work of a cautious and slightly revisionist defense of the literary canon, Charles Altieri's "An Idea and Ideal of a Literary Canon" (1983). Although much has been written about the issue since, this article is used frequently in teaching situations and for that reason alone deserves closer scrutiny. This piece addresses the example of Milton's *Paradise Lost,* which I mentioned above for this reason. It seeks to articulate the universal values on which canons are based and denies the political in what the author seems to consider conspiracy theories that historicize and pluralize such criteria.

Altieri's focus is literary, and therefore it appears not so shocking that his claims are exactly opposite to those of the article that follows his in the collection in which it was first published, Gerald Bruns's "Canon and Power in the Hebrew Scriptures" (1983). For Altieri, canons are heritages of cultural values that help produce "strong identities." This way of phrasing the issue of canons ties in with cultural memory, an issue to which I will return. He dismisses the political-historicizing theory advanced by new historicists such as Jerome J. McGann (1981), of the signature that John Guillory names the liberal critique (1995). Bruns claims the important politics that underlie canon formation, the very politics Altieri denies. The difference in status between literary and religious canons—the one produced in an ongoing and socially unlocated process, the other definitive and decided upon by religious leaders—although not addressed by either author, silently accounts for that opposition and mitigates it. To sharpen our focus, I will question the opposition.

Altieri sets forth an intelligent argument in favor of canons and of the possibility of articulating and promoting common principles of judgment on whose basis a form of valuable "idealization" is recognized (1983, 46). Thanks to that recognition, canonical texts will be preserved and read. This gives them the power to shape public moral identities through identification. He then proceeds to specify, according to the age-old fallacy of a form-content distinction, that the values inherent in canonical texts concern literary "craft" (form) and "wisdom" (content; 51). My argument so far urges us to question such distinctions, most notably when the structure or form of the texts turns out to sustain a meaning not otherwise strong enough to make.

Here I will only mention three disturbing problems with Altieri's article. First, Altieri's argument is entirely based on an unspoken, and certainly unargued, assumption that literary canons are important and productive enough to merit being defended, while nowhere telling us *why*. Second, he sketches the process of canon formation as an entirely rational, directed process, thus ignoring institutional powers and wider ideological issues that contribute more diffusely to that process, as well as the affective basis on which canons, both literary and religious, bind their readers. Third, his criteria remain profoundly, even literally, conservative. This makes them a priori unfit to help break open the self-evidence of conservatism that any discussion of the canon pursues. Instead of facing the authority that makes canons, it assumes, hence endorses, that authority.

In view of all this, the common denominator between Altieri and me is not only surprising but also a bit worrisome. Whereas I focus on women and Alitieri on literary masterpieces, I on speaking bodies and he on transhistorical values—in short, I on the political, he on the literary—we appear to share a significant negligence toward religion. As I discussed the bits from the Bible and the Qur'an as if they had nothing to do with religion, I took God as a literary character on a par with Jacob and Potiphar, whom he resembles in his favoritism toward Yusuf. This makes sense, it makes a point about texts, but it leaves a gap when I wish to connect culture to politics. Altieri's example, similarly, remains silent on the religious identity that his literary canon nevertheless promotes. Until I saw myself do the same thing, he got away with it too.

Not any longer. The point of this chapter is to reconsider that silence. I contend that facing authority—which is not the same as refusing it, only to denaturalize it and make it responsible—is a strategy most apt to understand canons, religious, literary and artistic, as attempts to establish a fundamentalist "truth" against literalist respect for the wholeness of the sign, attempts to make us separate signifier from signified. In other words, the authority "behind" canonization tempts its subjects to break the sign and thus disobey the book whose wisdom is, for believers as well as their "others," to impose the freedom to adhere—or not.

The first issue I wish to revisit in this context is *the relation between ethical and artistic merit.* As I mentioned earlier, when looking into the conjunction of Rembrandt's representations of the story with the later literary version, I was quite struck by the fact that Thomas Mann, in his preface, is explicitly attempting to overcome the mythical reification of misogyny he encountered in the traditions surrounding the episode. His "humanization of the figure of Potiphar's wife" is, in terms of the problematic of canons, a pretty uplifting political undertaking. In the name of that endeavor Mann claims literary success for the episode—the best of the book. Mann claims a "protofeminist," *humanist* ideology as an argument for aesthetic accomplishment. What he claims for his retelling of a story from the religious canon is literary canonicity on ethical and, I contend, political grounds.

When I first read this, I was taken aback by the argument. But instead of examining how this claim could be justified on principle, I cast it aside, typically, in a concessive subclause, by writing, "Although I am reluctant to endorse such a conflation of aesthetics and ethics . . ." (1991, 97) while the rest of my analysis remained silent on the aesthetic—say, the specifically literary—merit of Mann's defense of Potiphar's wife. Partly to revisit this earlier analysis in a self-reflection framed by historical change, I am writing this book today. At this point (and on the basis of the bond between literary and religious identity and between canon and identity that I am probing in this chapter), I would wish to revise this dismissal and withhold judgment on this general issue.

My previous reservation was related to the *ethical indifference* commonly held up in the face of artistic success. Such indifference has been displayed, for example, in enthusiastic receptions of wildly misogynist novels full of rape scenes presented as masculine value by Norman Mailer and Arthur Miller, an example that marks the beginning of feminist critiques of the literary canon by Kate Millet in the 1960s and 1970s (2000 [1970]). Or the naturalization of the literary value of South African literature during apartheid, in which racist representations of black people were not even noticed. Or the infamous case of Louis-Ferdinand Céline's brilliant but shockingly anti-Semitic novels.

This suspicion of ethical indifference was not wrong, and I still hold it. Now, though, I wish to take a different view. I will not retrospectively endorse the conflation but will first revise and then promote Mann's claim, otherwise. In my analysis in chapter 3 I prepared the ground for this work.

Usually the problem of the relation between ethics and aesthetics is resolved, albeit uneasily, by severing the link between them. It is generally acknowledged that some literature is politically disturbing yet aesthetically "great," and these problematic works have never, to my knowledge, been cast out of the canon. Nor have the less obviously problematic works of the accepted canon been examined for their problematic ethics until feminism and postcolonial thought took a closer look at them. Altieri, for example, would not subject *Paradise Lost* to a critical analysis regarding the ways in which it builds those strong identities at the cost of others. My earlier solution, which was to focus only on the ethical element, now strikes me as escapist. Now I would take the opposite perspective and examine how ethical *nonindifference*, far from being indifferent to aesthetics, informs the novel's artistic merit on its—the novel's—own aesthetic terms. This will be the first step in developing a notion of *literary* or *artistic identity*. It is only after that reflection that I feel equipped to further define the latter term, so as to be able to face authority from an ethical perspective.

To make this move, I have to insist that Mann's presence in his text, which is overt and powerful, alternating between earnest and ironic, cannot be decisive. According to George C. Rosenwald (1978, 545), Mann tried to put ethics before aesthetics. That may be the case according to the writer's stated intent, but this is not where I am looking for answers. I do not endorse the separation between ethics and aesthetic implied in such prioritizations. Mann's prose is utterly performative, as William E. McDonald has demonstrated (1999). In the sentence from Mann's preface the vindication is already broached, on two levels: that of the storytelling and that of the story as sequence of events (the *fabula*). In my earlier analysis I noted that "by writing about him, Mann includes Potiphar's presence in the story, signifying his absence differently in the adjective *pro forma*. As a husband, Potiphar is only a signifier, an empty form, and it is the absence of the signified that triggers the story and makes it 'mournful'" (1991, 96).

Back then, I was sensitive to the understanding Mann displayed for the woman's desire. This desire is the motor of the fabula, but the description of the character of Potiphar, however brief, gives the desire a reason, a motivation, an excuse. "Mournful" gratified me as an acknowledgment of her plight on the level of the story.

Now I am more sensitive to the underlying endorsement of monogamy, to the suggestion "with such a husband, what can you expect?" As I have argued elsewhere, monogamy is not indifferent to either religious or, I now add, literary identity, and biblical metaphors of "whoring" for religious unfaithfulness prove it. In an earlier literalist gesture, I argued that in parts of the Hebrew Bible the metaphor of whoring for "going after other gods" should be taken much more literally than is usually done. The verb *whoring* when used in the masculine form is not, or not only, metaphorical if we accept that it has a much more social, anthropological meaning than *prostitution*. The bond between the imaginary but obsessive concern for monogamy (of women) and the imagery of prostitution in biblical indictments of polytheistic wanderings was an important element in my study *Murder and Difference* (1988b) and more extensively in *Death and Dissymmetry* (1988a). The semantics of the verb *zanah* and the noun *zonah* around the notion of the stranger do bear out the ethnic protectionism that the alleged metaphor conveys.

This seemingly small philological issue has important consequences. One is, most obviously, the possibility that the anxieties surrounding monotheism and monogamy are deeply connected in all three canons of the Abrahamic monotheisms. This fits what I wrote in the previous chapter about the truth speak of the structure of chronology. Another one is the issue of (one-sided) monogamy itself, the anxiety about inheritance versus the hospitality that, in the Qur'an, extends to kinship. And then, the acknowledgment implied in the bond between the two monocultures (monotheism and monogamy) brings up the idea that women do have sexual desires. Sarah said it explicitly when she laughed at the messengers who predicted her late childbirth. "Can I have pleasure, being old, and my lord being old as well?" (Genesis 18:12). Mut stands in the lineage of this assertive Sarah.

In this respect, it is more disturbing that Mann's statement regarding the motivation of the woman's desire in her husband's inadequacy deprives that desire of its "desirousness." An implicit moral consideration—say, excusing her adulterous desire because of the husband's malfunctioning—overrules the simple but profoundly subversive fact that the desire both is inalienably hers and weakens her identity: it makes her, as the saying goes, weak in the knees. In other words, the figure of Mut-em-enet in Mann's novel and the woman in the Qur'an version on which it ostensibly draws, that is, both incarnations of Mut, insist—more than Mann takes credit for in his preface—on a desire that is hers while depriving it of her powers to act socially and morally according to the rules. This may sound like a lame excuse, lamer than her husband's inadequacy as a husband, but it is surely hers. And it is the site of the tangled relationship between elements that are usually distinguished, such as, first of all, body and spirit, and second, private and public, a relationship I wish to foreground.

The unexamined term here is *body* in Christianity's culturally specific sense. When Mut is weakened by desire, she is importantly not playing the game with spirit promoted by Christianty in its representations that narrativize the embodiment of spirit. Just think of the bodily iconography in Christian art, so thoroughly in opposition to Islamic and Judaic prohibitions of such representations. Suffering and—or as—sacrifice are valued through narratives such as the *Pietà* (Scarry 1985, 216). This scene stages nativity and death in conflation to convey the sense in which Christianity sees the bond between body and spirit. Loyal to the Abrahamic monotheory of procreation, Mary is body as a vessel for spirit, Christ is body in which spirit is *incarnated, placed*; together they promote the body as site of embodiment.

The antiquated Aristotelian gender division involved in the *Pietà* imagery is further enhanced—but again, *not* foregrounded, remaining unmarked—by the youthfulness of Mary in many such images, which suggests a heterosexual love relationship as the middle term between nativity and death. Representation, of the kind the more orthodox forms of Christianity and the other two monotheistic religions reject, is vitally important as a tool to promote a sense of the body that is specific, politically apt to enhance domination, and paradoxically at the same time invisible, because *unmarked*. Dyer argues that the representational "ideologeme" (my term, based on Jameson 1981) of incarnation

provides unmarked white bodies with self-evident power through
the conception of spirit it implies, in combination with the use to
which that spirit is put politically as "entrepreneurial" and imperialist (Dyer 1997, 14–40). This conjunction between a Christian
conception of body and an imperialist politics makes a critical reconsideration of both literary and religious canons such as the one
I am engaged in here urgent, relevant, and timely.

My little case study concerns desire. Why? Desire, I would
think, is the systematic opposite of embodiment. It is that happening between *state* and *act* that is, in Dyer's terms, *of* the body,
not localized *in* it. All psychoanalytical theory of desire aside, the
noun *desire*, like the noun *fire* which is its classical literalized metaphor, hovers between state and event. A new look at the scene in
Mann that "explains," by way of a "literary masterpiece" written
by a canonical white male author, what the novel's vindication of
the rights of women amounts to, may help to clarify how artistic
identity and religious canons can be inflected together. This may
result in opening up my own and Altieri's silencing of the religious element in this chapter's conceptual knot. At the heart of
that knot, and therefore hard to disentangle, lies authority.

I am alluding to the scene so central in this book, where the
bodiliness of desire and the impossibility to separate spirit and
body becomes painfully clear—in the most literal sense of the
adjective. It is the scene of the little knives that is absent from the
biblical story. Extensively represented in Mann's novel, it is present in that rival canon, the Qur'an, as it is in many *midrashim*
that, to Kugel's delight, precede the Qur'an. But I insist these exegetical exercises do not have the canonical authority by virtue
of which the Qur'an is, for its believers, the original truth speak.
Mann's novel, then, does more than vindicate the woman as if
he were her ideological *cavalier servant*, turning her into a near-
virgin by claiming her husband's inadequacy. In one sweep—a
complex but effective alternation of focalizing positions, distributed between Mut, the Yusuf figure called Osarsiph, and the other
women in town—the novel accomplishes its literary greatness, its
contribution to literary identity, and its "opening up" of the religious canon. Let me explain this judgment.

It is the scene of the vindication of Mut's desire. To assess what
Mann accomplishes here, the difference from the Genesis text is

important. As I have mentioned and wish to reiterate in the context of facing authority, in the Genesis text, after the fateful ultimatum that will lead Joseph to prison, the nameless woman calls upon "the men in the house" to slander him, using both their sense of social hierarchy and ethnic prejudice to entice the men's solidarity with her: "And she called unto the men of the house and said to them saying: see he made come to us a Hebrew man to mock us, he has come to me to lie with me and I called out in a loud voice" (39:14). In my earlier analysis I paid no attention to the woman's choice of arguments. It now strikes me that, to phrase it harshly for the sake of clarity, the woman appeals to racial sentiment and class subordination to disqualify her husband's management of the house in the eyes of his subordinates by promoting envy of the latter against the higher-placed foreign slave Joseph. This puts her in the category of an ill-understood Delilah, calling on the tribesmen to defeat Samson. It distinguishes her overly sharply from her narrative sisters Yael and Judith, who deploy the same feminine "devices" but stand on the ethnic "right" side.

The argument will be repeated to the husband, who, without discussion, gets furious and takes Joseph into custody. No wonder such a story has contributed to the further rigidifying of misogynistic mythology, as well as, let's not forget, to a further rigidifying of the opposition between the intended Hebrew readers of the story and their "others" to whom this woman ethnically belongs. Note that it is the husband whom she accuses of disrespect toward herself and the other men in the house. The Hebrew man is just an instrument. So are the other servants. The woman uses race and class to get to sex. Conversely, the story uses sex to disqualify femininity, while putting forward "self-evidently"—without foregrounding—race and class as well as the straitjacket of male bonding in a hierarchically organized society. The excuse a humanist feminist perspective could allege is that the woman's strategy appeals to the only instruments available in a predominantly men's world to a woman confined to the house. This is a well-known argument. It does not satisfy me. The argument, in any case, would not hold for the Qur'an version, where hospitality, not servitude, is central.

Mann's ethical nonindifference is artistically motivated as well as the other way around. My analysis so far has intimated that if framed within their own aesthetics, each of the three stories has literary brilliance. And in each case ethical issues are involved in that literariness. Similarly, Rembrandt's three images are artistically among the worldwide top works, if only because the artist is beyond questioning. Because the means of especially narrative literature touch upon the intricate connections between private and public aspects of subjectivity, attempts to pass off objectionable ethics under the cover of literary brilliance are doomed. So are attempts to separate the two, condemning a work on ethical terms while continuing to read it canonically on aesthetic premises, through *ethical indifference*.

In my discussion of chronology in Genesis and point making in the Qur'an, artistic principles came up that determine ways of storytelling in relation to the ideas the stories build and convey. That analysis was premised on the inseparable bond between form and content—a bond as tight as that between body and spirit. Here I will only touch upon aesthetical concerns in Mann's text. These are both explicit in the author's preface and, more important, known to the readers of the novel who share the canonical form of literary literacy within which the novel was conceived, written, and read. The authority of the literary canon and its principles passes off the canonical status as unquestionable.

The issue, as I have mentioned before, is the rhetoric of realism. To write a novel—hundreds of pages, realistic in detail, psychology, and all that that entails—Mann's vindication, he alleges, needs a richer source. As Mann complained, the biblical meager "what" was lacking the "how" and the "why": life's circumstantiality was missing (Yohannan 1982, 431). The "why" in Mann's complaint is a "why?" question of the type Kugel asked. Mann's expansion is not unlike the *midrashim* that fleshed out the biblical meager "what." As in Mann's novel, fantasy thus underlies much interpretation, scholarly or not. At first sight, this might seem to be a literary issue, and what Mann gives expression to is the novel's realistic needs in its status as a literary artifact. The circumstantial detail is a notable feature of realistic narrative and an important element in aesthetic judgments on the basis of such narratives that may decide their status in or outside the canon (but see Schor 1987). Realism in literature and art requires detail. Please keep in mind, though, that realism as a *belief* in the reality of the representation is also the ground both for fundamentalism and for the iconophobia in Judaism, Protestantism, and Islam. I submit that these two concerns bind the religious to the literary concerns.

That bond is this. What leads to *idolatry* in religion leads to *sympathy* in the novel, and the two are equally dangerous as enticements to transgression. The difference is the conception of the body—as site of embodied spirit versus a site defined by spirit. This bond between religious and literary taboos on the one hand and conceptions of body-and-spirit on the other becomes clearer when we realize that there is a legal point to Mann's complaint as well. Circumstantial evidence, although legally meager and problematic, is often the only evidence there is to indict or declare "not guilty." Hence the artistic consideration—how to gain a place in the literary canon by doing the aesthetically good job with details—*inevitably* entails considerations that bleed into the social domain, where politics and ethics meet before the law. This is the reason we must not forget that the Greek word *kanon* means "law."

Mann's search for circumstantial detail in a story where guilt is at stake is therefore in and of itself an act of merging aesthetics and ethics—an act, that is, *against the ethical indifference of aesthetics*. This is how his statement in the preface deserves to be endorsed, say, as a philosophical position. Against a Kantian disinterestedness, Mann, on the eve of unequaled crimes against humanity, proposes an aesthetic of ethical nonindifference.

Before returning to the historical moment, I will now argue two further points that follow from the need for ethical nonindifference as an (element of) aesthetics. First, according to this logic, *literariness*, not blind obedience to authority, is the tool for identity formation. Hence my insistence on literalism, a mode of reading that supports literariness. Second, religious canonicity is not premised on that formation but allows, even facilitates, it. I will argue these points by revisiting Mann's little scene in its search for detail.

Although, as Kugel has demonstrated, the scene had been floating around in exegetical texts within the Judaic tradition, I contend that Mann significantly, not coincidentally, found his most suitable circumstantial evidence in the rival text, the later and abducted version so to speak, to which its readers nevertheless give the authority of the "original," the only true because perfected version. Only after versioning-in the scene into the canonical text was the latter "perfect." The episode of Qur'an 12:23–35, where the follow-up of the seduction attempt is different and more extended than in Genesis, pitches one canon against another. Now authority is neutralized; both canons claim it, and hence it fades away. Yet the Qur'an is not a novel any more than Genesis is. While "detail" is added, part of the circumstantiality of Genesis is also eliminated. This is why I don't find the terms *gap* and *gap-filling* useful beyond what they betray of the critic's commitments. They fail to account for repression and elimination and allow only for supplementation. There is no equivalent to Genesis 39:14—no interaction with the other men in the house until the master of the house appears at the other side of the door and a witness steps forward, no racial slurs, no appeal to class subordination to solicit sympathy.

This omission, especially that of the ethnic denigration, is easily explained away by the respective ideological and religious identities of the intended readership and the context within which each text functions. I am most certainly not interested in further sharpening the divide between Judaism and Islam, the respective curators of these canonical legacies. Contemporary politics takes care of that, much to my dismay. For those interested in the enormous extent to which symbols, visual as well as literary, are shared by the two brother bands who, like Jacob's sons, are involved in world-threatening strife, I can only refer to two texts in particular: Bardenstein 1999 and Said 2000. These two texts have contributed a great deal to my own understanding of culture's contribution to this situation. I merely mention the omission to gloss Mann's seemingly *quantitative* complaint. The appeal for support and solidarity that in Genesis took the "argumentation" we saw figures in the Qur'an as well. But the people called upon are different. The social setting shifts. Mann's choice of the Qur'an episode to aesthetically "supplement" the meager Hebrew text is therefore not just supplementation or gap-filling but a selection of ethical concern—an act of ethical nonindifference. I will argue below that his choice is overdetermined by a particular care for keeping the ethical visible.

This selection focuses on the important difference between the two religious texts: in the Qur'an, the woman is not the only woman in the story. *In the city* she becomes subject to slander among her women friends (12:30). The scene is twice displaced, from men to women and from house to city. Significantly, the woman acquires a public status that enables her to act. And although according to the fabula she pulls the same trick on Yusuf as in Genesis and hence lends herself to the same misogynistic mythologizing, the story receives an instructive different twist that prevents such stabilization. The women in the city assume that the woman is going crazy with love (12:31). She acts in response to this "cabal," not in order to disqualify and harm Joseph nor to deny her desire but to gain literal *sym-pathy*, cosuffering from desire, and thus to constitute a community. Here is, finally, the passage of Qur'an 12:31, now as a whole:

> When she heard
> Of their cabal,
> She sent to them
> And prepared a banquet
> For them, and she gave
> Each of them a knife,
> And she said,
> "[Joseph,] shew thyself to them."
> And when they saw him,
> They were amazed at him,
> And cut their hands, and said,
> "God keep us! This is
> No man! This is no other
> Than a noble angel!"

Then she proceeds to confess to her friends that she did in fact seduce and trick him and that he did "firmly save himself guiltless" (12:32). Potiphar and "the men" in fact imprison Joseph for his own good, "for a time" (12:35).

When I first studied this case I was interested in Mann's appeal to the Qur'an to vindicate the woman. Now I wonder what the choice of that text offers more specifically in terms of the problematic of this chapter, in literary as well as in theoretical terms. What authority did he invoke, and to what purpose? As far as the text's literary status is concerned, first, and most obviously, there is more to the historical position of Mann's text than I realized, especially in terms of ethnicity, hence of one extremely important issue of identity. Moreover, this historical consideration—the novel's pre-Holocaust position—needs to be put in conjunction with my own moment, speaking as I do from a post-Holocaust time but also from a "global" moment of migration and cultural mixing, a time, moreover, when feminism allegedly has become another "post-". I will return to this in chapter 10.

Second, Mann's novel, by means of the—literary, realist—detail of oranges, does more than deploy, consider, and parody the rhetoric of realism as truth speak. In particular, the citrus fruit with its acid adds both more color and more pain. Pain is not here an overcoming of the body by a spirit only temporarily housed there but an endorsement of a nonsplit body of desire. Like the sign, the body is whole, with spirit an unalienable aspect of it. Physical pain, in other words, is here of a nature that, by its metaphorical acceptance of the woman's heartache, transforms her desire from the moral-political sphere to the realm of the body, in an acceptance that spirit and body are one. This implicates the body in the politics and makes the ethics un- or anti-Christian.

I did realize that this pain was important when I wrote:

> At dessert, oranges and very sharp little knives to peel them are distributed. And when the ladies are busy peeling their oranges, Osarsiph/Joseph comes in to serve wine. Sheer fright at the *sight* of such beauty makes all the women cut their fingers, some of them to the bone. "My loves, what ever has happened to you all? What are you doing? Your blood is flowing" is the reaction of the plotting, lovesick virgin. Her intentionally insincere exclamation receives sincerity from the contiguous comment in which the speaker fails to distinguish between himself and this woman. For the narrator continues: "It was a fearful sight." (Bal 1991, 116, quoting Mann 1983, 803)

Today, in a consideration of canonicity, this sharper pain, caused by the acid of the oranges, and the bloody visibility of it, appear more striking in terms of theorizing identity through identification as one form of "literary identity." This is aesthetically played out on the level of the "detail" of representation and ethically on the level of shifting the interpretation of the body, rubbing it against Christian conceptions. Christianity, let's keep this in mind, was the ethical-political-religious setting of Mann's writing. And it was in the name of Christianity that utter horror was perpetrated on Christianity's alleged others. Remember what I said earlier about suffering and sacrifice. Literary identity as bound up with representation is here elaborated *on the terms of,* yet in critical engagement with, Christian ideology: the same Christian ideology that sent missionaries to Islamic countries, holding back cultures that had not asked for such interventions. Later I will argue that this concern for representation is but one of its aspects, but in the face of the authority of the representational canons in which this story is laid down, it remains an important one.

Theoretically speaking, then, the two aspects of the differences among the versions that appear important are those I announced as the theoretical elaboration of the literary merit of ethical nonindifference. First, *literariness* is here the tool for identity formation. Second, religious canonicity is not premised on that formation but allows, even facilitates, it. Concerning the first point, the novelist practices a literary genre in which evaluation of character's action is much more common, but that aesthetically calls for such mitigating and complicating tropes as irony and such narrative devices as alternating, double, and ambiguous focalization. In this practice, he adequately walks the fine line between ethical and aesthetic work by mediating on the level of fantasy—of the imagination. As he creates an imaginary realm that readers and characters can inhabit, the appeal to other subjects here also appeals to different readers, all with their porous subjectivity. This potential for community, then, is why fantasy, discussed in chapter 3, is a key concept and why Spinoza is an important philosophical inspiration.

This emergence of community happens on the level of the fabula as well. The women friends feel the pain of their friend's desire themselves at the moment they cut themselves. This common pain produces community—literal, bodily community. Common ground is produced through heteropathic identification, to use Kaja Silverman's term—a form of identification where the subject, rather than absorbing the other's alterity to make her the same, extols it, idealizes it, and goes out of herself to share it

(1996). This is the meaning of the plural as well as of the "city" in "the ladies of the City." It is the polemical plural that responds to Potiphar's extension of "you." Although the banquet takes place within Mut's confined space of the house, the public life of the city enters that space, opening its walls and liberating her from confinement, hence facilitating contact. Mut's doors are opened, this time not by the authority who can canonize her to stand for all women but by the community of women in the city: plural but not universal.

The Qur'an text already did something like this. It was in this text that Mann found his circumstantial evidence, to which the oranges as, say, a modern "effect of the real" were easy to add (Barthes 1968). They are colorful, and in addition to their colorist attraction to imagine in contrast to the white robes soon to be colored red, they add "couleur locale" as a fruit of the subtropical regions. But the point I was not able to see when I first studied this is the importance of the conjunction of *pain* with *women* and *city* in this version. The recognition of women's public life is as important as their frail, threatened, but potentially salvaged solidarity on the basis of something so deceptively perceived as private as desire. It is in this semantic space that the identity produced on the imaginary level of literature can be mobilized for a perhaps "religious" identity. Not religious as in official, regulated Judaic, Christian, or Islamic religion, but in another sense to which I will revert in a moment.

This identification of women with one another so as to form a community is opposed to the identities defined by religious affiliation, that is, the submission to the authority of one canon over the two others. Instead there is this identity of, to put it a bit flippantly, women collectively, hence publicly, entitled to their desires even if it does not fit the public morality and hence has no canonical status. But the texts that offer it as a possibility do: Mann's novel in a secularized world has literary canonicity, the Qur'an in its religious function has canonical status. The two cases belong to their respective mainstreams—although it seems important that these two mainstreams are quite separate—and it seems a good guess that their canonical status is *not* due to their vindication of the rights of women to desire. In other words, if this entitlement to desire is ethically "good," we must see that neither the literary nor the religious canonicity can be confined to ethical "goodness" or "badness." Nor is the biblical story's canonical status imputable to the disturbing sentiments its more clearly wicked woman character appeals to in order to promote her case.

Ethical nonindifference—not culturally and historically specific goodness or evil—is involved in literary merit as modern Western culture has construed it and on which it has based its canonization process. Hence ethical nonindifference contributes to potential literary canonicity. But as the case clearly demonstrates, the canonization as either literary masterpiece or religiously institutionalized scripture is not directly based on the particular *ethical merit* of the positions represented.

The second point to which I was blind earlier and which I find important now, although I still feel ill-equipped to address it, concerns the element "religion." None of the passages around the story of Mut are explicitly religious in their "points." Nevertheless, I have argued that the scene with the little knives does revisit Christian ideology critically. Rather, one would be inclined to say, at least for the three religious canons, that these passages are ancient myths that ended up canonized for some reason that may have nothing to do with the laws of Judaism, Christianity, and Islam respectively. This very plausible lay view of things made it easy for me to discuss biblical texts in nontheological terms throughout my earlier work on the Bible. But since then I have learned from my feminist theologian friends that "religion" need not be like the institutionalized religions from which I long ago took leave. Also, I have become a bit more intrigued—albeit admittedly also worried—by what Hent de Vries calls "the turn to religion" (1999). I do not participate in this movement but acknowledge its presence and cultural significance. In the current historical moment of global migration, religion cannot so easily be bracketed as it might have seemed.

Jonneke Bekkenkamp has written extensively about the problem of canon and religion (1993). She always answers my questions about what religion could possibly mean for feminism if we do not limit it to the largely women-unfriendly institutionalized religions, with the etymological insistence on *binding*. If religion is what binds, it could well be one of those domains that mediate between the terms of the infelicitous but persistent binary oppositions private-public, individual-collective, body-spirit, and the like. With that understanding, what can the subversive literary identity of our woman figure(s) mean in religious terms, so that the canonical status of at least the Qur'an version may offer something that is not "merely" literary?

Let me rephrase this question in a way that foregrounds the contribution already inherent in literary texts—at least narrative texts—to what is religiously relevant. What would make the triple case of Mut's mishaps—her tricks, her powerlessness, and her desire—"religious"? Religious as in offering an *imaginary* realm in which such oppositions can be suspended, a realm that would be forbidden if the imagination were visually represented. First, the pain caused by the cutting knives (or was it by desire shared?) and exacerbated by acid oranges (or was it by colorful detail?) is a metaphor for the three elements of tricks, powerlessness, and desire, covered by such oppositions and covered over by their oppositional structure. The pain is a metaphor, however, to be taken as literally as whoring or "going strange," going with strangers, to bring the Dutch expression for adultery to resonate with the Jewish tradition that uses the same word for "whore" (in the feminine) as for "stranger" (in the masculine). "Pain" translates the way the irreducible difference and the subsequent loneliness of an individual, especially one not quite firmly positioned in mainstream society, *cuts*: it severs and hurts.

But second, the blood thus shed also stands for the hot blood of desire that is, as such, the movement out of the autistic self into a risky, dangerous, but fulfilling and indeed indispensable communion and communication with another. Blood gives body to the porous subjectivity of fantasy. Third, then, the pain or *pathos* is a *sym*-pathos, a pain that qua pain binds, by means of heteropathic identification, the lonely woman sick of unrequited love and her friends who a moment before had dropped her into the abyss of social loneliness like a hot potato. The blood for me also symbolizes a multiple "marriage," the emotional defloration of the women enslaved by imposed monogamy, potentially accepting the risks of their own desires in a social sphere where they are not alone with the one man who owns them. The women who have the guts to love Yusuf, the stranger. Through the knives, their woman friend "penetrates" their bodies, releasing the blood of the ruptured hymen. Theirs is a binding that does not cancel but temporarily suspends the self-evidence of monogamy—as well as, perhaps, its metaphorical counterpart, monotheism. Now, is such a binding religion? I don't know, but the place where I see that possibility opened is part of a religious canon that *as a whole* is indifferent to such issues and such plights. For if the religious canon does not foreground this form of identity-based "religion," the literary one does. Two forms of binding, then, can coexist.

This requires, first, mixing up the neat distinctions between religious and literary identities and canons. As for canons, second, I do recognize that religious canons are fixed forever and by political authorities, that they have oppressive power in that they police boundaries. Nevertheless, their texts' canonical status is also informed and strengthened if not determined by the kind of literary, aesthetic achievement that informs the looser and more changeable literary and artistic canons. Conversely, the literary features of the texts produce effects that are ethically nonindifferent, so that the neat distinction between the two types of canon falls apart. This has led to the political need to open up literary canons even if religious canons, different in that they are definite, are beyond such revisions. This is the reason why, third, the canon cannot be truly opened up through inclusions only. Revisionist interpretations of religious canonical texts must continue to be made. The novel and the Rembrandt images, each in its own way, do just that.

Perhaps paradoxically, the main motivation for turning religious canons into literary or artistic ones is, as I see it, to facilitate the "double binding." The enfolding of unofficial shared desire within official religion allows women to belong to their gender group as well as to their ethnic group with its religious identity, while also allowing insight into what is of their bodies. From a perspective not bound to established religion, the point is not to save the religious texts from ethical jeopardy—to argue, for example, that neither the Bible nor the Qur'an is an overall misogynist text while critiquing the way they are when and where they are—for that can lead to the kind of idealistic trappings I have called "the politics of coherence" (Bal 1988a). Neither the Bible nor the Qur'an is a unified text, nor is any single text ideologically unified anyway. Literalist reading will always demonstrate this. Instead, I find it important to save these religious canonical texts'

literariness itself from ethical indifference. This gesture opens up
the tight boundaries that separate and thus protect each from the
other. It binds the distinct domains of religion and literature on
the level not of their texts or the functions thereof, but of their
readings.

If "religion" may be extended to mean what I just said that the
cutting knives and the women's pain meant, then the literary aspect of our problematic is also up for reconsideration. Ultimately,
with "literary identity" I did not mean only what has come out so
far, the production through narrative and poetic art of identities
that would not have easy access to the public domain otherwise,
such as the group of Mut's friends or the male subordinates in the
Egyptian house in Genesis. That sort of identity is "literary" in
that it is fictional: while not actually present, it is an example, a
model, of what exists in a society or can be made to exist or at least
be *thinkable*. So far, in other words, I have based my argument on
a rather traditional representational conception of literature.

This conception remains important to the extent that what a
society considers imaginable can in fact happen. Moreover, the
other, more obviously and directly political sense of representation as "standing in for" is never entirely out of scope when we
talk about representation. Nevertheless, as is well known, literature is more than the sum of possible, thinkable, imaginable
representations, and so is visual art. Three additional aspects of
literature and art are relevant for a conceptualization of something
like "literary identity." It is an *institution*, it is a form of *agency*,
and it is a *frame*. What I understand by the concept of artistic or
literary identity is the composite result of the cultural promotion,
if not altogether imposition, through the authority of canons, of
the integrated effects of literature as representation—including
the intricacies of identification that representation entails: institution, agency, and framing. These aspects together are the subject
of the final chapter.

10

Dad Pains

Tony Tanner's commentary on the passage regarding sex in the city (versus in the field) in Deuteronomy contains the strong statement "Language has total authority, and within it individuals have total responsibility" (1979, 19). In contemporary news reports about Muslim hostility, this total authority of language is indicated as fundamentalism and the total responsibility of individuals as Islamic law or shari'a. This presentation is a bit one-sided if we consider the general validity of this claim and its source in the Bible. To become aware of that generality is only one step, but an indispensable one, toward a cure for that terrible power of canon, law, or rule, of legal excorporation (Tanner's term, 19) or social ostracizing. What we need to recognize is that authority hurts, and so do the fathers who claim to possess it.

French psychoanalyst Marie Balmary has written a series of books on Freud, the Bible, and contemporary culture that demonstrate the gain of reading the words, as I advocated in chapter 2, in order to get at fantasies, such as the ones I attempted to "show"—literally, as visions—in chapter 3. With great patience and ever-alert open-mindedness, Balmary explores how ancient and more recent authoritative texts suffer from the very authority that sustains their durable validity. She demonstrates, that is, how a certain kind of philology or loyalty to words as signs, and, I would add, to signs in general, helps to break open the dogmas of an ill-understood canonicity. I bring her intervention in against what I have termed fundamentalism. As is hopefully clear by now, this term refers to the reading posture that splits the sign in a signifier treated as a rigid denominator, much like a proper name, and a signified that logocentrically fixates what can respond to cultural life only if it remains fluid. It is, as I have argued with the help of Herman Beck (2001), an oppositional, authoritarian, and defensive mode of reading. Against this fundamentalism, Balmary proposes something that comes close to what I have termed *literalism*: a respect that honors the texts, all of them, while rigorously keeping open where the signs go. She follows, that is, the traces of earlier meanings, never loses sight of the sign's past, yet always remains open to the transformative work of time. This mode of reading is the best weapon against fundamentalism, as Balmary's magisterial and to my mind best book demonstrates, the early *Psychoanalyzing Psychoanalysis: Freud and the Hidden Fault of the Father* (1982).

In this book she argued that Freud's obsession with the son position made him blind to the ancient faults of the primal father, Oedipus's father Laios. Laios the homosexual rapist, the child molester, murderer, and abandoner of his son—in short, a monster of a figure—faded away, in the shadow of the son who committed his faults unconsciously, as if driven by a more ancient guilt.

Balmary then goes on to trace in Freud's own writing the repressed fears and pains connected to the father. This father was called Jacob, just like Yusuf's father. His mistakes, perhaps crimes, have left barely understandable symptoms that had great power and forcefully influenced psychoanalysis. Balmary's method is as Freudian as they come; as she states several times with some overinsistence, she is loyal to the master whose lessons she also turns against him. This, I propose, is the paradox of the relationship between canon and memory. At the beginning of her book, Balmary cites a patient, a young child, who said to her, "J'ai mal à mon père" (1986, 13). This phrase, which is not grammatically correct in French but astoundingly clear and precise, cannot be translated into English. "I hurt at my father" is equally ungrammatical, while "My father hurts [me]" is grammatical but less precise; it suggests acute pain instead of the chronic pain of Balmary's patient. It also suggests a father who beats or rapes instead of a father whose child suffers from the sheer relationship with the father it is doomed to maintain. A "father ache," like a bellyache, might be the best way to express it. In light of this, we can make more of the instructive analyses of the structural position of fathers and the consequences for male gender identity in the Bible such as those provided by Daniel Boyarin (1995).

In this final chapter, exploring a parallel to such a father ache or dad pain, I seek to expand the perspective on Yusuf and the pain caused when a woman transgresses all the laws by loving him. Yusuf the perhaps-adopted son of the household in Egypt hurts in prison, but not because of some action that is clearly illegal, criminal, or immoral. He is brought down because loving him was not allowed. In one version, the divine father would not have it; in another, the biological father appeared before Yusuf's mind's eye when he was tempted and thus visually prohibited the intercultural love. The social father held the strings of Yusuf's purse and career, and the fantasmatic father—bedpost or image—cast his imaginary gaze, enough to strike Yusuf with a fear of women.

Fathers and canons—social and textual authority—go hand in hand. But if the arch-patriarch, Abraham, is any indication, the power of the father is always derivative, tenuous, and grounded in total submission, a willingness to sacrifice the child. No wonder the child has "mal à son père"—suffers dad ache. The sacrificing of sons in Abraham's story follows the trajectory of their life development. Ishmael is sent away and almost dies as a baby, then again as a young boy. Isaac is almost killed as, I imagine, a preadolescent. Girls are also sacrificed, with less pomp and no rescue: Jephtah's daughter, the young woman in Judges 19, Samson's first wife—all marriageable or married without children. Clearly, there is a need to sacrifice as an entrance into adulthood (Bal 1988a). Daughters die of it, sons barely survive. The sacrifice of Jephthah's daughter as a case of the vested interest that narrative form has in solving social tensions has not escaped critical attention (see, e.g., Sjöberg 2004). That this is an issue of textuality and narrative as much as of social disturbance—in other words, that the form of chronology has a bearing on the subject matter and vice versa—is important for the purpose of this book.

Yusuf stands at the edge of adulthood as well. He doesn't die, not even nearly. Instead, symbolically at least he is born three times over. As I mentioned earlier, he is born of his mother first, then taken out of an empty well where he was put by his envious brothers because his father favored him, rescued by the Egyptians who bought him. Then he is taken out of the prison, another kind of pit, where Potiphar cast him. In all cases, the father can be said to have put him there. And the father is suffering the loss of the son who suffers from the father—from dad ache.

The question of the tenuous position of the father remains thus at the heart of such canonical stories, as if the cultures where these stories circulate need to make sure fathers don't take their authority for granted. The same holds for texts. Fundamentalism as I have described it at the end of chapter 3 is defensive. This defensiveness, I speculate, derives from fear: fear of the signs that remain stubbornly autonomous, refuse to be split. Clearly, the authority of texts is not as stable as the fearful might like. This fear at the heart of canonicity has, however, a counterforce to face. I wish to mobilize this counterforce by revisiting the issue of canon, now from the paradoxical perspective of *abstraction*—the potential for form. Canons are possible because, and only to the extent that, the signs they harbor remain possibilities, potentials, for useful forms of meaning-making in cultural contexts. Sacrifice is, then, no longer necessary. Instead, authorities under threat can face emerging authorities and align themselves with them, in order to establish new lines of force more suitable for the different times and places we now inhabit.

Canons are institutions as much as bodies of texts. Art and literature are also institutions, quite like institutionalized religions. Although canon formation occurs differently in each instance, both sets of institutions "live by" the deployment of some version of Louis Althusser's Ideological State Apparatuses. The phrase "live by" questions the self-evident power of their authorities. Institutions live, too; they transform themselves over time in relation to the subjects they subject by means of their apparatuses and the forms of interpellation these facilitate. Storytelling, frivolous as it appears, is one such form.[1]

Interpellation, in turn, works by virtue of its effectiveness in the formation of groups. This effect is at the heart of canon formation. John Guillory argued in his entry on canon in *Critical Terms for Literary Study* that the works in literary canons, far from representing from the start a body of texts sanctioned as great, initially served as textbooks for proper use of language (Guillory 1995). By the sheer fact that texts are more lasting than oral speech, the literary production of a culture stabilized language use, instilled proper grammar, and created a firm, class-bound distinction between literate and illiterate language. The identity that can be properly called "literary," then, is characterized as the civilized, literate, adapted, mainstreamed user of proper English, or Dutch for that matter.

No specific *literary* model is required, only a literary identity in that sense. The same holds for art, an institution that discriminates the cultured from the uncultured "mob." This is a cultural means to distinction that is profoundly political (Bourdieu 1984). It produces the kind of identity that promotes social success. And it includes things like naturalizing saying—to recall an old Dutch joke in anticolonial circles—as does an inhabitant of Curaçao, "The Rhine enters our country at Lobith." Geography books written for Dutch schools used to be simply transferred to the colonies, where "our" country was, equally simply, that foreign country the children had never seen. Such uses of *our* are interpellations in the same way as the *you* of Althusser's policeman; they are invitations to be a reluctant witness.

This institutional aspect of art and literature is obviously of the kind of exclusionary nature that liberal critiques of the canon indict. No critical analysis of specific canonical texts nor any amount of adding nonmainstream texts to the canon can really touch this effect of the canon. This is why analyses such as Charles Altieri's, for all their philosophical sophistication regarding the question why canons should have authority, can never satisfy the critique

1. The phrase "live by" resonates with George Lakoff and Mark Johnson's path-breaking cognitive approach to metaphor (1980; 1999), which is quite relevant to my attempts to make metaphors more "literal" (see chapter 3). Althusser's concept of Ideological State Apparatus (1969; 1971) remains important, as Kaja Silverman has argued for its twin concept "interpellation" (1992).

of the canon. For, as I noted above, his entire argument is based on the unexamined cultural need to have canons in the first place. He also, I must now add, connects canons to memory. His article develops from the opening statement that "if we are less in need of discovering new truths than of remembering old ones, there are obvious social roles canons can play as selective memories of traditions or ideals" (1983, 41). The premise of this statement, from which the argument then proceeds, is that such selection can be performed by and for a collectivity. In relation to this argument, my childhood memory of the Yusuf and Mut story remains stubbornly relevant. For it keeps raising the questions which group we are talking about, on what the authority of that group is based, and which canon therefore serves which social roles.

At this juncture another memory comes up, this time the memory of someone else as it links with my own. In an article published in *Atlantic Monthly* in 1943, during his exile in the United States, Mann evokes a rather triumphant memory quite like Yusuf's dreams of ears of corn bowing before him. The difference is that, unlike Yusuf, he kept silent about it. The authority, the teacher, the overdetermined importance of "authentic" names: it all harks back to my school mistress's moral lesson that made me a reluctant witness to my own abject status. I quote Mann's passage at some length because it puts another spin on Mann's metacommentary and its ironic truth claims; it demonstrates that irony is not so easy to take lightly.

> The narrative enters into the highly developed and sophisticated cultural sphere of the Nile Empire, which through *sympathy* and *reading* had been familiar to me since the time of my boyhood, so that I knew more about it than even the teacher who during Religion Class had questioned us twelve-year-old boys as to the name of the holy steer of the ancient Egyptians. I showed that I was eager to answer, and was called upon. "Chapi," I said. That was wrong in the opinion of the teacher. He reproached me for having raised my hand when I knew only nonsense. "Apis" was the right name . . . I knew better than the good man, but discipline did not allow me to enlighten him about it. I kept silent—and all my life I have not forgiven myself for this *silence* before *false authority*. (1943, 95; emphasis added)

The assembly of boys, like the assembly of girls, is being held spellbound by an authority that is false yet wins because the reluctant witness is silenced. The boy Thomas preferred to be publicly admonished rather than to question the authority that defined the collective of which he was a part. Social isolation is more terrifying than public shame. But this collectivity already presupposes its sociolinguistic streamlining, bringing me back to Altieri's argument.

More important still for my argument here is the way Altieri ignores the more diffuse authority of linguistic correctness and the class elitism that pertains to it, which *any* canon possesses. Less obviously, however—and this serves as a small cautionary footnote to canon bashing—the linguistic elitism produced by literary canons is also a means through which nonmainstream subjects can get access to the mainstream and thus further expand the company of the select happy few, perhaps even subvert it from within. Of course, I would not promote this possibility as a solution, but let it stand as something that canons—as long as and to the extent that they exist—cannot master, for all the authority that pertains to them. Exclusion is the form taken by the willingness to sacrifice what makes the authority an authority—or a father, a father. As a straitjacket for identity, then, canonical literature even in its most conservative guise has a permeable skin. For identity, like desire, is not confined to either spirit or body, despite the religious and cultural propaganda for embodiment and against the integration of body and spirit.[2]

Because of their institutional power, art and literature, moreover, are also forms of *agency*. Writing and reading, making and looking at images, are forms of acting. This aspect has been extensively argued by those who took up J. L. Austin's radical revision of the philosophy of language from representational model—the result of informational or constative language use—to performative act (Austin 1975). As I mentioned in chapter 6, Jonathan Culler, in one of his articles that make him so utterly useful—and I would say *generous*—as a scholar, follows the concept of the performative from philosophy in the 1960s, through literature in

2. An amusing version of this linguistic canonicty is discussed with great brilliance by Srinivas Avaramudan (2006).

the 1980s, to gender studies in the 1990s, and back to philosophy (Culler 2000). In the process, performativity, from a rather special category of words allowing special utterances that do not state but do things, became generalized to stand for an aspect of any utterance: the aspect of an utterance as an act. Generalizing further on the basis of the iterability on which all language use depends, Culler recalls that not performativity but its "standard" other constativity became a special case of a generalized performativity.

For the purpose of this book, the decisive move here has been Derrida's insistence on the citationality that enables and surrounds each speech act (1988). Austin explicitly excluded literature from the analysis because literary speech acts are not "serious." Derrida, on the contrary, shifting the focus from the speaker's intention to the social conventions that guarantee the very possibility of performing speech acts, made the iterability or citationality of any language use the standard, subordinating intention to the social—a view that Judith Butler has put to excellent use in her analysis of gender (1990; 1993). This citationality lies at the heart of literature's public status, its canon's institutional power, and its contribution to the shaping of identity. Without repetition, Butler says, no identity.

Mann's memory of false authority breaks into that silenced, inconspicuous, naturalized, ongoing repetition of the relation to authority. But as we have learned from, most prominently, Gilles Deleuze, repetition not only comes inevitably with difference; it *is* difference (1994). For a theory of cultural memory this is an indispensable insight. I dare say that I share this boy's experience, although not in the same emotional realm; I share this man's memory, from a range of moments where I too felt I knew better than the authority but couldn't say so. Can I really say this—can I "have" Mann's memory, and can this help somehow, somewhat, to partially suspend or even dispel the authority that holds sway over cultural memory?

Silverman seems to think so. In her analysis of Chris Marker's *Sans soleil* she quotes the voice-over in that film who opposes history to memory, in a way that would go against Jan Assmann's conflation of the two. The voice-over says: "That's how history progresses—plugging its memories as one plugs one's ears" (quoted in Silverman 1996, 188). This extraordinary metaphor

leads the critic to theorize what she calls "other people's memories." The figure of Krasna in Marker's film, Silverman writes,
suggests that "history represents less the 'hurt' . . . than the dis-
avowal of what 'hurts,' the assertion of unity and wholeness over
rupture and loss. However, although expelled from its human
residence, the foreclosed wound of the past somehow persists. It
languishes in the spiral of time, waiting once again to be granted a
locus which is finally more psychic than corporeal. To remember
is, in effect, to provide that psychic locus" (1996, 188–89).

The terms *wound* and *hurt* lead us back to Balmary's young
patient, hurting with dad ache. We can now add his hurt "at" his
father qua authority. Silverman makes the distinction between
remembering and remembering other people's memories in the
following words, which connect to the porous subjectivity Mann
was interested in staging: "If to remember is to provide the disem-
bodied 'wound' with a psychic residence, then to remember other
people's memories is to be wounded by their wounds" (Silverman
1996, 189).

Mann's memory affirms what George Rosenwald calls the
link between exile and the defense of truth (Rosenwald 1978,
546), and his act of thinking about Yusuf in his residence of exile
is an attempt to do just that. He imagines—in other words, he
imaginarily "images"—Yusuf's exile as a struggle to get out of,
or rid of, the wound of paternal authority. In this context the
brief moment when Yusuf was facing a woman who loved him
against the law is, for him, a cultural memory in the poignantly
precise sense of that term: personally hurtful, striking a wound,
yet potentially, once the wound has healed, opening up life beyond paternal authority. But such reparative memories also need
repetition-as-difference in order to stick. For that, Mann knew,
we need more than incidental flashes of possibility. The very
length of his monumental novel may well have something to do
with this realization.

In this view, from originating, founding act performed by a
willing, intentional subject, art and literature's performativity becomes an instance of an endless process of repetition; a repetition
that involves similarity and difference and that therefore both rel-
ativizes and enables social change and subjects' interventions—in
other words, agency. In collaboration with representation and

institutional power, this agency produces, shapes, perpetuates, but also potentially transforms what I call here *literary* or *artistic identity*. This brings me to the last aspect of literary identity: the *framing* that produces it and that at the same time it constitutes. It provides frames of reference through which subjects can make sense—of the world, their lives, and the literature they read.

Framing is a key concept here. As is well known, the concept of framing has been productively put to use in cultural analysis as an alternative to the older concept of context. Framing, then, accounts for the possibility of working with ignorance in approaching the texts of less familiar cultures without appropriating them.[3]

Framing is usually not noticed and is only rarely explicitly acknowledged. This absence of the term in the presence of the activity is perhaps what characterizes framing most significantly. This is, in the most profound sense, the point of the concept. The lack of commentary—or moralizing judgment—at key moments in the Yusuf story points to this kind of invisible framing. The women in the city, for example, just pop up, where they were uncannily absent in Genesis. The change from context to framing has not been one of terminology but of implications. I will briefly summarize three arguments in favor of its use over context.

The first argument pertains to context itself. Context, or rather, the self-evident, nonconceptual kind of data referred to as "context," is often invoked for the interpretation of cultural artifacts such as artworks in order to uncover their meaning. In effect, though, its deployment serves to confuse *explaining* with *interpreting*, and frequently origin with articulation (Pavel 1984). With this confusion, and in any endeavor of an interpretive, analytical nature, a whole range of presuppositions becomes important, whereby the term *context* loses both its specificity and its grounding. The perspective becomes unacknowledgedly deterministic. The unavowed motivation for the interpretation—indeed, the analytical passion—becomes entangled in a conflation of origin, cause, and intention. And this conflation may well be the most important damaging frame in the humanities. It is here that I see

---

3. One of the most influential formulations of this concept, usefully succinct, is Culler's "author's preface" to his volume *Framing the Sign* (1988). See also the chapter on framing in Bal 2002.

fundamentalism, as I have described it at the end of chapter 3, insinuate itself as a "normal" mode of reading.

The conflation of these three forms of beginnings—origin, cause, and intention—while betraying an ontological nostalgia, relies on a confusion of metaphysics, logic, and psychology. The first, metaphysics, is largely irrelevant for cultural analysis, the second is unattainable, and the third is unknowable. I contend that if the confusion and the passion are cleared away, the human scientist with interdisciplinary interests can pursue a much more exciting project, an analytical interpretation that avoids three sterile activities (paraphrasis, projection, and paradigmatic confinement) and that opens up a practice of cultural analysis that endorses its function as cultural mediation.

The second argument in favor of *framing* becomes clear from the simple facts of language. *Context* is primarily a noun that refers to something static. It is a "thing," a collection of data whose factuality is not in doubt once its sources are deemed reliable. *Data* means "given," as if context brings its own meanings, fixed and unquestionable. The sign is broken, the signifier made rigid, the meaning selectively and defensively given authority. The need to interpret these data, mostly acknowledged only once the need arises, is too easily overlooked. Contextualism shares this property with fundamentalism. In contrast, framing is an act. The act of framing produces an event. This verb form, as important as the noun that indicates its product, is primarily an activity. Hence it is performed by an agent who is responsible and accountable for his or her acts. This may be perceived as a burden by some—the scholar, after all, may become subject to what can be perceived as a form of policing—but to me this accountability is also liberating. It is, moreover, intellectually enriching, as it implies the necessity of self-reflection. Not to speak of the much more frightening, because "lawless," policing that goes on in the name of methodological obviousness, or dogma.

Furthermore, in a regress that might, in principle at least, be infinite, transitive verbs imply that the agent of framing can be, and is, framed in turn. In this way, the attempt to account for one's own acts of framing is doubled. First, one makes explicit what one brings to bear on the object of analysis: why, on what grounds, and to what effect. Then one attempts to account for one's own position as an object of framing, for the "laws" to which one submits. This double self-reflection, it seems, might help solve the problems of an unreconstructed contextualism as well as of a moralistic and naive self-reflexivity.

The third argument in favor of framing is the involvement of *time* in interpretation and analysis. *Framing* as a verb form points to process. Process both requires time and fills time, like the life of the sign according to Peirce. It is a factor of *sequence* and *duration*. And where there is duration, change occurs: differences emerge over time. Here lies the strength of the argument such as Amima Wadud's for a flexible reading of the canon (1999). This is also where history, inevitably and importantly, participates in any act of interpretation or analysis. One way of taking this simple fact through to its consequences is to enforce a reversed perspective on historical thinking, starting with and in the present. This is one distinction between cultural analysis and history, but a distinction, obviously, that does not free the one from entanglement with the other.

An important consequence of the fact that framing has its roots in time is the unstable position of knowledge itself. This might seem to lead to an epistemic aporia, since knowledge itself loses its fixed grounding. But a full endorsement of this instability can also produce a different kind of grounding, a grounding of a practical kind. Thus the case I present here, allegorically, begins and ends with a material practice. That practice, in turn, reaches out to cultural analysis, claiming to participate fully in the academic practices whose object it would otherwise powerlessly remain. Here the object, an image always mise-en-scène within itself as well as within its environment is put under pressure; its meaning is multiplied, its material existence is set up as troubled.

As I announced in my discussion of Mut-em-enet's social agency when she established shared desire, I need to return, in conclusion, to the historical consideration of the episode from *Joseph and his Brothers*—the novel's pre-Holocaust position—and the need to put it in conjunction with my own position. I am speaking from a post-Holocaust moment but also a "global" moment of migration and the subsequent questioning of the nation-state as well as of the unmarked predominance of Christianity in what is awkwardly called "the West." I must now tentatively articulate, through such a double historical consideration, how literary identity as I have come to define it—a product of the conjunction-in-performance of representation-with-identification, institution, agency, and framing—can inform religious canons and be sustained by them, without falling back into the paternal, hurtful nature of the canon as authority. For simplicity's sake I will henceforth speak of literary identity and implicitly include artistic identity. The argument may appear clearer if I remain within the domain of language, since this is Mann's domain, as well as that of his "sources."

There are two distinct levels at which I see literature's identity-shaping potential as having an impact on religious canons. I am not saying easily, but possibly. Both pass through history. By laying out these possibilities, I am also trying to reply to criticism leveled at my earlier work from the side of art history: that I ignored the historical and hence that my work was ahistorical. I have replied to that criticism at length in *Quoting Caravaggio* (1999) but there is more to say. The first level of literature's constructive power to shape identity is what Walter Benjamin would call allegory. History is a model whose otherness, compared to our contemporariness, informs what we can think, feel, and do. On this level, Mann's vindication of the female figure allegorically, obliquely, critiques the ideology of his time. Without using the term *allegory*, I wrote about this aspect in the earlier analysis in *Reading "Rembrandt"*:

> I would suggest that this comment on the Hebrew myth of the Jew in a foreign country, confronted by a foreigner in love with him, could only arise from a response to the historical moment. While Nazism, *with its neurotic ideology of maleness*, was beginning to make the limits between groups of subjects so absolute as to become those between life and death, the ambivalence, both sexual and ethnic, of the encounter between two ambivalent subjects became an acutely necessary alternative, an opportunity to dramatize the intensity of emotional community. (Bal 1991, 117, emphasis added)

Again, this interpretation of Mann's oblique critique of Nazism through the problematic of gender, in a move that is in turn allegorical, is not wrong; I would still maintain it. The relations between Nazism and gender essentialism are too important to ignore.

But it now seems that I passed over the importance of the simple, *literal*, and institutionally relevant fact of Mann's choice of canonical source: the Qur'an. From the perspective of today's concerns, where gender is much more tightly embedded within an interculturalist pluralization of religious canons, the choice seems tremendously important, as a contribution to the endeavor of opening up the canon—of reading the canonical texts before all, but as "abstract," in the sense of having potential for as yet unknown forms. This abstract reading fits my image of Mann, writing in full awareness that he was taking up "Jewish" matters at a time when "his godforsaken countrymen were exterminating this people" (Rosenwald 1978, 545). For Mann as an intentional writer probing the potential of porous subjectivity, myth was the productive alternative: "It is essential that myth be taken away from intellectual fascism and transmuted for humane ends. I have for a long time done nothing else" (1975, 103).

I acknowledge Mann's humanizing project in relation to the Jews. I consider his choice of the Qur'anic source in the particular episode where the other—the other woman—extends her subjectivity to the group that hosts her social identity an instructive case of mining cultural memory. Mann may have been less conscious of this implication, but it is equally humanizing. Even more humanizing, I would venture, because this implication extends the humanizing effect beyond the defense of a single group, albeit the most threatened and hurt one of the moment.

Above I suggested that the gendering of the people carrying wounds and whose wounds strike Mann as he remembers their memories is an allegorical move of great relevance. But is this not limiting the issue to the liberal critique again, and moreover, is it not an anachronistic fallacy? To begin with the latter: yes and no. It would be if I made this interpretive claim to explain Mann's choice qua conscious selection—his intention. But as Balmary learned from Freud how to read Freud, I learned from Mann how to read Mann—as an instance of the porous subjectivity he is imaginatively inventing. I write this in my post-Holocaust present time.

This contemporary interest can easily be reconciled, however, with the historical one. I would be inclined to argue that paradoxically but interestingly, Mann's foregrounding of the Islamic version denaturalized the primacy of Christianity and thus obliquely constituted a defense of the Judaic tradition that was under threat. Bringing in a canon that stands in tension with the Judaic one yet is also related, quite like a family member, is an effective—for apparently impartial—way of defending the Jews' right to difference, a difference anchored in a similarity that is vehemently denied. This is an adequate historical interpretation that has contemporary resonance through the allegorical union of differences.

The literary identity at stake contains sensitivity to difference of the kind that Mann's group of sympathizing women would allegorically embody. The religious canon, by the same token, is also momentarily broken open, not really extended, of course, but denaturalized as the only one. "Opening up the canon" is then not simply a matter of inclusion but of radically transforming what *canon* means. The literary identity helps the difference between the two canons to keep, so to speak, a foot in the door of each other's closed religious canon.

The one drawback of this historical interpretation is that women end up, as usual, as a metaphor for politics instead of participants in it. To alleviate this problem, we can examine a second level at which the constructive power of literary identity on religious canons can be seen. This level is historical in a different sense; the one I have called preposterous. It consists of reversing the usual relation between past and present and articulating how the present reenvisions the past. From such a perspective, it is all the more urgent to reconsider the Qur'an version first of all literally as a contribution, from *within* a powerful religious canon, to the literary one—Mann's novel. And through the latter's shaping of literary identity, it again helps open up not the religious canon, which is closed by definition, but the religious sensibility itself—the binding, community-making form of identification called heteropathic (Silverman 1996).

The desiring woman in the story, in this preposterous appropriation of pre-Holocaust revisionism of religious canons, is no longer the symbol or emblem of political critique but an agent of revision. The distinction demonstrates that the literary categories in which we think themselves partake of the ideology of embodiment that keeps *white identity*—now specified in relation to such troubling categories as "autochthonic" and "allochthonic" inhabitants of Europe—invisible because defined by a spirit that is in but not of the body, to reiterate Dyer's phrase. Allegory as a rhetorical figure is itself a case of such ideology that separates form, representation, from meaning.

Some people might think this view is correct but vastly exaggerates the influence of literature on social reality. Of course, literature does not act alone, nor does visual art; the point is that they can act, they do act, and in specific ways that "introduce the 'not-me' into my memory reserve" (Silverman 1996, 185). And such acts of heteropathic recollection enhance what, across canons and their (false) authorities, we can share by sympathizing or co-suffering. This leads me to the moment during which I am writing this book—a moment in relation to which the Holocaust has rewritten Western expectations and hopes, its trust in a narrowly defined reason. From after that moment, past for me, future for the creators of the artifacts discussed here, the "point" of literature must be assessed anew.

A powerful example of the positive potential of such a literary identity to help produce agency has been suggested by various Holocaust scholars. Inmates of concentration camps, so the story goes, derived strength, possibly even survival, from the silent recitation of poetry (e.g., Roder 1999). This statement, impossible to verify empirically, is based on testimonies of camp survivors, and on that basis I will assume its truth. The question that matters here is, what does this alleged fact teach us about the meaning of *literary identity*?

I think it is of crucial importance to distinguish an elitist-humanist interpretation of this fact from a performative one. Both are based on an ethically nonindifferent aesthetics, which makes it easy to conflate them, but the difference is radical for an assessment of their respective impacts on the status of canons. George Steiner, for example, would stand for the elitist-humanist interpretation. Alleging Liana Millu's 1947 testimony *Smoke over Birkenau*, J. H. de Roder ironically depicts Steiner's humanistic ideal of the classically educated subject, his head filled with poetry that makes him unassailably strong and morally superior (1999, 4). Since not only the uneducated died in Auschwitz, this moralizing elitism is blatantly inadequate.

For camp inmates, a performative view of the importance of poetry—not at all, by the way, exclusively canonical—would go in an altogether different direction. Literature's contribution to the strengthening of the subject under extreme duress would reside not in its passive absorption and subsequent recitation but in its active performing of literature that remained resilient in the subjects' cultural memories. The "reading," performed under specific conditions by subjects belonging to specific, historically determined identities—to simplify, say, not Jews but Jewish inmates—produced, rather than reproduced, the "literary identity" that was helpful.

In his study of contemporary art and thought on the Holocaust, Ernst van Alphen has analyzed the negative, destructive effect of depriving subjects of the frames that they ordinarily have at their disposal to make sense—those frames that remain unspoken because they are self-evident, until they are taken away. In other words, trauma—the inability to experience, form memories, and live through events as contributions to the ongoing formation of one's identity—is an assault on subjectivity that consists of depriving subjects of the frames of reference that are required for processing events into experiences (Alphen 1997; esp. 1999).

Van Alphen explains that the nature of what happened to inmates in the camps led to a *semiotic incapacitation*. He distinguishes four types of deficient framings: ambiguous actantial position, when one is neither subject nor object of the events, or one is both at the same time; the total negation of any actantial position or subjectivity; the lack of a plot or narrative frame by means of which the events can be narrated as a meaningful coherence; and the unacceptability of plots or narrative frames that are available or are inflicted, as they do not do justice to the way in which one partakes in the events (1999).

The ensuing analysis of trauma demonstrates negatively what happens if one denies access to frames, including, importantly, those frames that shape canons. Such frames are institutional and hence limiting. However, they are also indispensable mediations between idiosyncratic, potentially psychotic individuality and community. A community is required, precisely and in accordance with a performative view of language, to make sense of things. Those inmates who felt reciting poetry helped them were able to activate the frames offered by literature, not to replace the frames that were denied them but to make sense at all and thus stay semiotically alive in the face of attempts to cause their semiotic, social, and physical death. Literary identity in this sense can ultimately become a matter of life and death.[4]

Instead of using women as allegories for male concerns, and with the preposterous help of a willfully anachronistic interpretation much as Mann interpreted the Qur'an for his time, in his novel but not in his preface, I can now propose a view of the literary identity based on ethical nonindifference, an aesthetic for our time. For that proposal I return one last time to Dyer's critique of racial whiteness as unmarked. Before going into the specifics of the bond between Christianity, whiteness, and colonialism, Dyer writes about the importance to overcome such splits in general: "There is specificity to white representation, but it does not reside in a set of stereotypes so much as in narrative structural positions, rhetorical tropes and habits of perception" (1997, 12). In other words, in those invisible frames. Thomas Mann did a thorough job of vindicating the stereotype of the mythical wicked stepmother, but I have argued that he did a whole lot more. To do that, he deployed precisely the three means Dyer mentions. In the elaboration of Mut-em-enet's narrative structural position, her agency, he also liberated her from confinement in her allegorical role, and by forcing the reader, emblematized by the woman's friends, to experience *sym-pathy*, he changed those habits of perception, informed by Christian iconography, that allowed readers take distance from her as a nonreal, allegorical, trope for something else, as embodiment of a spirit.

From a much more pedestrian memory I recall a conversation with cab driver in Paris. When I apologized for having kept her waiting, she said it was no problem. She always spent her waiting time listening to a language course.

"What language are you studying?"

"Arabic."

"But isn't that your native language?"

"No, I only speak Moroccan Arabic. What I need is literary Arabic." "What do you need that for?"

"To listen to poetry. How else can I stand living here?"

---

4. This phrasing alludes to Orlando Patterson's seminal study of slavery as social death (1982).

DAD PAINS227

This is, of course, far less dramatic than the recitation of poetry by camp inmates. But it is happening today. I am not claiming identity or even continuity between these two moments. The present may simply serve as a magnifying glass for the past—but then also for the future that is already becoming in this memory.

Mann produced a female figure at history's most fraught and violent time, as his contribution to a life-with-desire because it is of the body. To perform that feat, he proceeded to undercut the tight bond between monotheism, monogamy, and masculinity by depicting for our imagination the "adulterous" woman as a figure who *produces*, in her rather nasty, painful agency limited but also enabled by institution and framing, the condition of possibility to think canons differently. If that is possible, the story of Mut and Yusuf has served its most productive function. It will then have demonstrated its "abstraction": against the fundamentalism of the fraught father who hurt his son, it will have allowed the woman who loves Yusuf to stay put. She may have fallen in love in most risky and unfortunate ways, but she does not, in the end, fall out of the story.

REFERENCES

Abu el-Haj, Nadia. 2002. *Facts on the Ground: Archaeological Practice and Territorial Self-Fashioning in Israeli Society*. Chicago: University of Chicago Press.

Adorno, Theodor W. 2003. In *Can One Live after Auschwitz? A Philosophical Reader*, ed. Rolf Tiedemann, trans. Rodney Livingstone and others. Stanford, CA: Stanford University Press.

Ahmed, Leila. 1992. *Women and Gender in Islam: Historical Roots of a Modern Debate*. New Haven, CT: Yale University Press.

Aichele, George. 1995. *The Postmodern Bible: The Bible and Culture Collective*. New Haven, CT: Yale University Press.

Alpers, Svetlana. 1983. *The Art of Describing: Dutch Art in the Seventeenth Century*. Chicago: University of Chicago Press.

Alphen, Ernst van. 1992. *Francis Bacon and the Loss of Self*. London: Reaktion Books.

———. 1997. *Caught by History: Holocaust Effects in Contemporary Art, Literature, and Theory*. Stanford, CA: Stanford University Press.

———. 1999. "Symptoms of Discursivity: Experience, Memory, Trauma." In *Acts of Memory: Cultural Recall in the Present*, ed. Mieke Bal, Jonathan Crewe, and Leo Spitzer, 24–38. Hanover, NH: University Press of New England.

———. 2005. *Art in Mind: How Contemporary Images Shape Thought*. Chicago: University of Chicago Press.

Alphen, Ernst van, Mieke Bal, and Carel Smith, eds. 2008. *The Rhetoric of Sincerity*. Palo Alto, CA: Stanford University Press.

Althusser, Louis. 1969. *For Marx*. Trans. Ben Brewster. London: New Left Books.

———. 1971. "Ideology and Ideological State Apparatuses (Notes towards an Investigation)." In *Lenin and Philosophy and Other Essays*, trans. Ben Brewster, 127–86. London: New Left Books.

Altieri, Charles. 1983. "An Idea and Ideal of a Literary Canon." In *Canons*, ed. Robert von Hallberg, 41–64. Chicago: University of Chicago Press.

Appadurai, Arjun. 2000. "Grassroot Globalization and the Research Imagination." *Public Culture* 12 (1): 1–19.

Ardener, Shirley, ed. 1981. *Women and Space: Ground Rules and Social Maps*. New York: St. Martin's.

Aravamudan, Srinivas. 2006. *Guru English: South Asian Religion in a Cosmopolitan Language*. Princeton, NJ: Princeton University Press.

Assmann, Jan. 2006a. *Religion and Cultural Memory*. Trans. Rodney Livingstone. Stanford, CA: Stanford University Press.

———. 2006b. *Thomas Mann und Aegypten. Mythos und Monotheismus in den Josephromanen*. Munich: C. H. Beck.

Attridge, Derek. 1999. "Innovation, Literature, Ethics: Relating to the Other." *PMLA* 114 (1): 20–31.

Austin, J. L. 1975 [1962]. *How to Do Things with Words*. Cambridge, MA: Harvard University Press.

Aydemir, Murat. 2007. *Images of Bliss: Ejaculation, Masculinity, Meaning*. Minneapolis: University of Minnesota Press.

Bach, Alice. 1997. *Women, Seduction, and Betrayal in Biblical Narrative*. Cambridge: Cambridge University Press.

Bakhtin, M. M. 1981. *The Dialogic Imagination: Four Essays*. Trans. Caryl Emerson and Michael Holquist. Austin: University of Texas Press.

Bal, Mieke. 1986. *Femmes imaginaires: L'ancien Testament au risque d'une narratologie critique*. Utrecht: Hes.

———. 1987. *Lethal Love: Literary-Feminist Readings of Biblical Love Stories*. Bloomington: Indiana University Press.

———. 1988a. *Death and Dissymmetry: The Politics of Coherence*. Chicago: University of Chicago Press.

———. 1988b. *Murder and Difference: Gender, Genre, and Scholarship on Sisera's Death*. Trans. Matthew Gumpert. Bloomington: Indiana University Press.

———. 1996 [1985]. *Narratology: Introduction to the Theory of Narrative*. Toronto: University of Toronto Press.

———. 1997. *The Mottled Screen: Reading Proust Visually*. Trans. Anna-Louise Milne. Stanford: Stanford University Press.

———. 1999. *Quoting Caravaggio: Contemporary Art, Preposterous History*. Chicago: University of Chicago Press.

———. 2001. "Legal Lust: Literary Litigations." In "Writing against Legal Racism: Law and Literature Explorations," ed. Judith Grbich and Peter Hutchings. Special issue, *Australian Feminist Law Journal* 15:1–24.

———. 2002. *Travelling Concepts in the Humanities: A Rough Guide*. Toronto: University of Toronto Press.

———. 2006 [1991]. *Reading "Rembrandt": Beyond the Word-Image Opposition*. New York: Cambridge University Press; reprint Amsterdam: Amsterdam University Press.

————. 2006a. *A Mieke Bal Reader.* Chicago: University of Chicago Press.

————. 2006b. "The Pain of Images." In *Beautiful Suffering: Photography and the Traffic in Pain,* ed. Mark Reinhardt, Holly Edwards, and Erina Duganne. Chicago: University of Chicago Press and Williams College Museum of Art.

Bal, Mieke, Jonathan Crewe, and Leo Spitzer, eds. 1999. *Acts of Memory: Cultural Recall in the Present.* Hanover, NH: University Press of New England.

Bal, Mieke, and Dimitris Vardoulakis. In prep. "A Rembrandt for Our Time."

Balmary, Marie. 1982. *Psychoanalyzing Psychoanalysis: Freud and the Hidden Fault of the Father.* Baltimore: Johns Hopkins University Press.

————. 1986. *Le sacrifice interdit: Freud et la Bible.* Paris: Grasset.

————. 1999. *Abel, ou A traversée de l'Eden.* Paris: Bernard Grasset.

Bardenstein, Carol B. 1999. "Trees, Forests, and the Shaping of Palestinian and Israeli Collective Memory." In *Acts of Memory: Cultural Recall in the Present,* ed. Mieke Bal, Jonathan Crewe, and Leo Spitzer, 148–68. Hanover, NH: University Press of New England.

Barlas, Asma. 2002. *"Believing Women" in Islam: Unreading Patriarchal Interpretations of the Qur'an.* Austin: University of Texas Press.

Barthes, Roland. 1968. "L'effet du réel." *Communications* 4:84–89. (English: 1986. "The Reality Effect." In *The Rustle of Language,* ed. Roland Barthes, trans. Richard Howard, 141–54. New York: Hill and Wang.)

————. 1972. *Mythologies.* Trans. Annette Lavers. London: Jonathan Cape.

————. 1974. *S/Z.* Trans. Richard Miller. New York: Hill and Wang.

————. 1977. *Fragments d'un discours amoureux.* Paris: Editions du Seuil.

Beal, Timothy K. 1997. *The Book of Hiding: Gender, Ethnicity, Annihilation, Esther.* London: Routledge.

————. 2002. *Religion and Its Monsters.* London: Routledge.

Beck, Herman L. 2001. "The Borderline between Muslim Fundamentalism and Muslim Modernism: An Indonesian Example." In *Religious Identity and the Invention of Tradition,* ed. Jan Willem van Henten and Anton Houtpen, 279–91. Assen, Netherlands: Van Gorcum.

Bekkenkamp, Jonneke. 1993. *Canon en keuze: Het bijbelse Hooglied en de "Twenty-one Love Poems" van Adrienne Rich als bronnen van theologie.* Kampen, Netherlands: Kok Agora.

Benesch, Otto. 1970. *Collected Writings,* vol. 1, *Rembrandt.* London: Phaidon.

Bennett, Jill. 2005. *Empathic Vision: Art, Politics, Trauma.* Stanford, CA: Stanford University Press.

Benveniste, Emile. 1971. *Problems in General Linguistics.* Trans. Mary Elizabeth Meek. Coral Gables, FL: University of Miami Press.

Bhabha, Homi K. 1994. "The Commitment to Theory." In *The Location of Culture,* 19–39. London: Routledge.

Biezenbos, Lia van de. 1995. *Fantasmes maternels dans l'oeuvre de Marguerite Duras.* Amsterdam: Rodopi B. V.

Bleeker, Maaike. 2006. "Theatricality and the Search for an Ethics of Vision." *Performing Arts Journal MASKA* 21 (Winter): 41–45.

————. In prep. "Theatres of Truth."

Bloom, Harold. 1980. *A Map of Misreading.* Oxford: Oxford University Press.

Boer, Inge E., ed. 2004a. *After Orientalism*. Amsterdam: Rodopi.

———. 2004b. *Disorienting Vision: Rereading Stereotypes in French Orientalist Texts and Images*. Amsterdam: Rodopi.

Bollas, Christopher. 1987. *The Shadow of the Object: Psychoanalysis of the Unthought Known*. New York: Columbia University Press.

Borch-Jacobsen, Mikkel. 1988. *The Freudian Subject*. Trans. Catherine Porter. Stanford, CA: Stanford University Press.

Bourdieu, Pierre. 1984 [1979]. *Distinction: A Social Critique of the Judgement of Taste*. Trans. Richard Nice. Cambridge, MA: Harvard University Press.

Boyarin, Daniel. 1995. *Carnal Israel: Reading Sex in Talmudic Culture*. Berkeley: University of California Press.

Brenner, Athalya. 1997. *The Intercourse of Knowledge: On Gendering Desire and "Sexuality" in the Hebrew Bible*. Leiden: Brill.

———. 2005. "Lust Is My Middle Name, I Have No Other: Madame Potiphar." In *I Am . . . : Biblical Women Tell Their Own Stories*, 50–57. Minneapolis: Fortress.

Brenner, Athalya, and Jan-Willem van Henten. 1998. "Madame Potiphar through a Culture Trip, or, Which Side Are You On?" In *Biblical Studies / Cultural Studies: The Third Sheffield Colloquium*, ed. J. Cheryl Exum and Stephen D. Moore, 203–19. Sheffield, UK: Sheffield Academic Press.

Bronfen, Elisabeth, and Misha Kavka, eds. 2000. *Feminist Consequences: Theory for the New Century*. New York: Columbia University Press.

Brooks, Peter. 1984. *Reading for the Plot: Design and Intention in Narrative*. New York: Alfred A. Knopf.

Bruns, Gerald L. 1983. "Canon and Power in the Hebrew Scriptures." In *Canons*, ed. Robert von Hallberg, 65–84. Chicago: University of Chicago Press.

Bryson, Norman. 1983. *Vision and Painting: The Logic of the Gaze*. London: Macmillan.

Buck-Morss, Susan. 1994. "The Cinema Screen as Prosthesis of Perception: A Historical Account." In *The Senses Still: Perception and Memory as Material Culture in Modernity*, ed. C. Nadia Seremetakis, 45–62. Chicago: University of Chicago Press.

Butler, Judith. 1990. *Gender Trouble and the Subversion of Identity*. New York: Routledge.

———. 1993. *Bodies That Matter: On the Discursive Limits of "Sex."* New York: Routledge.

———. 1997. *Excitable Speech: A Politics of the Performative*. New York: Routledge.

———. 2000. *Antigone's Claim: Kinship, Aberration, and Psychoanalysis*. New York: Columbia University Press.

Culler, Jonathan. 1981. *The Pursuit of Signs: Semiotics, Literature, Deconstruction*. Ithaca, NY: Cornell University Press.

———. 1988. *Framing the Sign: Criticism and Its Institutions*. Norman: University of Oklahoma Press.

———. 2000. "Philosophy and Literature: The Fortunes of the Performative." *Poetics Today* 21 (3): 48–67.

———. 2006. *The Literary in Theory*. Stanford, CA: Stanford University Press.

Dabashi, Hamid. 2000. "In the Absence of the Face." *Social Research* 67 (1): 127–85

Delaney, Carol. 1989. "The Legacy of Abraham." In *Anti-covenant: Counter-Reading Women's Lives in the Hebrew Bible*, ed. Mieke Bal, 27–42. Sheffield, UK: Sheffield Academic Press and Almond Press.

———. 1991. *The Seed and the Soil: Gender and Cosmology in Turkish Village Society*. Berkeley: University of California Press.

———. 1998. *Abraham on Trial: The Social Legacy of Biblical Myth*. Princeton, NJ: Princeton University Press.

Deleuze, Gilles. 1994 [1968]. *Difference and Repetition*. Trans. Paul Patton. London: Athlone.

Derrida, Jacques. 1976 [1967]. *Of Grammatology*. Trans. Gayatri Chakravorty Spivak. Baltimore: Johns Hopkins University Press.

———. 1985. "Racism's Last Word." *Critical Inquiry* 12 (Autumn): 290–99.

———. 1988. *Limited Inc*. Trans. Samuel Weber. Evanston, IL: Northwestern University Press.

———. 1990a. "Force of Law: The 'Mystical Foundation of Authority.'" Trans. M. Quaintance. *Cardozo Law Review* 11 (919): 921–1045.

———. 1990b. *Mémoires d'aveugle*. Paris: Réunions des Musées Nationaux and Musée du Louvre.

———. 1995. *The Gift of Death*. Trans. David Wills. Chicago: University of Chicago Press.

Derrida, Jacques, and Anne Dufourmantelle. 2000. *Of Hospitality: Anne Dufourmantelle Invites Jacques Derrida to Respond*. Stanford, CA: Stanford University Press.

Doi, Takeo. 1973 [1971]. *The Anatomy of Dependence*. New York: Kodansha.

Duras, Marguerite. 1965. *Le vice-consul*. Paris, Gallimard.

———. 1987. *La vie matérielle*. Paris: P.O.L.

Dyer, Richard. 1997. *White*. London: Routledge.

Eco, Umberto. 1976. *A Theory of Semiotics*. Bloomington: Indiana University Press.

Fabian, Johannes. 2001. *Anthropology with an Attitude: Critical Essays*. Stanford, CA: Stanford University Press.

Fanon, Frantz. 1986 [1952]. *Black Skin, White Masks*. Trans. Charles Lamm Markmann. London: Pluto.

Felman, Shoshana.1982. "Psychoanalysis and Education: Teaching Terminable and Interminable." *Yale French Studies* 63:21–44.

———. 1983. *The Literary Speech Act: Don Juan with J. L. Austin, or Seduction in Two Languages*. Ithaca, NY: Cornell University Press.

Fisher, Helen. 1992. *The Anatomy of Love: The Natural History of Monogamy, Adultery, and Divorce*. New York: W. W. Norton.

Freud, Sigmund. 1953 [1900]. *The Interpretation of Dreams*. London: Hogarth.

———. 1950 [1913]. *Totem and Taboo*. New York: Routledge and Kegan Paul.

Frosh, Stephen. 2005. "Fragments of Jewish Identity." *American Imago* 62 (2): 179–91.

Fuchs, Esther. 2000. *Sexual Politics in the Biblical Narrative: Reading the Hebrew Bible as a Woman*. Sheffield, UK: Sheffield Academic Press.

Gatens, Moira, and Genevieve Lloyd. 1999. *Collective Imaginings: Spinoza, Past and Present*. New York: Routledge.

Ghoussoub, Mai. 1987. "Feminism—or the Eternal Masculine—in the Arab World." *New Left Review* 161 (1): 3–18.

Glissant, Eduouard. 1981. *Le discours antillais*. Paris: Editions du Seuil.

Gravett, Sandie. 2004. "Reading 'Rape' in the Hebrew Bible: A Consideration of Language." *Journal for the Study of the Old Testament* 28 (3): 279–99.

Guillory, John. 1995. "Canon." In *Critical Terms for Literary Study*, ed. Frank Lentricchia and Thomas McLaughlin, 233–49. Chicago: University of Chicago Press.

Habermas, Jürgen. 1972 [1968]. *Knowledge and Human Interests*. Trans. Jeremy J. Shapiro. London: Heinemann.

Hammami, Reza, and Martina Rieker. 1988. "Feminist Orientalism and Orientalist Marism." *New Left Review* 1 (170): 93–106.

Hartman, Geoffrey H. 2001. "Tele-suffering and Testimony in the Dot Com Era." In *Visual Culture and the Holocaust*, ed. Barbie Zeliger, 111–26. New Brunswick, NJ: Rutgers University Press.

Heck, Paul. 2005. "Can Christians Believe in the Prophecy of Muhammad?" Manuscript.

Herman, David. 2002. *Story Logic: Problems and Possibilities of Narrative*. Lincoln: University of Nebraska Press.

Hertog, Cornelis den. 2006. "The Want-to-Be of the Divine Name: A Psychoanalytical Reading of Exodus 2.23–4.17." *Journal for Lacanian Studies* 4 (1): 76–98.

Hirsch, Marianne. 1992–93. "Family Pictures: *Maus*, Mourning, and Postmemory." *Discourse* 15 (2): 3–29.

———. 1999a. *The Familial Gaze*. Hanover, NH: University Press of New England.

———. 1999b. "Projected Memory: Holocaust Photographs in Personal and Public Fantasy." In *Acts of Memory: Cultural Recall in the Present*, eds. Mieke Bal, Jonathan Crewe, and Leo Spitzer, 3–23. Hanover, NH: University Press of New England.

Hirsch, Marianne, and Evelyn Fox Keller, eds. 1990. *Conflicts in Feminism*. New York: Routledge.

Huntington, Samuel. 2001. *The Clash of Civilizations*. New York: Free Press.

Jameson, Fredrick. 1981. *The Political Unconscious: Narrative as a Socially Symbolic Act*. Ithaca, NY: Cornell University Press.

Janssen, Yolande. 2006. *Stuck in a Revolving Door: Secularism, Assimilation, and Democratic Pluralism*. Amsterdam: Amsterdam School for Cultural Analysis.

Johnson, Barbara. 1980. *The Critical Difference: Essays in the Contemporary Rhetoric of Reading*. Baltimore: Johns Hopkins University Press.

———. 1998. *The Feminist Difference: Literature, Psychoanalysis, Race, and Gender*. Cambridge, MA: Harvard University Press.

Jomier, Jacques. 1964. *The Bible and the Qur'an*. Trans. Edward P. Arbez. San Francisco: Ignatius.

Kaltner, John. 1999. *Ishmael Instructs Isaac: An Introduction to the Qur'an for Bible Readers*. Collegeville, MN: Liturgical.

Keller, Evelyn Fox. 1992. *Secrets of Life, Secrets of Death: Essays on Language, Gender, and Science.* New York: Routledge.

Kenney, Joseph M. 1983. "Apotheosis and Incarnation Myths in Mann's *Joseph und Seine Bruder.*" *German Quarterly* 56 (1): 39–60.

Kermode, Frank. 1966. *The Sense of an Ending: Studies in the Theory of Fiction.* Oxford: Oxford University Press.

Kirk, Geoffrey S. 1972. "Aetiology, Ritual, Charter: Three Equivocal Terms in the Study of Myth." *Yale Classical Studies* 22:83–102.

Koelb, Clayton. 1978. "Mann's Use of Hebrew in the *Joseph* Novel." *Monatshefte* 70:148–49.

Kugel, James L. 1990. *In Potiphar's House: The Interpretive Life of Biblical Texts.* San Francisco: HarperSanFrancisco.

LaCapra, Dominick. 2001. *Writing History, Writing Trauma.* Baltimore: Johns Hopkins University Press.

La Caze, Marguerite. 2005. "Love, That Indispensable Supplement: Irigaray and Kant on Love and Respect." *Hypatia* 20 (Summer): 92–114.

Lakoff, George, and Mark Johnson. 1980. *Metaphors We Live By.* Chicago: University of Chicago Press.

———. 1999. *Philosophy in the Flesh: The Embodied Mind and Its Challenge to Western Thought.* New York: Basic Books.

Lang, Berhard. 1985. *Anthropological Approaches to the Old Testament.* Philadelphia: Fortress.

Laplanche, Jean. 1996. "Psychoanalysis as Anti-hermeneutics." Trans. Luke Thurston. *Radical Philosophy* 79:7–12.

Lawrence, Bruce B. 1998. "From Fundamentalism to Fundamentalisms: A Religious Ideology in Multiple Forms." In *Religion, Modernity, and Postmodernity,* ed. Paul Heelas, 88–101. Oxford: Blackwell.

Lawrence, Karen R. 1992. *Decolonizing Tradition: New Lives of Twentieth-Century "British" Literary Canons.* Urbana: University of Illinois Press.

Luxemburg, Jan van. 1992. *Rhetoric and Pleasure: Readings in Realist Fiction.* Berlin: De Gruyter.

Maleuvre, Didier. 2005. "Art and the Teaching of Love." *Journal of Aesthetic Education* 39 (Spring): 77–94.

Mann, Thomas. 1978 [1934]. *Joseph and His Brothers.* Trans. Helen Tracy Lowe-Porter. New York: Alfred A. Knopf.

———. 1943. "The Joseph Novels." *Atlantic Monthly* 171:92–100.

———. 1975. *Mythology and Humanism: The Correspondence between Thomas Mann and Karl Kerényi.* Ithaca, NY: Cornell University Press.

McDonald, William E. 1999. *Thomas Mann's "Joseph and His Brothers": Writing, Performance, and the Politics of Loyalty.* New York: Camden House.

McGann, Jerome J. 1981. "The Meaning of *The Ancient Mariner.*" *Critical Inquiry* 8 (Autumn): 35–67.

McHale, Brian. 1987. *Postmodernist Fiction.* London: Methuen.

Melas, Natalie. 1995. "Versions of Incommensurability." *World Literature Today* 69 (Spring): 275–80.

———. 2007. *All the Difference in the World. Postcoloniality and the Ends of Comparison.* Stanford, CA: Stanford University Press.

Meltzer, Françoise. 1987. *Salome and the Dance of Writing*. Chicago: University of Chicago Press.

Millet, Kate. 2000 [1970]. *Sexual Politics*. Urbana: University of Illinois Press.

Moaddel, Mansoor. 1998. "Religion and Women: Islamic Modernism versus Fundamentalism." *Journal for the Scientific Study of Religion* 37 (1): 108–30.

Neuwirth, Angelika. n.d. "Structural, Linguistic, and Literary Features." Manuscript.

Niditch, Susan. 1993. "War, Women, and Defilement in Numbers 31." *Semeia* 61:39–57.

Nietzsche, Friedrich. 1974 [1882]. *The Gay Science*. Trans. Walter Kaufmann. New York: Vintage.

Norman, Julie. 2005. "Rape Law in Islamic Societies: Theory, Application and the Potential for Reform." Lecture presented at the Center for the Study of Islam and Democracy Sixth Annual Conference, Washington, DC, April 22–23.

Overholt, Thomas W. 1985. "Prophecy: The Problem of Cross-Cultural Comparison." In *Anthropological Approaches to the Old Testament*, ed. Bernhard Lang, 60–82. Philadelphia: Fortress.

Patterson, Orlando. 1982. *Slavery and Social Death: A Comparative Study*. Cambridge, MA: Harvard University Press.

Pavel, Thomas. 1984. "Origin and Articulation: Comments on the Papers by Peter Brooks and Lucienne Frappier-Mazur." *Style: Psychopoetics at Work* 18 (3): 355–68.

Peacock, James L., and Tim Pettyjohn. 1995. "Fundamentalisms Narrated: Muslim, Christian, and Mystical." In *Fundamentalisms Comprehended*, ed. Martin E. Marty and R. Scott Appleby, 115–34. Chicago: University of Chicago Press.

Peeren, Esther. 2005. *Bakhtin and Beyond: Identities as Intersubjectivities in Popular Culture*. Amsterdam: Amsterdam School for Cultural Analysis.

Peters, Francis E. 2003. *Islam: A Guide for Jews and Christians*. Princeton, NJ: Princeton University Press.

Pollock, Griselda. 1999. *Differencing the Canon: Feminist Desire and the Writing of Art's Histories*. London: Routledge.

Qurashi, Asifa. 1997. "Her Honor: An Islamic Critique of the Rape Laws of Pakistan from a Woman-Sensitive Perspective." *Michigan Journal of Law School* 18 (2): 287–315.

Racine, Jean. 2001 [1677]. *Britannicus, Phaedra, Athaliah*. Trans. C. H. Sisson. Oxford: Oxford University Press.

Rahv, Philip. 1953. "The Myth and the Powerhouse." *Partisan Review* 20:635–48.

Rajan, Rajeswari Sunder. 1993. *Real and Imagined Women: Gender, Culture, and Postcolonialism*. New York: Routledge.

Rimmon, Shlomith. 1977. *The Concept of Ambiguity: The Example of James*. Chicago: University of Chicago Press.

Roder, Jan H. de. 1999. *Het schandaal van de poëzie: Over taal, ritueel, en biologie*. Nijmegen, Netherlands: Vantilt and de Wintertuin.

Rosello, Mireille. 1998. *Declining the Stereotype: Ethnicity and Representa-tion in French Cultures*. Hanover, NH: University Press of New England.

Rosenwald, George C. 1978. "The Art Work as a Force in the Artist's Life." *Psychoanalytic Study of the Child* 33:519–62.

Said, Edward W. 1978. *Orientalism*. New York: Pantheon.

———. 2000. "Invention, Memory, and Place." *Critical Inquiry* 26 (Winter): 175–92.

———. 2004. *Freud and the Non-European*. London: Verso and Freud Museum.

Salomon, Nanette. 1991. "The Art Historical Canon: Sins of Omission." In *(En)Gendering Knowledge: Feminism in Academe*, ed. Joan E. Hartman and Ellen Messner-Davidow, 222–36. Knoxville: University of Tennessee Press.

Scarry, Elaine. 1985. *The Body in Pain: The Making and Unmaking of the World*. Oxford: Oxford University Press.

Scholz, Susanne. 2000. *Rape Plots: A Feminist Cultural Study of Genesis 34*. New York: Peter Lang.

Schor, Naomi. 1987. *Reading in Detail: Esthetics and the Feminine*. New York: Methuen.

Sells, Michael. 1991. "Sound, Spirit, and Gender in Surat al-Qadr." *Journal of the American Oriental Society* 11:239–59.

Silverman, Kaja. 1992. *Male Subjectivity at the Margin*. New York: Routledge.

———. 1996. *The Threshold of the Visible World*. New York: Routledge.

Sjöberg, Mikael. 2004. *Wrestling with Textual Violence: A Case Study of the Jephtah Narrative in Antiquity and Modernity with Specific Regard to Gender*. Uppsala: Uppsala Universitet.

Smart, Carol. 1989. *Feminism and the Power of Law*. New York: Routledge.

Smith, C. E. 2008. "The Rhetoric of Justification." In *The Rhetoric of Sincer-ity*, ed. Ernst Van Alphen, Mieke Bal, and Carel E. Smith. Stanford, CA: Stanford University Press.

Sonbol, Amira. 2000. "Rape and Law in Modern Ottoman Egypt." In *Women and Sexuality in Muslim Societies*, ed. Pinar Ilkkaracan, 309–26. Istanbul: Women for Women's Human Rights.

Spivak, Gayatri Chakravorty. 1993. "More on *Power/Knowledge*." In *Outside in the Teaching Machine*, 25–52. New York: Routledge.

———. 1999. *A Critique of Postcolonial Reason: Toward a History of the Vanishing Present*. Cambridge, MA: Harvard University Press.

Stock, Brian. 1983. *The Implications of Literacy: Written Language and Models of Interpretation in the Eleventh and Twelfth Centuries*. Prince-ton, NJ: Princeton University Press.

Stoler, Ann Laura. 2002. *Carnal Knowledge and Imperial Power: Race and the Intimate in Colonial Rule*. Berkeley: University of California Press.

Sturken, Marita. 1999. "Narratives of Recovery: Repressed Memory as Cultural Memory." In *Acts of Memory: Cultural Recall in the Present*, ed. Mieke Bal, Jonathan Crewe, and Leo Spitzer, 231–48. Hanover, NH: University Press of New England.

Tanner, Tony. 1979. *Adultery in the Novel: Contract and Transgression*. Baltimore: Johns Hopkins University Press.

Teubal, Savina J. 1990. *Hagar the Egyptian: The Lost Tradition of the Matriarchs*. San Francisco: Harper & Row.

Tully, James. 1995. *Strange Multiplicity: Constitutionalism in an Age of Diversity*. Cambridge: Cambridge University Press.

Valentiner, W. R. 1957. *Rembrandt and Spinoza: A Study of the Spiritual Conflicts in Seventeenth Century Holland*. London: Phaidon.

Vardoulakis, Dimitris. 2004. "The Critique of Loneliness: Towards the Political Motives of the Doppelganger." *Angelaki: Journal for the Theoretical Humanities* 9 (2): 81–101.

Venuti, Lawrence. 1996. "Translation, Philosophy, Materialism." *Radical Philosophy* 79:24–34.

Vickery, John B., ed. 1966. *Myth and Literature: Contemporary Theory and Practice*. Lincoln: University of Nebraska Press.

Vlies, Inge C. van der. 1993. *Grenzen aan het recht*. Zwolle: W. E. J. Tjeenk Willink.

Vries, Hent de. 1999. *Philosophy and the Turn to Religion*. Baltimore: Johns Hopkins University Press.

Wadud, Amima. 1999. *Qur'an and Woman: Rereading the Sacred Text from a Woman's Perspective*. New York: Oxford University Press.

Wagtendonk, Kees. 1985. "Van de bijbelse Josef tot de Joesoef van de Islam." In *Beginngen bij de letter Beth: Opstellen over het Bijbels Hebreeuws en de Hebreeuwse Bijbel voor Dr. Aleida G. van Daalen*, ed. Th. K. A. Deurlo and F. J. Hoogenwoud, 131–38. Kampen, Netherlands: Kok.

Weber, Samuel. 2000. "Psychoanalysis and Theatricality." *Parallax* 16 (3): 29–48.

Wesseling, Elizabeth, and Robert Zwijnenberg, eds. 2007. *Art in Time: On the Use and Abuse of Anachronism in the History of Art*. London: Equinox.

White, Christopher. 1969. *Rembrandt as an Etcher: A Study of the Artist at Work*. 2 vols. London: A. Zwemmer.

Yates, Frances Amelia. 1966. *The Art of Memory*. Chicago: University of Chicago Press.

Yohannan, John D. 1982. "Hebraism and Hellenism in Thomas Mann's Story of Joseph and Potiphar's Wife." *Comparative Literature Studies* 19 (4): 430–41.

Young-Bruehl, Elisabeth. 2003. "Where Do We Fall When We Fall in Love?" *JPCS: Journal for the Psychoanalysis of Culture and Society* 8 (2): 279–88.

Zornberg, Aviva Gottlieb. 1995. *Genesis: The Beginning of Desire*. London: Doubleday.

INDEX OF NAMES AND TITLES

INDEX OF TERMS AND CONCEPTS